WOOD, CONCRETE, STONE, AND STEEL

WOOD, CONCRETE,

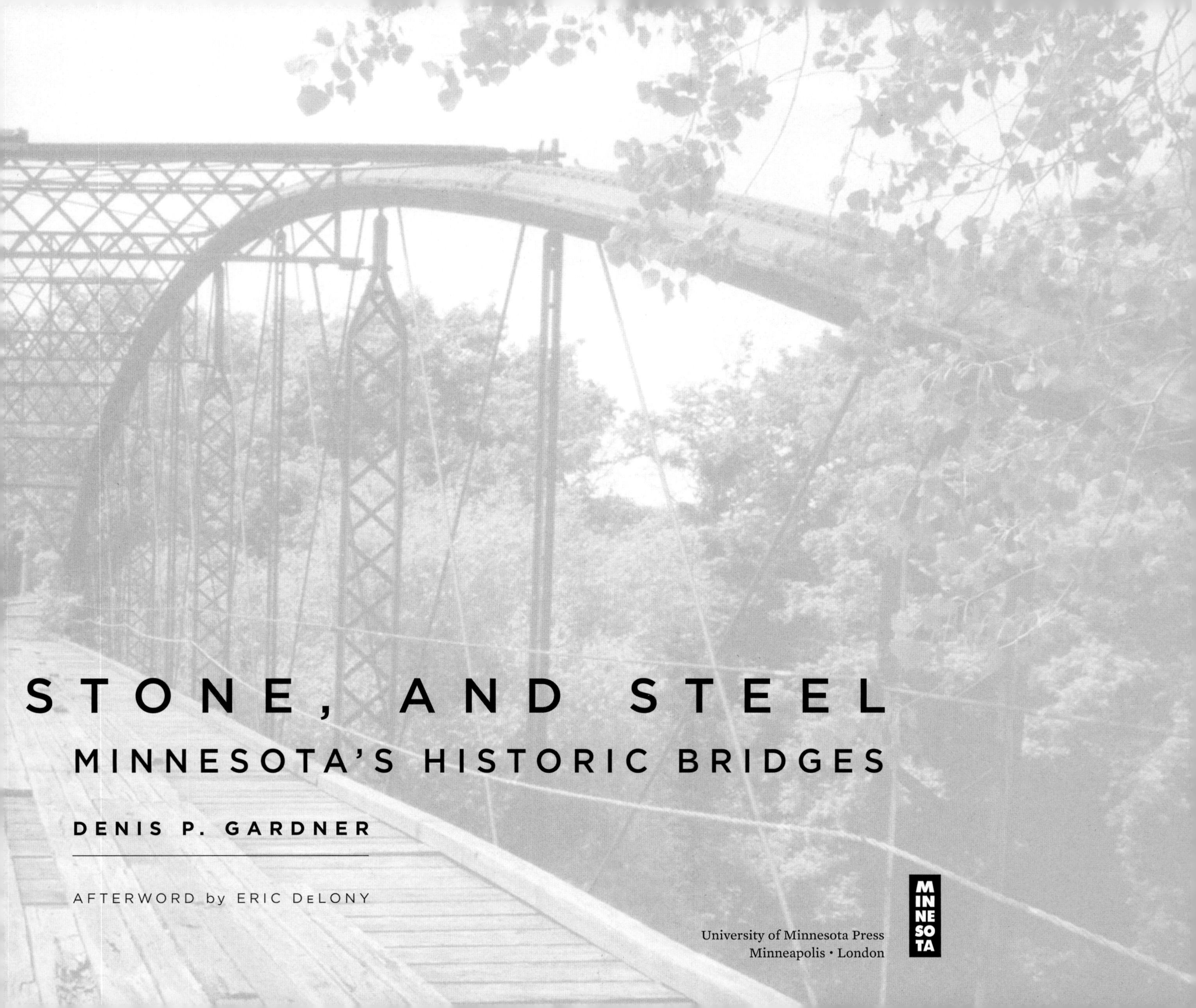

STONE, AND STEEL
MINNESOTA'S HISTORIC BRIDGES

DENIS P. GARDNER

AFTERWORD by ERIC DeLONY

University of Minnesota Press
Minneapolis · London

Frontispiece: Kern Bridge over Le Sueur River, South Bend Township (south of Mankato), built 1873.

Truss drawings created by Parrot Graphics

Photographs in "Minnesota's Historic Bridges" courtesy of the Minnesota State Historic Preservation Office of the Minnesota Historical Society.

Design and production by Mighty Media, Inc.

Index by Eileen Quam

Published by the University of Minnesota Press
111 Third Avenue South, Suite 290
Minneapolis, MN 55401-2520
http://www.upress.umn.edu

Library of Congress Cataloging-in-Publication Data

Gardner, Denis P.

Wood, concrete, stone, and steel : Minnesota's historic bridges / Denis P. Gardner ; afterword by Eric DeLony.

    p.   cm.

Includes index.

ISBN 978-0-8166-4666-1 (hc : alk. paper) —
ISBN 978-0-8166-4667-8 (pb: alk. paper)

1. Historic bridges—Minnesota. 2. Bridges—Minnesota—Design and construction—History. I. DeLony, Eric. II. Title.

TG24.M47G37 2008

624.209776—dc22

2008007776

For my mother, for a life well lived

There can be little doubt that in many ways the story of bridge building is the story of civilization. By it we can readily measure an important part of a people's progress.

—Franklin D. Roosevelt, "New York Speaks," *New York Times,*
October 18, 1931

CONTENTS

PREFACE

Hon. K. Nelson, Alexandria.

Sir, I beg leave to inquire of you whether there is any bridges to be built in your county and if there is who can I write to in regard to them.

I am prepared to build iron, combination or wood bridges of any description desired and prices to defy competition, while satisfaction is warranted in every instance.

CHARLES FILTEAU was a late-nineteenth-century bridge builder based in Minneapolis when he penned this note.[1] In 1877, a year after he mailed the letter, he constructed a railroad bridge across the Mississippi River between Minneapolis and St. Anthony. Only a few years later, he built a railroad bridge over the Red River of the North at Grand Forks, North Dakota. By the late 1880s, however, Filteau no longer advertised his services, implying that he had left the regional bridge-building scene.[2]

Filteau's letter sheds at least some light on the nascent bridge-building process in nineteenth-century Minnesota. It was not a formal process—well, not entirely formal. When Minnesota became a territory in 1849, the territorial government authorized county commissioners to maintain roadways and build bridges. Counties often simply hired a local farmer to erect a bridge over a river, stream, or ditch; the structure usually did not last long. By the 1860s and 1870s, it was not uncommon for county governments to receive solicitations from bridge builders like the one from Filteau. These contractors had at least some formal training in building bridges and sometimes in designing bridges. Often this experience was gained by working for the railroad, the one enterprise that was almost always building a bridge somewhere. Still, some of these early builders were not engineers: more accurately, they were not engineers as we think of the profession today. Nevertheless, these early builders brought a level of professionalism to the bridge-building process.

Essentially, the process evolved into one where local governments (usually counties and townships) advertised for the erection of a bridge within their jurisdiction. Regional bridge builders submitted bids for the construction, and the county or township board almost always embraced the builder who charged the least. This must have caused at least a modicum of trepidation as farmers with laden wagons eyed swiftly moving spring currents and bridge after bridge built by the lowest bidder. And with no standardization in the bridge-building process, frail crossings were hardly a rarity. This became ever more an issue as Minnesota's rising population forced greater traffic demands on the state's thrifty bridges.

Heavier and stronger crossings became the norm in the early twentieth century when the state gained control over bridge construction and developed standard plans and specifications for bridges. Perhaps the state was late to the party, but local governments probably were not anxious to relinquish their rights to the state and, truthfully, the state was not anxious to accumulate debt. In 1858, the year Minnesota became a state, the state legislature inserted a provision into the constitution that stated, "The State shall never contract any debts for work of internal improvement or be a party in carrying on such works." This provision freed the state of any financial obligation for transportation infrastructure improvements. As Minnesota's population continued to swell, however, it became increasingly apparent that local governments were not going to be able to build and maintain reliable transportation infrastructure without help from the state. As the state assumed authority over much of the public construction, standardization was inevitable.

Minnesota does not have many bridges remaining from the state's prestandardization period, and most but not all of these early bridges are featured in the main sections of this book. The others can be found in "Minnesota's Historic Bridges," a list of all of the state's known historic bridges at the time of this writing. The term *historic* must be clarified: most of the extant bridges in this book are historic as defined by criteria established by the National Park Service, the administrator of the National Register of Historic Places, a repository of buildings, structures, districts, sites, and objects considered historic because they meet federally established criteria.[3]

This book was originally intended to highlight historic bridges still decorating Minnesota. It is important to showcase these structures because we are rapidly losing them, and Minnesotans should be aware of the rare structural history that is disappearing almost without the populace realizing it. Ultimately, the book evolved into more than just a record of extant bridges. Several of the bridges described here have been gone for some time but still deserve attention, a conclusion I embraced once I realized that some bridges are such a significant part of Minnesota's story that I would be banished from the state if I did not acknowledge them. For instance, it is insolent to pen a book on Minnesota bridges and not include the Hastings Spiral Bridge, a crossing that has been gone for several decades now.

After considerable thought, it seemed most appropriate to organize this book according to the material employed for construction rather than by bridge type or geographic location. Bridge construction evolved in part because of the introduction of new building materials; for example, bridge building began with wood and stone and progressed to iron and steel and then to concrete. Thus Minnesota's arch bridges began in stone, graduated to iron and steel, and then became some of our most prominent present-day bridge forms in concrete. Clearly, this method of parceling the book also has chronological appeal. Each chapter is generally chronological as well—that is, bridges are mostly featured in the order they were constructed. However, it was impossible to be entirely chronological and maintain the nuance of the narrative.

Most of this book features roadway bridges, but a number of railroad bridges are also included. Minnesota's roadway bridging story has been thoroughly studied, but almost no study has been completed on the state's railroad bridging history. This results from the fact that railroads are private entities, and the public cannot simply impose on the railroads because we desire to know more about the history of the state's railroad bridges. We need permission for such an endeavor, and perhaps the future will bring it. Some of the rail-

road bridges that have been substantially documented will be found in this book.

Finally, I never intended to end this preface with a discussion of the Interstate Highway 35W Bridge over the Mississippi River in Minneapolis, but life sometimes surprises by pitching a curve that makes the knees buckle. The draft of this book had already been delivered to the publisher when this substantial bridge fell down, bringing death and injury to many motorists.

While this book chiefly was written to document and celebrate Minnesota's historic bridges, my publisher and I recognized that we needed to acknowledge the Interstate Highway 35W Bridge, for its failure raises a serious question, namely, what should we do about our aging bridges? The obvious answer might be to replace them, but perhaps a better solution is to replace the system that has allowed much of our bridge infrastructure to deteriorate to the point where so much needs replacing. I address this issue briefly in the bridge preservation section of this book, but with the recent collapse of this major bridge through Minneapolis, it seemed appropriate to pause to consider the importance of investing in routine maintenance, which may preserve many of the notable bridges described in this book, as well as lives and money.

After perusing the pages of this work, perhaps readers will understand why many bridge historians and preservationists think as we do. In truth, we are practical people, realizing that it is not always necessary to build new if we can maintain the old. Moreover, we can continue to bask in the cultural heritage of the old—and that means something.

ACKNOWLEDGMENTS

A DECADE AGO, I was certain that this book was soon to be written. Jeffrey A. Hess and Charlene K. Roise, two professional historians based in the Twin Cities, appeared destined to pen an ode to the North Star state's bridging heritage. It never happened. Through no fault of these potential authors, circumstance reversed itself and the expected narrative never came about. But interest in the subject did not wane, and after all these years I find myself completing a work about many of the bridges that have graced Minnesota's landscape.

Several people and organizations deserve credit for this book's publication, including editor Todd Orjala and the University of Minnesota Press. Orjala has been intrigued by Minnesota's bridging story for some time and has long wanted to produce a book on the subject. Charlene Roise and Jeffrey Hess also deserve recognition; they are responsible for teaching me much of what I know about the history of bridges in the state. Hess is also responsible for the written context on Minnesota's masonry bridges, which he completed in the late 1980s and serves as the de facto story on stone arch bridge building in the state. Fredric L. Quivik, with aid from Dale L. Martin, provided the context on Minnesota's iron and steel bridges, and Robert M. Frame III wrote the context for reinforced-concrete bridges. Much of what we know about Minnesota's bridging history stems from the efforts of Frame, who conducted early study on the subject. All of this work can be found at the Minnesota State Historic Preservation Office (SHPO) at the Minnesota Historical Society, a unique body charged with overseeing much of the preservation activities in Minnesota.

I owe a nod to the SHPO as well. As with my first book, *Minnesota's Treasures: Stories behind the State's Historic Places*, the SHPO offered considerable aid, providing information and advice whenever these were sought. While all of the staff there contributed to my endeavor to one degree or another, Dennis Gimmestad, the government programs and compliance officer,

was particularly helpful: he substantially clarified the complicated deliberations that have surrounded the future of the Stillwater Bridge. Susan Roth, Minnesota's National Register historian, is once again the person at the SHPO for whom I am most grateful: as with my previous book, Susan offered sage advice and gentle criticism, ensuring that the narrative touched pertinent points. Kristen Zschomler and Mn/DOT (Minnesota Department of Transportation) deserve recognition. Zschomler, a historian and archaeologist within the cultural resources unit of the state agency, was quick to offer any aid that Mn/DOT could provide. I am also thankful for the help of Peter L. Wilson, a senior engineering specialist within the bridge inspection unit of Mn/DOT: he frequently answered my technical inquiries while also providing historical information for several bridges.

Many historic images were procured from the Minnesota Historical Society, an organization with such a wealth of historical information that researchers of Minnesota subjects should feel compelled to use its resources. Other historical organizations that helped me include the Northeast Minnesota Historical Center at the University of Minnesota Duluth and the Goodhue County Historical Society in Red Wing.

I am indebted to my brother, Robert W. Gardner Jr., who took photographs of a number of bridges. His long hours on the road greatly lightened my load, and I will always be grateful for his kindness. I also appreciate the support of my frequent traveling companion as I motored across the state photographing so many interesting bridges that most Minnesotans never get a chance to see. Perhaps it seems odd that a historian-photographer would take his mother into the field, but it shouldn't: my mother always had a curious mind and a desire to see what was beyond the fence. I hope readers enjoy that same curiosity and desire.

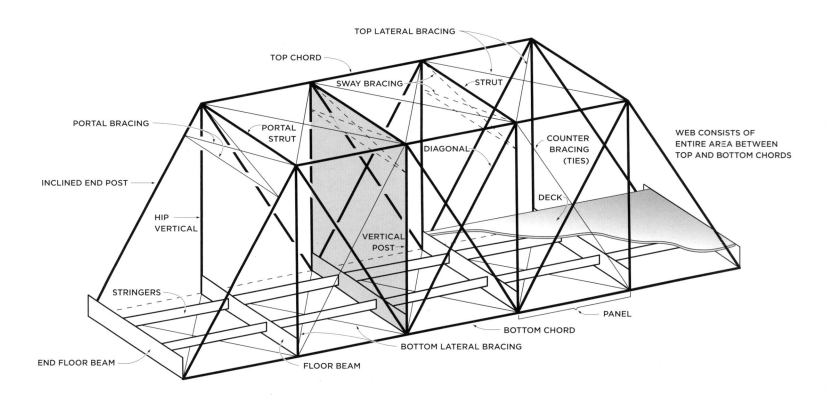

TOP LATERAL BRACING

TOP CHORD

SWAY BRACING

STRUT

PORTAL BRACING

PORTAL STRUT

DIAGONAL

COUNTER BRACING (TIES)

WEB CONSISTS OF ENTIRE AREA BETWEEN TOP AND BOTTOM CHORDS

INCLINED END POST

DECK

HIP VERTICAL

VERTICAL POST

STRINGERS

PANEL

END FLOOR BEAM

BOTTOM CHORD

FLOOR BEAM

BOTTOM LATERAL BRACING

TRUSS BRIDGES

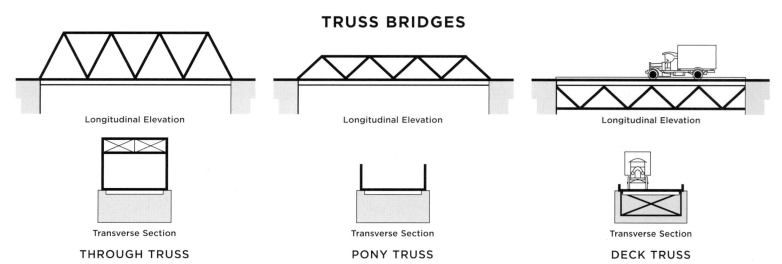

Longitudinal Elevation

Longitudinal Elevation

Longitudinal Elevation

Transverse Section

Transverse Section

Transverse Section

THROUGH TRUSS

PONY TRUSS

DECK TRUSS

GUIDE TO BRIDGE TRUSSES

KING POST
(Wood)
A traditional truss type with its origins in the Middle Ages.
Length: 20–60 feet, 6–18 meters

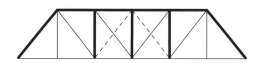

PRATT
1844–20th Century
Diagonals in tension, verticals in compression (except for hip verticals adjacent to inclined end posts).
Length: 30–250 feet, 9–75 meters

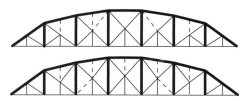

PENNSYLVANIA (PETIT)
1875–Early 20th Century
Top: A Parker with sub-struts.
Bottom: A Parker with sub-ties.
Length: 250–600 feet, 75–180 meters

WARREN
(with Verticals)
Mid-19th–20th Century
Diagonals carry both compressive and tensile forces. Verticals serve as bracing for triangular web system.
Length: 50–400 feet, 15–120 meters

TOWN LATTICE
(Wood)
1820–Late 19th Century
A system of wooden diagonals with no verticals. Members take both compression and tension.
Length: 50–220 feet, 15–66 meters

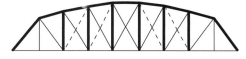

PARKER
Mid-Late 19th–20th Century
A Pratt with a polygonal top chord.
Length: 40–250 feet, 12–75 meters

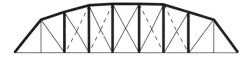

CAMELBACK
Late 19th–20th Century
A Parker with a polygonal top chord of exactly five slopes.
Length: 100–300 feet, 30–90 meters

DOUBLE INTERSECTION PRATT
(Whipple, Whipple-Murphy, Linville)
1847–20th Century
An inclined end post Pratt with diagonals that extend across two panels.
Length: 70–300 feet, 21–90 meters

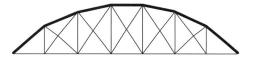

BOWSTRING ARCH-TRUSS
1840–Late 19th Century
A tied arch with the diagonals serving as bracing and the verticals supporting the deck.
Length: 50–130 feet, 15–40 meters

WOOD

BRIDGES

Over 100 sleighs, it is said, were in a line, embracing between five and six hundred persons.... As sleigh after sleigh in compact array passed over the wiry fabric not a muscle of that fairy-like creation moved to show that it labored under the burden.... To sum it all up, there is no breach of good taste, no effort at pretension; and the tout ensemble pleases the eye of everyone.

—"Grand Celebration," *St. Anthony Express*, January 27, 1855

1

New York engineer Thomas Musgrove Griffith's "fairy-like creation" was a wagon bridge over the Mississippi River, spanning the distance from Nicollet Island to what would become the city of Minneapolis. Griffith's bridge was special because it was a rare mid-nineteenth-century example of a suspension span. And it was notable for another reason as well: it was the first bridge to reach across the Mississippi River.[1]

The bridge was constructed in 1854, although the formal opening was not until early 1855. Minneapolis was more than a decade away from incorporating as a city. It would not even become a township until May 1858, which would seem to make the crossing, located on present-day Hennepin Avenue, somewhat premature. The land on the west side of the Mississippi River, opposite the community of St. Anthony, belonged to the U.S. government, which had acquired it from the local American Indian population years earlier. But for those with manifest destiny on the mind, a wide river and the government property that formed the Fort Snelling Military Reservation were hardly obstacles. This insatiable urge to squat on the west bank of the river was fed in part by entrepreneurs like Franklin Steele, who seemed to recognize that the geographic blessing known as the Falls of St. Anthony (situated just below Nicollet Island) would transform Minneapolis into a flour-milling colossus. Steele, believing it was only a matter of time before the west bank officially opened to white settlement, formed the Mississippi Bridge Company with several partners in early 1852. In little more than two years, the company's fanciful bridge was spanning the river. The toll to pass over the structure was five cents for pedestrians and twenty-five cents for a wagon and team.[2]

It is difficult to apply a particular style to the structure engineered by Griffith, but its wood suspension towers and arching cables exuded a kind of rustic elegance. If it were built today, it would fall under the

Designed by New York engineer Thomas Musgrove Griffith and opened in 1855, the first bridge spanning the Mississippi River at what would become Hennepin Avenue was a suspension span, an especially rare bridge type for frontier Minnesota. *Photograph by Edwin D. Harvey, ca. 1865; courtesy of the Minnesota Historical Society.*

heading of roadside architecture, a somewhat fuzzy term for structures that are deliberately conspicuous and have a certain whimsy. Sheathed in wood boarding, the framed suspension towers rested on stone foundations near either end of the 620-foot bridge. Thick wire cables hung between the towers, spanning the river. The cables passed through the tops of the towers and then downward into limestone anchorages several feet underground. The cables supported numerous wire lines that vertically extended to the seventeen-foot-wide wood deck. In essence, the anchored cables carried the deck via the vertical wire lines. This was impressive bridge engineering for frontier Minnesota, but those responsible for the structure understood that the bridge was more than a means to cross the river: it symbolized the promise of the future, a promise that would arrive so quickly that Griffith would return to Minneapolis two decades later and engineer anew.[3]

In part, Griffith's wood crossing was unique because it was out of place. Almost all bridges in Minnesota at that time were rude timber structures, most rather small. In comparison, the Mississippi River crossing above the falls was frontier finery. Griffith's substantial bridge was joined a few years later by a large timber truss over the Mississippi River at Wabasha Street in St. Paul. But honestly, suspension structures almost always reflect a stylishness that is lacking in trusses, and the bridge in St. Paul offered few charms. One observer from the period remarked that the crossing was "a most distressingly untraditional bridge, all on the oblique and very awkward, like a great clumsy fire-escape propped up against a high wall." The Wabasha Street Bridge was rebuilt in the 1870s but remained a peculiar-looking timber object. Later that decade, it was rebuilt again, this time as an iron bridge, which lasted until 1889, when St. Paul once more shaped a new bridge over the Mississippi River at Wabasha Street, an interesting iron structure that stood for over a century.[4]

For many years, the crossing at Wabasha Street in St. Paul was an ungainly looking structure that reached over the Mississippi River in a series of steps. St. Paul completed four different bridges at the site before erecting the current structure. Here the city is erecting the first iron bridge at the site, although the approaches (the sections that look like steps) are still formed of wood because they have not yet been rebuilt of iron. *Photograph by Truman Ward Ingersoll, ca. 1879; courtesy of the Minnesota Historical Society.*

This timber beam-span bridge was completed over a canal near Detroit Lakes in the late 1800s and is an example of the crude bridges common to Minnesota during the period. *Photograph ca. 1895; courtesy of the Minnesota Historical Society.*

perpendicular to a road or trail. This type of bridge was often used over soft, spongy areas where vehicles such as oxcarts or coaches were likely to get stuck. Sometimes corduroy bridges were elevated over a stream or river. This type of crossing's major shortcoming was the jarring ride delivered to travelers, many of whom probably needed a spinal adjustment upon passing over such a bridge. Additionally, corduroy bridges became slippery during wet weather, clearly a hazard to horse, ox, or human. To alleviate both these dilemmas, corduroy bridges were sometimes covered with gravel or turf. Today this bridge type can occasionally be found on hiking or bicycle trails. Measuring about a quarter-mile long, the corduroy bridge in Rhode Island's George Washington State Park may be one of the longest of its type in the nation.[5]

For most of Minnesota's early settlers, stylishness in bridge design was inconsequential as they merely required stable crossings to carry them over the many rivers, streams, and marshy areas impeding their paths. Ugly or no, most timber crossings satisfactorily accomplished the task. Timber bridges were popular in mid- to late-nineteenth-century Minnesota because wood was a readily available building material in many areas. By erecting wood crossings, Minnesotans were simply repeating the bridge-building practice that began on the Eastern Seaboard and moved west with migration. One type of timber crossing common to many parts of early Minnesota was the corduroy bridge. In fact, there were probably many corduroy bridges on the Red River Trails, which were relatively crude fur-trading passageways that were established at least by the 1830s and extended from St. Paul northwest to the Red River Valley and Canada. A corduroy bridge is a primitive construction that consists of laying logs

Although rudimentary, the corduroy bridge was not the most common bridge type in early Minnesota. That distinction goes to the timber beam span, a crossing type that is perhaps the oldest bridge structure known to history. Indeed, simply felling a tree and positioning it over a stream makes a timber beam-span bridge. As settlement in Minnesota increased, dropping tree trunks across streams or rivers gave way to more refined beam spans, although most were still crude by today's standards. Often resting on a substructure of timber piles driven into the earth or riverbed, many early beam spans presented a somewhat perilous profile. An example was located at Detroit Lakes. History seems to recognize the structure simply as the Canal Bridge, but it is uncertain what canal it crossed and when precisely it was constructed. Nevertheless, it is a good representation of the modest timber beam spans found in many parts of Minnesota in the mid- to late nineteenth century.[6]

Timber beam spans are still constructed, but they are often located on hiking, bicycle, and snowmobile trails. In the first half of the twentieth century, the Minnesota Department of Highways erected many timber beam spans to carry automobiles as well, even though timber was not widely embraced as a building material for highway bridges by this time. Northern Minnesota was the recipient of a large number of timber beam spans. The early twentieth century found northern Minnesota undergoing substantial settlement, and the state was forced to rapidly complete a transportation infrastructure. In a region flush with timber, it is not surprising that the state helped solve its construction needs by employing timber structures. Still, timber highway bridges were usually a second choice as the state almost always demanded steel or reinforced-concrete crossings when practicable.[7]

While they were never as common as in northern Minnesota, timber beam-span highway bridges still occasionally were erected in the southern part of the state. One example is still standing just west of the Twin Cities on a road that accommodates ever-increasing traffic. Located immediately north of the community of Maple in Carver County, Bridge No. 5837 carries County State Aid Highway 10 over a former route of the Burlington Northern Railroad (BN). Although the design was subject to the approval of the state, engineering drawings for the bridge were completed by the Great Northern Railway, which became part of the BN in 1970. The bridge was constructed in 1939 by Fielding and Shepley, a St. Paul contracting company founded by Michael F. Fielding and Louis E. Shepley in 1893. Interestingly, it appears that this was one of the last bridges constructed by the firm, or at least one of the last bridges built under the founding moniker.[8]

In the first half of the twentieth century, timber beam-span bridges were not a favorite of the Minnesota Department of Highways. However, the crossing type was still occasionally built, such as this extant structure near Maple erected in 1939. *Photograph taken in 2005.*

The oldest remaining timber bridge in Minnesota, the Zumbrota Covered Bridge graduated from stagecoaches and wagons to early automobiles. Erected in 1869, the bridge now carries pedestrians over the North Fork of the Zumbro River in Zumbrota. *Photograph taken in 2005 by Robert W. Gardner Jr.*

The timber bridge north of Maple was part of the Railroad Grade Separation Program as established in the Emergency Relief Appropriations Act of 1935. The purpose of this program was to eliminate many of the nation's dangerous railroad-roadway intersections. This was usually accomplished by elevating the roadway over the rail line. Part of the funding for building the timber bridge over the rail line near Maple came from the Public Works Administration (PWA). The PWA was a federal relief initiative of President Franklin Roosevelt. Federal relief efforts were a staple of Roosevelt's New Deal policy for America. The farsighted chief executive understood that pouring federal dollars into government programs, including transportation infrastructure

projects, was a means of salving a nation suffering the economic wounds of the Great Depression. Numerous improvement endeavors received federal dollars and millions of unemployed entered the workforce through government initiatives like the Civilian Conservation Corps, Civil Works Administration, National Youth Administration, Works Progress Administration, and, of course, the PWA. Although the Great Depression was one of the most economically wrenching periods in America's history, it was also an era of unrivaled infrastructural development.[9]

The timber bridge near Maple was but one Minnesota bridge project that received federal aid under Roosevelt's New Deal. In fact, scores of Minnesota

Perhaps the only railroad covered bridge completed in Minnesota, this bridge was erected by the Duluth, Red Wing and Southern Railroad over the North Fork of the Zumbro River not far from Zumbrota. *Photograph ca. 1900; courtesy of the Goodhue County Historical Society, Red Wing, Minnesota.*

bridges erected during the 1930s and early 1940s were a result of federal relief efforts. Many of these are especially handsome, a hallmark characteristic of federal relief bridges. The timber beam span near Maple is an exception, however. Although its railings of metal pipes and concrete posts hold some visual interest, the bridge mostly looks ordinary.

This trait in no way applies to the oldest wood bridge remaining in Minnesota. Completed in 1869, Minnesota's only extant covered bridge spans the North Fork of the Zumbro River in the small town of Zumbrota in Goodhue County. The intriguing Zumbrota Covered Bridge was not always singular, however. By the 1880s, Minnesota featured a handful of covered bridges. A covered wagon bridge was situated near a mill above Vermillion Falls on the Vermillion River in the community of Hastings. Another covered wagon bridge spanned the Root River in the tiny town of Whalan, only a few miles east of Lanesboro. Yet another covered wagon bridge was located at Waite's Crossing, a popular Sauk River crossing point near St. Cloud that was named for Henry Chester Waite, a prominent St. Cloud personality with a large farm near the bridge site. At least some of Waite's farm eventually became part of the community of Waite Park, adjacent to St. Cloud. Minnesota had at least one railroad covered bridge as well. Constructed by the Duluth, Red Wing and Southern Railroad, it was positioned over the North Fork of the Zumbro River not far northwest of Zumbrota.[10]

The American covered bridge finds its origins in the northeastern part of the country. Timothy Palmer, Ithiel Town, Squire Whipple, Theodore Burr, William Howe, Stephen H. Long, and Thomas and Caleb Pratt all hailed from the region. All were early designers of wood bridges, many as covered structures. Interestingly, some of these designers would become better recognized for their bridge designs in iron and steel.

Wood covered bridges are often thought romantic, sometimes even romantically macabre, as confirmed by Henry Wadsworth Longfellow in *The Golden Legend*, "The grave itself is but a covered bridge, leading from light to light, through a brief darkness." Romantic notions were largely secondary for these early bridge designers, however. Since wood bridges rarely survive for many years, Timothy Palmer, Ithiel Town, and the rest realized that encapsulating a bridge's timber

support structure within a shell substantially increased the useful life of the bridge.[11]

The timber support structure is a truss. A truss is merely a framework of diagonal, vertical, and horizontal structural members that are primarily in tension or compression. The members can be of virtually any material, although wood, iron, and steel are common. In essence, this framework acts like a beam, similar to a beam for a timber beam-span bridge. Trusses became popular because they could span greater distances than beam-span bridges. Put another way, they could reach farther over a waterway, railway line, or roadway before requiring substructure support. This is important when the number of piers at a bridge site must be limited, such as a site spanning a navigable waterway. Most trusses are either high trusses or low trusses. In Minnesota, high trusses are often referenced as through trusses and low trusses as pony trusses. With a through-truss bridge, the members that make up the truss encompass the entire roadway or railway, but with a pony-truss bridge, structural members are not positioned overhead. There are many variations of these trusses, since early bridge designers continually sought to produce examples better than their competition.

Historically, one of the most common types of trusses employed for wood covered bridges has been the Town lattice, named for its designer, Ithiel Town. Born in 1784, Town was an architect from New Haven, Connecticut. He patented the Town lattice truss in 1820. Town was not a bridge builder, however, preferring instead to promote and sell rights to build his design. This remarkably simple design consists of many intersecting diagonal wood planks. In other words, the web, which is that portion of a truss between the top and bottom chords, resembles a lattice. The lattice truss was relatively easy to build, but it had a tendency to warp because of the thinness of the web and its lack of posts. Town solved the problem by doubling the web. Basically, he created a lattice behind a lattice, for which he was awarded a patent in 1835.[12]

Not surprisingly, the 120-foot-long Zumbrota Covered Bridge is a Town lattice. Curiously, it features vertical posts. Perhaps the posts were added at a later date to provide additional support. The covered bridge replaced a timber beam span that was erected at the site in 1857 to facilitate stagecoach traffic between

Dubuque, Iowa, and St. Paul. The bridge often required repair, however, so in 1869 a carpenter-member of the Strafford Western Emigration Company, an enterprise established by New England immigrants that founded Zumbrota in the mid-1850s, constructed the current covered bridge. While the truss was completed in 1869, it was not encapsulated with a gable roof and board-and-batten siding until 1871.[13]

The bridge carried stagecoach, wagon, and eventually automobile traffic over the river at Zumbrota until 1932, when the state highway department completed a new bridge at the site. The Zumbrota Covered Bridge was moved to the Goodhue County Fairgrounds, serving as an exhibit and storage building. It is possible that the vertical posts were installed in the truss at this time, perhaps to ensure the structure's cohesiveness during the move. By 1970 the bridge was looking grim, but the Zumbrota Covered Bridge Society spearheaded a drive to relocate the bridge to a park near its original site and rehabilitate it. The unique structure remained in the park until 1997, when it was moved a short distance south and once again placed over the North Fork of the Zumbro River, near its initial location. Now serving as a pedestrian crossing, the bridge's appearance is largely unchanged from its original construction, although today it rests atop steel girders.[14]

In 1870, just a year after the truss was finished at Zumbrota, the Northern Pacific Railway (NP) began its long construction journey from Carlton, immediately southwest of Duluth, to the Pacific Coast. Minnesota had witnessed modest railroad construction during the previous decade, but the NP inaugurated a period of phenomenal railroad development. By the early 1900s, the state would be a dense network of rail lines. With the rail lines came countless bridges. Minnesota's history is filled with many interesting examples, including one erected over America's most famous river by the NP.[15]

It took the NP until 1883 to reach the Pacific, but its

The Zumbrota Covered Bridge employs Ithiel Town's lattice design. *Photograph taken in 2005 by Robert W. Gardner Jr.*

bridge across the Mississippi River in central Minnesota was completed only a year after the railroad initiated construction at Carlton. The infant community established at the bridge site was simply called The Crossing, but it was soon rechristened Brainerd. The bridge the NP raised at Brainerd was a large timber truss, but not a Town lattice. Instead, the NP erected a Howe truss, the most popular type of truss bridge for railroad lines in the last half of the nineteenth century. Many large roadway bridges erected during this period were also Howe trusses, such as the bridge "all on the oblique and very awkward" that was raised over the Mississippi River at Wabasha Street in St. Paul.[16]

The Howe truss was named for its creator, William Howe. Howe was a millwright born in Spencer, Massachusetts, in 1803. Although he received a patent for his truss type in 1840, his design was almost identical in appearance to a wood-truss design produced by Colonel Stephen H. Long. Long's early career was as a mathematics instructor at Dartmouth College, but he ultimately proved an adventuresome spirit and became a

The bridge the Northern Pacific Railway erected over the Mississippi River at Brainerd in 1871 was a Howe truss, America's most common railroad truss type in the last half of the nineteenth century. *Photograph by William Henry Illingworth, ca. 1873; courtesy of the Minnesota Historical Society.*

topographical engineer. In 1817, under orders of the War Department, he ascended the Mississippi River from St. Louis in search of a suitable location for a military post. He soon found the perfect site, an elevation overlooking the junction of the Minnesota and Mississippi rivers. Here Fort Snelling was erected in 1819, although at that time it was named Fort St. Anthony. Long returned to Minnesota in 1823, exploring up the Minnesota River to the Red River Valley. Seven years later, he patented his timber truss, which he subsequently improved. After Howe developed his similar truss design, Long became incensed and claimed patent infringement. Little seems to have come of it.[17]

Essentially, the Howe truss was a rectangle with webs formed of a multitude of crossed diagonals in compression, interrupted by vertical members in tension. While the truss designs created by Howe and Long took up load stresses differently, it was the material of the vertical members that most obviously distinguished Howe's truss from Long's. Long employed timber verticals, but Howe used iron verticals. The latter realized that iron was better than wood at absorbing tensile stresses. Additionally, the turnbuckles and bolts that were part of the iron tension members allowed the verticals to be adjusted as the truss's timber components seasoned. Howe's design represents a step toward all-metal truss-bridge construction, and he is considered one of the prominent personalities in the history of bridge design.[18]

The Howe truss at Brainerd was one of the first structures completed during the NP's massive construction program of the early 1870s. In effect, the railroad began building the community of Brainerd by erecting its economic foundation, a large complex of maintenance shops designed to maintain the line's rolling stock. As operating and engineering headquarters for the entire line, Brainerd became a magnet for those seeking employment with the NP. In turn, others established commercial enterprises to serve the rapidly growing town's citizens. Regrettably, good times in Brainerd did not last long, as Jay Cooke and Company, the financial muscle behind the NP, failed in 1873, leading to a national financial crisis. Work on the NP's route toward Puget Sound came to a halt, as did most work at Brainerd. Eventually, the financial outlook for the country and the NP improved, but not before the

railroad and the citizens of Brainerd suffered another setback. On July 27, 1875, the substantial timber bridge over the Mississippi River collapsed, taking an engine, tender, caboose, and over twenty cars with it. Sadly, several people on the train died, including the engineer and the fireman.[19] The day of the accident, the front page of the *St. Paul Daily Dispatch* announced, "Down to the Death on Northern Pacific: Bridge over Mississippi Gives Way at Brainerd." The story read:

Shortly after nine o'clock this morning a dispatch was received at the office in this city of General Manager Mead, of the N. P. R. R. which stated that the west bound freight train, No. 5, which left Brainerd at 7:45 A.M. had gone through the bridge over the Mississippi river and that several persons had been killed.... [It was] a wooden truss ... 622 feet in length and 80 feet above the level of the river. It was built in the summer of 1871 by the Northwestern Construction Company, and was supposed to be one of the costliest of the structures along the line. The fact that it has played out in less than five years is conclusive proof that it was originally either imperfectly constructed or that the material used therein was unfit for the purpose and should not have been allowed.

The failure of the bridge at Brainerd was not altogether extraordinary, since many Howe trusses gave way during the major railroad construction period of the mid- to late 1800s. Still, it is unlikely that the material employed for building these trusses was unfit for the purpose or that there was an inherent flaw in Howe's design. In truth, most Howe trusses failed because of poor construction, a subject addressed by bridge historian David Plowden in his popular *Bridges: The Spans of North America*: "The tremendous demand for new [Howe] bridges placed increasing emphasis on speed of construction. Quality often suffered, and with alarming frequency bridges would come tumbling down.... Most of these catastrophes were due to faulty construction rather than to any inadequacy in Howe's design." The NP soon replaced its crossing over the Mississippi River with a truss made entirely of iron, a type of construction that was just beginning to gain acceptance for bridge building in Minnesota at that time.[20]

A variant of the timber truss the NP built at Brainerd in summer 1871 was erected at Carver later that year. Carver sits on the banks of the Minnesota River about twenty-five miles southwest of the heart of Minneapolis, although it is currently being enveloped by a

The Northern Pacific Railway's bridge at Brainerd collapsed in 1875. Howe trusses failed at an alarming rate, but these bridge failures had less to do with Howe's design than with railroad companies rushing bridge construction so the rail line could quickly be pushed forward. *Photograph by Caswell and Davy, 1875; courtesy of the Minnesota Historical Society.*

The timber-truss bridge across the Minnesota River at Carver was an arched swing span. Apparently the M&StL concluded that an arched top chord rather than a horizontal top chord was best suited for the stresses placed on a swing-span bridge. A swing span is a type of movable bridge with a main span that pivots atop a central pier. This type of bridge was important on the Minnesota River during much of the nineteenth century because the waterway was navigable—that is, the waterway was plied by freight-carrying vessels. To allow ships to move from one side of the bridge to the other, the main span was rotated, or swung, out of the way.[22]

Downstream of Carver, the Milwaukee and St. Paul Railway featured a virtually identical bridge at the foot of Fort Snelling. It was completed about four or five years before the crossing at Carver. In 1874, the Milwaukee and St. Paul Railway became the Chicago, Milwaukee, and St. Paul Railway, which history has commonly recognized as the Milwaukee Road. Its timber bridge below Fort Snelling was eventually replaced with a steel swing span. It is unclear precisely how long Carver retained its arched timber-truss swing span, but by the early 1890s it had been replaced by a trussed swing span formed of iron or steel. This bridge also no longer exists, but another railroad bridge presently reaches over the Minnesota River at the site. Surprisingly, perhaps, two of the stone piers original to the 1871 bridge are still standing, adding substructure support to the current bridge.[23]

A year after the M&StL passed through Carver, the Hastings and Dakota Railway (H&D) followed. This railroad began its existence in 1857 as the Hastings, Minnesota River and Red River of the North Railroad, but ten years later it had evolved into the H&D. It was as the H&D that it initiated construction of rail lines. Its purpose was to link the agriculturally fertile areas just to the south, southwest, and west of Minneapolis and St. Paul with eastern markets via Hastings. Adjacent to the Mississippi River, about fifteen miles southeast of St. Paul, Hastings had been a major milling and grain distribution center almost from its founding as a village in 1853. Wheat arriving in Hastings by wagon from the surrounding region was milled, stored, and shipped downriver by steamboat. But the community's livelihood was threatened in the mid-1860s with the construction of the Minnesota Central Railway from

sprawling Twin Cities metropolitan area. For most of its existence, however, it was a small, rural community. The timber-truss bridge over the Minnesota River at Carver was erected by the Minneapolis and St. Louis Railway (M&StL), a company that began as the Minnesota Western Railroad in 1853. Like all of the other railroads incorporated in Minnesota in the 1850s, dreams were larger than financial reality allowed, and the Minnesota Western never laid any trackage during the decade. Nor did it build any trackage the following decade, remaining merely a paper railroad. Finally, in 1871, soon after the company became the M&StL, it started construction. One of the railroad's principal aims was to reach the southern and eastern parts of the country via St. Louis. It accomplished this by building southwest from Minneapolis before swinging southward over the Minnesota River at Carver. It intersected the St. Paul and Sioux City Railroad at Sioux City Junction (renamed Merriam Junction in 1875) a few miles southwest of Shakopee in late 1871. Toward the end of the decade, the line reached Albert Lea, where it merged with the Burlington, Cedar Rapids and Northern Railway, a line that connected to St. Louis and Chicago.[21]

Completed over the Minnesota River by the Minneapolis and St. Louis Railway in 1871, the timber bridge at Carver was an arched swing span, a movable bridge type that rotated, or swung, open to allow steamboats to pass from one side of the bridge to the other. *Photograph taken in 1871; courtesy of the Minnesota Historical Society.*

The timber railroad bridge erected by the Milwaukee and St. Paul Railway over the Minnesota River below Fort Snelling was almost identical to the bridge completed at Carver some years later. Note the open swing span. *Photograph ca. 1885; courtesy of the Minnesota Historical Society.*

Minneapolis and St. Paul south toward the Iowa border. This line absorbed much of the agricultural largesse once destined for Hastings. As a result, leaders in Hastings founded the H&D as a competitor to the Minnesota Central, ensuring the agricultural relevancy of the river town.[24]

Between 1867 and 1872, the H&D built its line from Hastings to Carver to Glencoe. As construction moved westward from Hastings, it quickly reached the Vermillion River. The bridge the H&D completed over the rocky gorge was a timber pony truss. A pony truss was acceptable at the site because the H&D erected a substantial substructure at either end of the bridge. A simple crossing, the Vermillion River Bridge was nevertheless pleasing sitting atop this towering foundation formed of a timber framework. It was completed

The Hastings and Dakota Railway built a timber pony truss across the bluffs of the Vermillion River in Hastings in 1868. The train in the photograph may be the John B. Alley, the railroad's first engine. *Photograph by Benjamin F. Upton, ca. 1870; courtesy of the Minnesota Historical Society.*

in 1868, a short time before the company's first railroad engine was placed in service. In mid-October 1868, the John B. Alley made its maiden run of roughly one mile from Hastings to the Vermillion River Bridge, where it met a host of local children waiting excitedly for a promised ride back into town.[25]

Although the H&D opted for a pony truss with a substantial timber-frame substructure, the railroad could have completed a through-truss bridge that would have reached farther over the Vermillion River and may have required a less extensive foundation. Even more, the H&D could have erected a deck truss, a truss type less common than pony or through trusses, yet suited to site conditions like those found at the Vermillion River at Hastings. A deck truss is much like a through truss, except the truss is below the bridge's deck rather than above it. In appearance,

then, a deck truss is the reverse of a through truss. A deck truss is only practical at sites with substantial vertical clearance between the lower chord of the truss and the high-water mark of a river; if a deck truss will obstruct a river, there is little point in erecting this type of bridge. Because there was considerable clearance at the Vermillion River at Hastings, the timber pony truss erected by the H&D was eventually replaced with a timber deck truss. It appears that the change came around 1880, but well before this the H&D had sold its Hastings–Glencoe route to the Milwaukee Road. The Milwaukee Road sheathed the bridge's webs in a wood covering, ostensibly to help protect the timber truss from the elements. The curious-looking bridge was gone by the turn of the twentieth century, when a metal-girder crossing occupied the site.[26]

A timber deck truss without the jacket was completed across the gorge of the Pigeon River in Cook County in 1917. As with the timber bridge at Brainerd, the Pigeon River Bridge linking northeastern Minnesota with Ontario, Canada, reflected William Howe's design. Built to carry automobile traffic, the roughly 110-foot-long Pigeon River Bridge was an especially late Howe truss, for by the early twentieth century, bridge designs in steel were already commonplace. A Howe truss was likely adopted because the bridge site was located within timber country. Moreover, the crossing was not sanctioned by either Minnesota or Ontario, so it is unlikely that government specifications ruled the design process. The bridge was born out of frustration, as exasperated citizens and commercial interests on either side of the border grew weary of waiting for Minnesota and Ontario to erect a bridge to join the two sides. A partnership that included the Lakehead Rotarians on the Canadian side and the Duluth Rotary Club on the American side, as well as Cook County, pooled funds for constructing the bridge.[27]

Locally known as the Outlaw Bridge, apparently because the structure was not officially authorized, the crossing's formal opening on August 18, 1917, was a gala affair. The bridge was festooned with flags and bunting as more than 250 Canadians, including a band of pipers, traversed the structure en route to celebrations in Grand Marais. The cavalcade paused to mingle with Americans at the bridge site and survey what everyone's efforts wrought. Surely anxious glances were cast at the

The crossing that replaced the pony truss at the Vermillion River was probably completed by the Milwaukee Road about 1880. It was a deck truss sheathed in timber siding. *Photograph by Henry Hamilton Bennett, ca. 1880; courtesy of the Minnesota Historical Society.*

The Pigeon River Bridge (Outlaw Bridge) was not officially sanctioned by either the American or Canadian governments. Nevertheless, in 1917, local groups on both sides of the border pooled resources to build a bridge joining Minnesota with Ontario. *Photograph ca. 1920; courtesy of the Minnesota Historical Society.*

steeply-inclined ramps at either end of the crossing, as revelers contemplated the coming adventure of winter travel over the Pigeon River. Bridge-building funds had been limited, however, so the pitched ramps were a cost-effective substitute to gently rising approaches. Minnesota and Ontario assumed control of the bridge not long after it was finished. It was razed in favor of a steel through truss in 1930.[28]

Those on opposing sides of the Pigeon River were hardly the first to seek a union, a tangible connection with others not part of their immediate communities. Three decades earlier, the tiny town of Kenyon became significantly tethered to the rest of the world with the arrival of the Minnesota and North Western Railroad (M&NW).[29] Kenyon, located in southwestern Goodhue

County, south of the Twin Cities metropolitan area and about fifteen miles west of Zumbrota, became part of the railroad set on September 23, 1885:

They strained to hear. Some knelt down beside the tracks to hear the vibration of the wheels against the steel rails. Then far off in the distance they could hear the faint sound of a whistle. The sound kept getting louder. Finally the little steam engine could be seen chugging across the high wooden trestle bridge spanning the [North Fork of] the Zumbro River north of town.... A cheer went up from the crowd and men waved their hats. It was an exciting and historic moment. The first passenger train to arrive in Kenyon pulled up to the station.... A new day had dawned for the little hamlet.[30]

The "high wooden trestle bridge" was a substantial structure that not only spanned the North Fork of the Zumbro River but also the valley bisected by the waterway. A timber trestle is formed of a framework of timber bents. A bent is a collection of generally vertical timber piles or posts topped with a horizontal timber cap and usually bound together by diagonal timber planks, which provide bracing. Sometimes bracing also extends longitudinally between the outside piles of adjacent bents. Timber stringers rest atop the bents and support the railroad ties that carry the metal rails. Historically, timber trestles have been immensely popular with railroads.

The M&NW became the Chicago, St. Paul and Kansas City Railway (CStP&KC) in late 1887, about two years after Kenyon's eight-hundred-foot-long timber trestle was completed. Six years after that, the Chicago Great Western Railway (CGW) gained control of the CStP&KC. In 1898, the CGW filled in the entire Kenyon trestle bridge with earth, while installing a stone culvert to carry the river through the earthen embankment created from the fill. A large timber-trestle bridge can still be found at Kenyon today, but it is not the one buried in the embankment and it never belonged to the CGW. Measuring roughly three hundred feet in length, the timber trestle of the Milwaukee Road spans a pasture at the eastern side of the small town. The trestle was completed during the first decade of the twentieth century, when the Milwaukee Road built a branch through Kenyon. Eventually the Milwaukee Road stopped passing through the Goodhue County community, as did the town's major railroad line, the CGW. The Milwaukee Road trestle bridge slowly deteriorates, but

The large timber-trestle bridge at Kenyon was built over the North Fork of the Zumbro River by the Minnesota and North Western Railroad about 1885, but the structure was buried in earth fill in 1898 by the Chicago Great Western Railway. *Photograph by George P. Nelson, ca. 1890; courtesy of the Goodhue County Historical Society, Red Wing, Minnesota.*

The extant timber trestle at the east side of Kenyon was constructed by the Milwaukee Road during the first decade of the twentieth century. *Photograph taken in 2006.*

it remains one of the few visual reminders of the days when large timber trestles were once commonplace in parts of Minnesota.[31]

Perhaps timber trestles are unique wood bridges because the railroads never allowed them to fall entirely from fashion. Sure, the large ones are mostly gone, or have been replaced piece by piece with metal members, but perusing railroad tracks today often leads to the small ones. These, too, have largely been replaced piece by piece over the years, but with timber members. The route of the current Dakota, Minnesota and Eastern Railroad across southern Minnesota, a line originally constructed by the Winona and St. Peter Railroad in the late 1800s, is an example of a rail line that continues to feature many minor timber trestles.

The most fantastic-looking timber bridge to ever punctuate Minnesota was not a timber trestle or even a timber truss, although it was a covered bridge. Even today, wood bridges are common to park settings, and the crossing erected by John Busha was hosted by just such a venue. Completed in 1898, Busha's pedestrian bridge decorated Duluth's Lester Park northeast of downtown. Resembling a pagoda, the structure is identified in history annals as the Lester Park Rustic Bridge. It replaced a footbridge over some Lester River rapids that washed out about 1896 or 1897. Part French and part Ojibwe, Busha was a Civil War veteran who recruited his sons, Abraham and George, to help him build the picturesque structure. Formed of peeled cedar, Busha erected the bridge with two levels. The bottom level carried foot traffic over the river, but it also held picnic tables. The top level was a promenade punctuated at its center by a pavilion with a flagpole. On warm days, Duluthians would lounge atop the bridge or peek

over its railings at the rapids below. The bridge was especially busy on summer holidays. Busha, drawing on his Indian heritage, formed numerous Ojibwe designs in the bridge's railings, dramatically enhancing the crossing's aesthetic allure. Regrettably, the top portion of the bridge was in such poor condition by the second decade of the twentieth century that it was removed. The remainder of the crossing was razed in 1931. Minnesota has yet to witness another wood bridge that matches the artistic sophistication of Busha's structure in Lester Park.[32]

The heyday of wood bridge construction in Minnesota was exceedingly brief. Minnesota became a state in 1858, and when settlement exploded in the 1870s and 1880s, demanding numerous bridges, many were formed entirely of metal. Even so, this development was more than two decades behind the East, which had been welcoming metal crossings as early as the 1840s. Minnesotans were not naïve, however, and many understood that wood could not match metal as a bridge-building material. It simply required a little time for the engineering and construction conventions in the East to move west. But when it finally arrived, Minnesotan's embraced the new convention and filled the state with almost every manner of bridge that could be raised in iron or steel.[33]

STONE

BRIDGES

Yesterday ... [Thomas M. Griffith] gave satisfaction to crowds in Minneapolis, now become a city numbering forty thousand inhabitants, by opening for travel a magnificent suspension bridge more glorious than the first, whose place it has taken by aid of what Milton calls the "wondrous art pontifical." From this time forward the structure becomes historic, and the prominent object in the city. It will be associated with all the varying emotions of humanity. The commercial man will recall it with its long line of wagons bearing the products of our various manufactories. Some will have it photographed upon their brain in connection with the slow-moving funeral cortege, bearing parent or child to the last earthly resting places. The placid man of a midsummer's night will hear ascending from its footwalks the whisper of a true lover's heart in some gentle maiden's ear, and see her shy, drooped, modest face. Not many years will roll by before it will become a "Bridge of Sighs," and in a whirl of passion or despair some poor unfortunate, unwilling to fade and rot ... will plunge from its parapets into the roaring waters of the Falls of Saint Anthony.

—"Griffith, Pontifex," *Minneapolis Tribune*, February 23, 1877

Newspapers in late-nineteenth-century Minnesota, as in many places, welcomed florid prose. Even while describing transportation infrastructure, journalists longed for the romantic. Perhaps the poetic voice of the *Minneapolis Tribune* passage quoted as the epigraph of this section is understandable, for by 1877, Minneapolis had traded its frontier fortress spanning the Mississippi River for a quixotic medieval castle.

At least by 1873, Minneapolis, a community with a fading memory of its squatter origins, wanted a new bridge over the Mississippi River at Hennepin Avenue. Two years later, the city awarded construction of the crossing to George McMullen, a contractor based in the Twin Cities whom the *Minneapolis Tribune* referred to as a "master mason." McMullen agreed to erect a stone suspension bridge designed by Thomas Griffith, the same New York engineer responsible for the wood suspension bridge completed in 1854. Perhaps it seems odd that only two decades after it opened the wood suspension bridge was thought obsolete, but Minneapolis was growing quickly by the mid-1870s and had recently swallowed the community of St. Anthony as proof of this maturation. Traffic between St. Anthony and Minneapolis was hindered by the modest dimensions of the wood crossing, and the wood bridge, barely above flood stage, was annually threatened by spring flows.[1]

George McMullen had just begun to quarry stone for the new bridge when the city council halted the work. Minneapolis paused to reconsider the structure's design: did the community need another suspension bridge? The city pondered erecting an arch bridge made of iron, but the pondering eventually gave way to the original stone suspension bridge design. The crossing was completed in early 1877, although not before the bridge was almost lost to fire in January of that year. The roadway surface was made of pine blocks set on end within a sludge-like coating of oil that had been smeared over the deck substructure while warm. As a kettle of boiling oil was carried onto the deck to cool, it was upset and spread over several feet of the untreated wood deck, igniting a blaze. Fortunately, a workman managed to push the kettle over the edge of the bridge onto the ice, while other laborers smothered the fire with their coats.[2]

Costing about $200,000, the finished bridge looked like something out of a fairy tale. Raised well above the river, it measured about 670 feet in length, with a width of 20 feet. The 111-foot-high limestone towers, roughly twice as high as the towers erected for the wood suspension bridge, resembled castle battlements. Indeed, an observer may almost have expected King Arthur and his knights to ride through the arched opening of either tower. The crossing, larger than its forerunner, operated in the same manner as the wood suspension bridge: large cables draped between the towers held smaller cables that supported the wood deck. Again, the larger cables were buried into anchorages at either end of the bridge.[3]

An incredible structure to behold, the second suspension bridge at Minneapolis, like the first, was an exception in Minnesota. Furthermore, the vast majority of stone bridges in Minnesota, as elsewhere, sprung from an arch, a graceful structural form common to the ancient world. The Romans erected countless semicircular arches, which explains why this arch type is also known as a Roman arch. An arch works through arch action: The vertical forces of a load moving over an arch bridge are transferred through the arch and into the abutments at either end of the arch. The arch is resisting the forces of the load moving over it by pressing against its abutments—that is, the arch is pushing back. The arch is found in other structures besides bridges, of course; numerous buildings incorporate arches of one kind or another. Dams are also sometimes formed from an arch. The Lanesboro Stone Dam in southern Minnesota, for instance, is an arch that has been resisting the hydrostatic forces of the South Branch of the Root River for almost a century and a half.[4]

Generally, stone arch bridges, both highway and railroad, have been thought somewhat rare in America; not as rare as stone-towered suspension bridges, certainly, but infrequent nevertheless. Prominent historian Carl W. Condit provides the reasoning for this view: "The arch bridge of stone has always been a costly type, with the consequence that in the United States, where wages are high and materials abundant, the form has never been as popular as it has been in Europe."[5] This argument is reinforced by bridge historian David Plowden:

One of the most visually impressive bridges ever raised in Minnesota, the second crossing at Hennepin Avenue in Minneapolis was a suspension span harkening to the medieval. Completed in 1877, the bridge was engineered by Thomas Musgrove Griffith, the same engineer who designed the first suspension bridge at the site. *Photograph by William H. Jacoby, ca. 1887; courtesy of the Minnesota Historical Society.*

Psychologically Americans were as temperamentally unsuited to build with stone as it was economically unfeasible for them to do so. Stone bridges are by nature strong and require little or no maintenance. Their disadvantage is the time it takes to build them, piece by piece, each stone needing to be quarried, dressed and individually fitted.... With few exceptions, impatient America [did not] take the time to lay up a stone bridge where an alternative was available.[6]

The stone arch bridge has not only been thought rare in this country, but its construction is believed to have mostly ceased by the end of the nineteenth century. Interestingly, it now appears that stone arch bridge building was not as rare as initially believed and,

at least in certain regions of the country, the erection of a surprising number of stone arch roadway bridges has been found to antedate the turn of the twentieth century. Historian Jeffrey A. Hess explains, "[The] traditional view of American masonry-arch bridge construction has been challenged ... by statewide, historic, highway bridge surveys in Pennsylvania and Wisconsin.... The authors of the Pennsylvania report declare: 'Although both nineteenth- and twentieth-century bridge historians have stated that early stone masonry structures are poorly represented in America, this survey revealed a large number of early stone arch [roadway] bridges.'" Hess also notes that the studies in

Erected over Garvin Brook near Stockton in Winona County in 1882, the Arches, a double arch completed by the Winona and St. Peter Railroad, is one of the finest stone arches remaining in Minnesota. *Photograph ca. 1905; courtesy of the Minnesota Historical Society.*

Wisconsin and Pennsylvania demonstrated that many of the bridges surveyed were built early in the twentieth century. In fact, subsequent study of Minnesota's stone arch roadway bridges also revealed that many were raised during the first part of the 1900s. Still, this is not to say that most stone arch roadway bridges in America were built after the turn of the twentieth century. Moreover, stone arch roadway bridges never dotted the landscape like the metal bridges and reinforced-concrete crossings that followed. Even so, some findings suggest that historians may wish to revisit commonly accepted notions about stone arch bridge building in America.[7]

Our understanding of stone arch bridge history is shaped, at least in part, by the railroads. Without doubt, the majority of stone arch bridges were erected by railroads. In large measure, this came about because the railroads often had more money than the local governments responsible for erecting wagon or automobile bridges; as both Condit and Plowden observed, stone arches are not cheap. Further, the railroads needed bridges that could support the weight of a railroad engine and train, and stone arches are quite strong. The railroads were practical, however, often completing relatively strong bridges out of cheaper building material like wood or metal. Still, the practical railroad recognized the cost-benefit of discovering stone building material in the vicinity of a bridge site.[8]

As with stone arches built on roadways, it seems most of the railroad stone arches were likely completed before the twentieth century. But, again, it is somewhat surprising to discover that a significant number of stone arches were also erected in the early part of the 1900s. For example, the Winona and St. Peter Railroad (W&StP) completed many stone arches on its line bisecting southern Minnesota en route to South Dakota. By the beginning of the twentieth-first century, seventeen of these bridges were extant, and just over half had been built during the first two decades of the twentieth century. While many of these twentieth-century bridges are quite handsome, such as the finely-crafted Bridge No. 540 at Lamberton in Redwood County, the most impressive stone arch crossing on the line remains the Arches, a nineteenth-century double arch spanning Garvin Brook.[9]

The Arches was constructed in 1882 near Stockton in southeastern Minnesota's Winona County, one of the

Although foliage has grown up around it, the Arches looks as if it could stand for another century or more, but its future may be threatened by redevelopment of the rail line. *Photograph taken in 2005 by Robert W. Gardner Jr.*

most picturesque parts of the state. The bridge replaced a timber railroad trestle that was built on the site several years earlier by the W&StP. The W&StP was formed in 1862 to connect the fertile lands of southern Minnesota and South Dakota to Winona, thus opening western markets for the Mississippi River community. By the time the limestone crossing was built, however, the W&StP was owned by the Chicago and North Western Railway (C&NW). Although the C&NW acquired the W&StP in 1867, the W&StP continued to operate under its own corporate name into the early 1900s.[10]

The Arches blends harmoniously into a verdant landscape framed by limestone bluffs and outcroppings. The bridge was part of a larger improvement project the W&StP initiated in the 1880s, replacing a number of its faltering timber trestles with stone arches. Facilitating this effort was Stockton Quarry, which was located a short distance west of the Arches bridge site. Stone harvested from the quarry was delivered to the construction site by a railroad engine and flatcar. Masons carved the stone into wedge-shaped blocks, commonly known as voussoirs. Wedged together, the voussoirs formed the barrel of each arch. The keystone at the crown of the arch ring on the south side of the westernmost arch was embellished with the date 1882. The spandrel, which is the space above and between the arches, was filled with earth and other materials. In essence, the tops of the arches and the stone sidewalls, or spandrel walls, served as a basin, within which earth was poured. Atop this fill material, the railroad laid its tracks. Historically, this filled-spandrel construction has been the most common way to build an arch bridge.[11]

Regrettably, the Arches, having decorated the landscape of southeastern Minnesota for more than 120 years, is now threatened with demolition, as are some of the other arches on the old W&StP line across southern Minnesota. Recent interests wishing to rehabilitate the railroad route apparently do not believe that many of the arch bridges are important to the continuation of the line.[12]

While potential demolition looms for one of Winona County's structural icons, there is no such threat to a stone arch crossing in Minneapolis that was completed only one year after the Arches. Simply known as the Stone Arch Bridge, the structure is one of the most fantastic stone arches in America. Along with the immense Richardsonian Romanesque–style mansion on Summit Avenue in St. Paul, the Stone Arch Bridge serves as a monument to James J. Hill and his Great Northern Railway (GN). Plowden acknowledges the magnificence of what Hill accomplished in the Stone Arch Bridge:

With the crossing of the Mississippi River just below St. Anthony's Falls … Hill built a bridge in the manner of a triumphal arch. This is the Great Stone Bridge [Stone Arch Bridge], a tour de force in every sense of the word. For the last 817 feet of its western end, the bridge is constructed on a sweeping six-degree curve. The problem of building a masonry bridge on such a curve was almost without precedents.… Doubtful engineers tried to dissuade Hill from attempting it. A bridge like that would never sustain the required load, they said. But Hill, encouraged by Colonel Charles C. Smith, who was to direct the work … remained adamant. Years later, the man whose life was filled with achievements, admitted "the hardest undertaking I ever had to face was the building of the Great Stone Arch Bridge."[13]

Hill's crossing was completed a short distance downriver of Thomas Griffith's second Hennepin Avenue Bridge, and it is the only stone arch bridge to span any part of the Mississippi River. The two impressive crossings must have wowed visitors to late-nineteenth-century Minneapolis, a city that was not yet far removed from its humble frontier days. Chiefly associated with the GN, the Stone Arch Bridge was actually constructed by the Minneapolis Union Railway. Established in late 1881, the railroad was one of Hill's interests. At the time, the railroading tycoon was managing the St. Paul, Minneapolis and Manitoba Railway (StPM&M), a company incorporated in 1879 to assume the routes of the floundering St. Paul and Pacific Railroad. The StPM&M became the principal component of the GN when the latter was organized in late 1889. Along with numerous other rail lines, the Minneapolis Union Railway officially became part of the GN in 1907.[14]

The primary purpose of the Minneapolis Union Railway was to establish a link between St. Paul and that portion of Minneapolis on the west side of the Mississippi River. By the early 1880s, the population of Minneapolis was about forty-five thousand and growing quickly. The major portion of the town was on the west side of the river, but the main railroad links were on the east side of the waterway. Hill realized Minneapolis needed a rail line to carry passengers to a railroad depot near the city's core. At that time, the core of Minneapolis was Bridge Square, a site near the Hennepin Avenue Bridge. The Stone Arch Bridge served as the line's final leg into Bridge Square.[15]

Work on the crossing began in January 1882, soon after the formation of the Minneapolis Union Railway. Hill had a problem, however. The site for the bridge's east approach was below the Falls of St. Anthony, while the site for the bridge's west approach was just above the falls. Hill could not simply erect a diagonal bridge connecting the two points, for the falls blocked the way. And although Hill could have designed the bridge to span the river just above the falls, making the connection from one bank to the next simpler, the weight of the structure may have undermined the falls. Since Minneapolis was becoming the milling capital of the world by the early 1880s, due in a large degree to the Falls of St. Anthony, Hill had little desire to erect a bridge with the potential to destroy the geographic cash cow. Hill's engineer, Charles C. Smith, solved the

Completed in 1883 by the Minneapolis Union Railway, an interest of James J. Hill's, the Stone Arch Bridge was designed to skirt the downstream edge of the Falls of St. Anthony and then sweep northward into the Union Depot near the Hennepin Avenue Bridge. *Photograph ca. 1890; courtesy of the Minnesota Historical Society.*

These two photographs show how timber forms were fashioned to shape the arches of the Stone Arch Bridge. *Photographs by Elmer & Tenney and Henry R. Farr, ca. 1882; courtesy of the Minnesota Historical Society.*

problem by building a roughly $700,000 bridge that skirted the southern edge of the falls at a diagonal, but near the river's west bank swept northwest, paralleling the river and leading Hill's rail line directly into his Union Depot, which he erected just below the west end of the Hennepin Avenue Bridge in 1885, two years after the Stone Arch Bridge was finished.[16]

The monumentality of the Stone Arch Bridge is extraordinary. Rising about eighty feet above the riverbed, it is an astounding 2,100 feet long. The bridge was originally formed of twenty-three arches varying from forty to one hundred feet in span. The stone used to build the structure was quarried from various locations, including Sauk Rapids and Mankato, Minnesota, as well as Stone City, Iowa, and Bridgeport, Wisconsin. Limestone for the bridge was also quarried near the construction site. Soon after it was completed, the state railroad commissioner gushed, "One of the finest stone viaducts in the world … [the bridge] is constructed for a thousand years, and with its massive masonry and lofty arches recalls the solidity of Roman antiquity." The railroad commissioner would not be the only gusher. More than a century later, Daniel L. Schodek, in his book *Landmarks in American Civil Engineering*, remarked, "Although it seemed extravagant at the time, James Hill's insistence on hand-laid solid stone and an artful curve, like his vision of American expansion westward, seems to have paid off. A marvel when constructed in 1882–1883, the Stone Arch Bridge with its massive masonry and graceful arches is a wonderful survivor of an ambitious era."[17]

Hill's epic bridge has undergone some change over the years. During the first decade of the twentieth century, the bridge was reinforced with concrete fill and metal anchor rods. The most obvious alteration occurred in the early 1960s, when two of the arches near the structure's west end were cut away and replaced with a section of steel deck truss. The modification came about to allow boats to reach the government lock at the foot of the Falls of St. Anthony. Although the bridge remains one of the country's most impressive stone arches, the 1960s alteration is a wound that will never mend. Additional modification came in the 1990s. By this time the GN was a distant memory, and Hill's landmark crossing, no longer servant to passenger trains rolling toward Minneapolis, became

a pedestrian and bicycle bridge. Thankfully, Minneapolis—indeed, Minnesota—had comprehended the historic significance of the bridge and rehabilitated it for the pleasure of future generations.[18]

While it is not surprising that Hill and his railroad contemporaries erected the majority of stone arch crossings in Minnesota, it may be surprising to learn that the state's oldest known stone arch bridge is not a railroad structure. Upon reflection, however, this should not be surprising in the least. Completed in 1863, five years before Lanesboro erected its remarkably durable arched dam, and two decades ahead of Hill's stone arcade across our nation's grandest river, the Point Douglas–St. Louis River Road Bridge was erected over Brown's Creek, at the northern edge of the St. Croix River community of Stillwater.[19]

The Point Douglas–St. Louis River Road Bridge is a remnant of one of Minnesota's earliest road-building programs. By 1850, Minnesota, freshly christened a territory of the United States but still eight years from statehood, featured few land transportation corridors. The railroads were two decades away from concerted construction of rail lines. The main land routes through

This present-day view of the Stone Arch Bridge shows the steel deck-truss section that was incorporated in the original bridge in the 1960s.

Built as a component of one of Minnesota's military roads, the Point Douglas–St. Louis River Road Bridge spanning Brown's Creek at the northern edge of Stillwater is probably the oldest bridge still standing in the state. *Photograph taken in 2006.*

sota Territory, the House Committee on Roads wrote, "That same fostering care which has always been extended to the new Territories of the country may, in the opinion of the committee, well be manifested towards Minnesota, in opening and improving thoroughfares as may be necessary for her protection …" But the committee finished its thought when it continued, "… and useful in advancing her settlements."[21]

The appropriation from the government was initial funds for construction of five military roads in Minnesota Territory. One road was to run along the east bank of the Mississippi River from Point Douglas, at the mouth of the St. Croix River, to Fort Ripley. Another route would traverse the distance from the mouth of the Swan River, near present-day Little Falls, to Long Prairie, while a third route would parallel the west bank of the Mississippi River from Mendota to Wabasha. A fourth military road was to run from Mendota to the mouth of the Big Sioux River, near Sioux City, Iowa. The last route was planned to span the distance from Point Douglas north to the Falls of the St. Louis River, near Lake Superior. Later the ending point for the road was changed to the mouth of the St. Louis River on Superior Bay, at the head of Lake Superior. It was this last road that necessitated the Point Douglas–St. Louis River Road Bridge over Brown's Creek at Stillwater.[22]

Little is known of the bridge. Its completion date implies that it was not the first bridge at the site, for the bridge was erected thirteen years after Sibley began acquiring funds for the military roads. It would seem that a cohesive road, including bridges, would have been in place sooner than 1863. In truth, however, the Point Douglas–St. Louis River Road was never finished as a military road. In large part, this was because of the stinginess of Congress, which seemed to believe that $10,000, $15,000, or $20,000 toward one road or another was enough to complete the road. It wasn't, of course, and Sibley, as well as the representative who succeeded him, had to go back to a tightfisted Congress

the territory were the Red River Trails. Put plainly, the small settlement population in Minnesota was not cohesively linked, stunting travel, communication, and commerce. Henry Hastings Sibley, a fur trader who became Minnesota's first territorial delegate to Congress, aided transportation links by convincing the federal government to fund a series of military roads in Minnesota Territory. Congress passed the Minnesota Road Act in July 1850, providing $40,000 for road construction.[20]

As the term implies, military roads were ostensibly for military purposes, such as moving the army from one point to the next quickly: forcing the army to beat its way through wood and brush during periods of crisis was unacceptable. Truthfully, though, military roads were more often used by settlers traveling from one population center to the next, or for helping settle previously unsettled areas. Politicians understood this, even though they often couched their approval of military roads in national security language. For example, in 1850, as Sibley lobbied for military roads in Minne-

The Point Douglas–St. Louis River Road Bridge was eventually incorporated into a milling operation, but the mill had been gone a decade or so by the time this photograph was taken. *Photograph ca. 1940; courtesy of the Minnesota Historical Society.*

year after year and ask for more money, which was not always forthcoming. In any event, two-thirds of the Point Douglas–St. Louis River Road was largely complete by 1858, one year after government appropriations for military roads ceased, and the same year Minnesota became a state. And even though this is five years before the bridge was finished over Brown's Creek, the historical evidence seems to indicate that the Point Douglas–St. Louis River Road Bridge was the first crossing at its site.[23]

What is known about the Point Douglas–St. Louis River Road Bridge is that it is a small stone arch that was erected using locally quarried limestone. The builders were local men Fredrick Curtis and Michael Hanly. It appears, however, that the Board of County Commissioners for Washington County was not entirely satisfied with the work of Curtis and Hanly, for it refused to accept the duo's effort. Eventually the bridge was used, implying that the board and the two builders resolved the issue. Not so, according to Tom Curtis, grandson of Fredrick. In 1974, eighty-two-year-old Tom Curtis, a retired stonemason and local historian, argued that his grandfather and Michael Hanly were never paid for their work. Curtis concluded that costs for the bridge probably totaled about $500. More than a century later, after compounding interest, Curtis believed that the relatives of the two bridge builders were owed about $200,000. The historian made the argument tongue-in-cheek, though, as he never submitted a bill to local officials. And even though he protested to a journalist that he was serious about collecting the fee, that journalist observed that the "twinkle" in the elderly gentleman's eye belied his intentions.[24]

The Point Douglas–St. Louis River Road Bridge was used at least until 1891, when a wider, wood bridge was built about two hundred feet to the east and the road adjusted to pass over it. In 1905, a man named John Kaplan incorporated the bridge into a three-story mill he erected on the site. But the mill did not succeed, and it was removed in 1927, leaving only the bridge. An artifact of the government road network of the mid-1800s, the Point Douglas–St. Louis River Road Bridge is now part of private property. It may be the oldest extant bridge of any type in Minnesota.[25]

Like the Point Douglas–St. Louis River Road Bridge,

the double-arched Seventh Street Improvement Arches is an extremely rare crossing. Featuring a strange moniker, the Seventh Street Improvement Arches was named for the improvement of St. Paul's Seventh Street in the 1880s. The bridge spans the former line of the St. Paul and Duluth Railroad just east of a busy downtown, but most automobile drivers have no idea that they are passing over an exceptional bridge as they motor to and from the Dayton's Bluff area. The Seventh Street Improvement Arches is special because of its helicoid design. Standing beneath the bridge peering through either arch, an observer immediately notices that the stone courses forming the barrels of the arches spiral. In other words, the stone courses create a helix. Whereas the barrels of most stone arches are made of wedge-shaped voussoirs—stones that, in a way, resemble the pieces of a pie—the stone voussoirs for a helicoid arch look something like slightly twisted rectangles. Put another way, the roughly rectangular stone voussoirs are slightly warped. Placing rectangular, slightly warped stone voussoirs of the same dimensions end to end creates a spiraling stone course. By forming many parallel spiraling stone courses, engineers can erect a substantially skewed stone arch bridge. Since Seventh Street passed over the tracks of the St. Paul and Duluth Railroad at a sixty-three-degree angle, a skewed bridge was precisely what was needed when engineer William Albert Truesdell began improving Seventh Street in the 1880s.[26]

In his 1909 obituary, Truesdell was described by the *Association of Engineering Societies* as a "bluff, undiplomatic, outspoken man of rigid standards [who] seldom smiled, and yet had a kindly manner, revealing a character which commanded respect, admiration, and affection." He was remarkably intelligent as well, for the Seventh Street Improvement Arches is major engineering. The bridge is so exceptional, in fact, that it is the only bridge of its type ever built in Minnesota. Even more noteworthy, it is one of only a handful of such bridges known to exist in America. One reason for this is that few engineers in late-nineteenth-century America knew how to build a helicoid arch, a bridge type pioneered in Europe by English architect Peter Nicholson. The fact that the skewed bridge is still standing, and obviously supporting far more traffic than Truesdell ever imagined when he completed the struc-

One segment of the Seventh Street Improvement Arches appears here. *Photograph ca. 1900; courtesy of the Minnesota Historical Society.*

Designed by William Albert Truesdell and completed in 1884 as part of St. Paul's Seventh Street improvement, the Seventh Street Improvement Arches is a singular bridge in Minnesota. This view illustrates how the stone courses of each arch spiral. *Photograph taken in 2006.*

neering sophistication of Truesdell's effort, is nevertheless an impressive stone arch bridge. The crossing's dull appellation is the result of Minnesota's numbering system for bridges. Many bridges, perhaps most, have a locally common, or historic, name—such as the Arches. Regrettably, the historic name often does not make it into the written record, and so bridges are frequently referenced by a state number, a designation bereft of charm, distinctiveness, and description.

Situated in a hilly, somewhat isolated area a few miles west of Winona, Bridge No. L1409 passes over Garvin Brook, the same stream spanned by the Arches, which is only about five miles southwest. Unlike the Arches, however, Bridge No. L1409 is not a railroad structure. Instead, it is a highway bridge carrying a gravel roadway. The rather narrow, forty-five-foot-long crossing is formed of a single, segmental arch. A segmental arch differs from a semicircular arch because its intrados (the lower surface of the voussoirs forming the curve of the arch) is less than half a circle. In other words, the rise of a segmental arch is less than the rise of a semicircular arch. Completed in 1895, roughly a dozen years after the Seventh Street Improvement Arches, the segmental-arched Bridge No. L1409 is Minnesota's best remaining example of a country stone arch bridge.[28]

Most stone arch highway bridges in Minnesota can be placed in one of three broad categories: country, city, or park. Country stone arches are defined as those masonry-arch bridges "built by either unincorporated towns or small rural villages on remote farm roads." City stone arch bridges were built mainly in Minneapolis, St. Paul, Duluth, and Carver. When these city bridges were erected in the late nineteenth and early twentieth centuries, each community was a regional trade center. With the exception of Carver, they remain so. Obviously, park stone arch bridges were raised in parks. Since country stone arches supported less traffic than city stone arches, their construction was often less robust. Moreover, many country stone arches crossed narrow waterways, such as brooks that ran dry in summer months, and so necessitated relatively petite bridges. Additionally, the aesthetics of most country stone arches did not match that of city stone arches, where bridges frequently reflected civic pride. Park stone arch bridges, often found within parks inside

ture in 1884, is testament to the engineering acumen of the man who seldom smiled. The Seventh Street Improvement Arches, a structural marvel declared a national historic civil engineering landmark by the American Society of Civil Engineers, is the only bridge known to have been designed by Truesdell. Odd.[27]

Bridge No. L1409, although unable to match the engi-

municipal boundaries, were usually designed to be especially fetching.[29]

Not surprisingly, the majority of country stone arch highway bridges were built in southeastern Minnesota, one of the state's most geographically stony regions. Many crossings built in this part of the state about the time of Bridge No. L1409 were a result of the Good Roads Movement, a late-nineteenth- and early-twentieth-century coalition of politicians, motorists, bicyclists, and farmers who advocated improved rural roadways and bridges. Minnesota's Good Roads Movement officially began in St. Paul in January 1893, when more than four hundred delegates from throughout the state gathered for a two-day convention. The state's civil engineers threw their support behind the movement two years later. The Good Roads Movement claimed a significant victory in 1898, when a state tax for county bridge construction under the guidance of a state highway commission was approved, although the commission was not formally organized until 1905.[30]

The uniqueness of Bridge No. L1409 is derived from its size. Whereas most country stone arches rarely exceeded fifteen feet in length, Bridge No. L1409 was three times longer, rivaling some stone arches constructed in urban centers. Furthermore, while most country stone arches were formed of rubble masonry, Bridge No. L1409 was crafted with rough-faced ashlar (dressed stone). This aesthetic clearly trumped that of most country stone arches. The crossing was designed by Fred H. Pickles, the county surveyor for Winona County in 1895 and 1896, and it was built for $1,340 by local stonemason Charles Butler. Other architectural and engineering works in Minnesota by either Pickles or Butler have yet to be discovered.[31]

Sadly, Bridge No. L1409 was forced to demonstrate the strength of its arch in summer 2007, when extreme flooding in southeastern Minnesota punished many bridges. Bridge No. L1409, more than a century old, was bludgeoned by rushing water that carried away its span-drel walls and the earth fill that supported the roadway. Even so, its arch was so strong that it remained in place. What will happen to this principal part of the bridge is uncertain. Perhaps it can be incorporated into a new bridge at the site, but it will not be surprising if it is removed to make way for a less-distinct crossing.

The country stone arch trend in southeastern Minnesota continued into the early twentieth century. Twenty years after Bridge No. L1409 was built, Houston County, immediately south of Winona County, erected Bridge No. L4013, a stone arch over Riceford Creek in Black Hammer Township, about eight miles west of the county seat, Caledonia. Situated in a wooded area, the bridge's length is typical of most country stone arches; it measures only about twelve feet long. Nevertheless, the modest-dimensioned bridge is distinctive.[32]

Bridge No. L1409 was erected over Garvin Brook in Winona County in 1895. The bridge was substantially damaged by severe flooding in 2007, yet its principal structural component, the arch ring, defiantly resisted the onslaught. *Large photograph taken in 2005 by Robert W. Gardner Jr. Inset photograph taken in 2007 by David F. Kramer, Winona County Highway Department.*

In the early twentieth century, the newly-formed Minnesota Highway Commission (MHC) created a series of standard plans for bridges, including designs for beam spans, plate girders, reinforced-concrete slabs, and concrete girders, as well as standard drawings for through trusses and pony trusses. MHC reports reveal little evidence of standard plans for stone arches, however. Since stone arches have been a somewhat rare bridge type in America, this is probably not surprising. But a standard plan did exist and likely was created specifically for stone-rich southeastern Minnesota. In 1915, the plan was employed by Alfred J. Rasmussen, the local MHC field engineer, when Houston County requested he design a bridge to span Riceford Creek in Black Hammer Township. The bridge that was

Houston County's Bridge No. L4013 is a small stone arch built over Riceford Creek in Black Hammer Township in 1915. Although discovering a standard plan for stone arch bridges in Minnesota would be a surprise, this crossing apparently had one, for the bridge design was repeated several times in various locations in southeastern Minnesota. *Photograph taken in 2005 by Robert W. Gardner Jr.*

approved was a short-span stone arch with well-defined impost ledges (the support point, such as the top of a wall or column, from whence an arch springs). The impost ledges, although aesthetically pleasing, were likely practical features intended solely to support the centering (temporary framework) used to form the bridge's arch.[33]

Although archives have been loath to give up a hard copy of a standard stone arch plan, one existed because the bridge built in Black Hammer Township was essentially replicated in other counties in southeastern Minnesota. Clearly, engineers in the southeastern corner of the state had a standard stone arch design that they shared. Whether the MHC officially developed it or it was created by the commission's field engineers operating in southeastern Minnesota is uncertain, however. In the late 1980s, during his study of the state's stone arch highway bridges, historian Jeffrey A. Hess summed up the historic significance of Bridge No. L4013, "The structure is important as the only surviving, authenticated example of an early twentieth-century, state-designed, stone arch bridge." Unfortunately, the historically significant crossing has received minimal maintenance over the years, evident by the joints around the voussoirs, which are largely absent of mortar. Still, the ninety-year-old bridge was well constructed, and so exhibits little settling.[34]

Almost at the other end of Minnesota, the Stewart Creek Stone Arch Bridge is better known and better cared for than the largely unseen crossing in Black Hammer Township. Erected over Stewart Creek on Duluth's Skyline Parkway, a scenic thoroughfare overlooking much of Duluth and Lake Superior, the bridge is part of the city's park system. Little building information exists for this structure, however, for both the engineer and the contractor are unknown. One of only a few park stone arch bridges in Minnesota, the Stewart Creek Stone Arch Bridge was erected around 1925, about the time Skyline Parkway was extended in the southwestern part of the city, thus implying that the crossing was part of boulevard construction.[35]

As with other park stone arches, the Stewart Creek Stone Arch Bridge was designed to be especially handsome. The bridge's attractiveness is derived from its rawness, a kind of crudity that makes it one of the most visually appealing stone arches in Minnesota. Hess

One of the few park stone arches in Minnesota, the Stewart Creek Stone Arch Bridge was erected around 1925 over Duluth's Stewart Creek. The bridge exudes a rawness uncommon to many stone arches—an appealing aesthetic. *Photograph taken in 2006.*

these walls. The dark-shaded bridge's most novel feature is its stone railings surmounting the arch. Resembling large, jagged teeth, the railings complete the brawny and craggy bridge, enhancing its brutal allure.[38]

The crossing on Skyline Parkway, seemingly hewn from the earth with a sledgehammer, dramatically contrasts with another park stone arch bridge. Commonly known as Split Rock Bridge, this structure appears as if it has been crafted with delicate instruments. Despite its moniker, the bridge is not linked to Split Rock Lighthouse, the striking and popular maritime signal beacon surveying Lake Superior from atop a rocky cliff near Beaver Bay. In fact, the two structures could hardly be farther apart and still be in the same state. Located in Pipestone County in southwestern Minnesota, about eight miles south of the community of Pipestone, Split Rock Bridge carries County Road 54 over Split Rock Creek.

A constituent of Split Rock Creek State Recreational Reserve, Split Rock Bridge may be the most beautiful stone arch crossing in Minnesota. Completed in 1938, exceptionally late for a stone arch bridge, the structure is composed of pink Sioux quartzite, Mother Nature's stunning geological gift to southwestern Minnesota. Indeed, the city of Pipestone was virtually raised on Sioux quartzite, and the stone seems to emit a mauve shimmer as the setting summer sun falls upon the fabulous Pipestone County Courthouse. The same holds for Split Rock Bridge, which also benefits from the pleasing aesthetic of randomly coursed ashlar. Framed by flared and stepped

describes the bridge's appearance as "Picturesque," a term credited to Andrew Jackson Downing, a prominent nineteenth-century landscape architect.[36] In his bridge study, the historian quotes the landscape architect:

The Picturesque is seen in ideas of beauty manifested with something of rudeness, violence, or difficulty. The effect of the whole is spirited and pleasing, but parts are not balanced, proportions are not perfect, and details are rude. We feel at the first glance at a picturesque object, the idea of power exerted, rather than the idea of beauty which it involves.[37]

Perhaps there is no better description of the Stewart Creek Stone Arch Bridge as it leaps a rocky ravine cleaved by Stewart Creek. Embraced by wooded park land, the thirty-foot-long, single-span structure is formed of gabbro, a greenish stone common to northeastern Minnesota. The crossing's elliptical arch (an arch forming a semi-ellipse, or, broadly, half an oval) springs from rubble abutments rising several feet above grade, thus the bridge's arched opening is reminiscent of a towering stone gateway. The spandrel walls, crudely coursed with irregularly shaped stone blocks, extend to the bridge approaches to form retaining walls. Gabbro boulders define the roadway immediately above

Finished by the Works Progress Administration in 1938, Split Rock Bridge over Split Rock Creek south of Pipestone may be the most beautiful of Minnesota's stone arch bridges. *Photograph taken in 2005.*

wing walls, the lines of the fifty-foot-long bridge are broken only by the graceful curve of its segmental arch. Lamentably, the crossing's appearance is marred somewhat by efflorescence, as water-soluble salts leach from the stone at different points on the bridge.[39]

This wonderful bridge exists because it was part of a federal relief effort. It was erected by the Works Progress Administration (WPA), which came into existence in 1935 and was renamed the Work Projects Administration in 1939. Its primary purpose was to put the employable, yet unemployed, to work in relatively modest projects benefiting society. The bridge the WPA finished over Split Rock Creek was but a piece of a larger project. In the mid-1930s, the WPA built a masonry dam across Split Rock Creek, an obstruction that created a modest lake that formed the core of Split Rock Creek State Recreational Reserve. The bridge was erected just downstream of the dam and lake. While

it was not unusual for federal relief bridge projects to incorporate stone, usually the building material was intended only as a facing. But since Pipestone County had a rich stone tradition, Split Rock Bridge was meant to showcase the local masonry heritage. At a time in America when load-bearing stone arch bridges were mostly memory, the WPA opted for such a structure over Split Rock Creek.[40]

Pipestone County highway engineer Elmer Keeler prepared the plans for the $46,000 bridge. He was aided by Albert G. Plagens, a consulting architect from New Ulm, Minnesota. Work began in 1937, about the time the dam was completed, and was finished one year later. As a final touch, the stone parapet in the southeast wing wall featured a stone commemorative plaque inscribed Split Rock Bridge, Works Progress Administration Project, 1938.[41]

One of the notable masonry structures in Minne-

sota, Split Rock Bridge was probably the last stone arch bridge to be built in the state. Although other bridges resembling stone arches were erected, mainly by federal relief entities like the WPA, these attractive crossings featured arches formed of metal or reinforced concrete. As Minnesota's last hurrah at stone arch bridge building, Split Rock Bridge is an exquisite nod to one of America's most endearing bridge types.

An especially late version of a stone arch bridge, Split Rock Bridge likely employed stone because of the rich stone-carving tradition of Pipestone County. *Photograph taken in 1938; courtesy of the Minnesota Historical Society.*

IRON AND STEEL

BRIDGES

And I think how many thousands
Of care encumbered men,
Each bearing his burden of sorrows,
Have crossed the bridge since then.

Mr. Longfellow was not thinking of our steel arch bridge when he wrote his somber poem. If he had taken this as a point of view, he would have sung a different song. The thousands who crossed the bridge would not all have been loaded up to the muzzle with care and sorrows. There are several sad persons in Minneapolis and some of them go across the bridge occasionally, but the majority of Minneapolitans are light hearted and happy, especially just at the time they cross this bridge, which is in itself a source of pleasure and pride.

—"A Bridge Count," *Minneapolis Tribune*, February 7, 1891

The first longitudinal section of the third bridge at Hennepin Avenue in Minneapolis was completed adjacent to the second Hennepin Avenue Bridge in 1888. *Photograph ca. 1889; courtesy of the Minnesota Historical Society.*

Few newspaper articles today begin with verse. Perhaps present-day journalists are more objective, less apt to interject emotion into a story. But in Minneapolis in the early 1890s, the city's population was bursting in all directions, as was the built environment necessary to support the population. It was a time when the community was morphing so quickly into a sophisticated, major metropolitan city that excitement, pride, and partiality ruled. In truth, the third Hennepin Avenue Bridge at Minneapolis was such a lovely piece of infrastructural art that, maybe, traversing it actually made some feel rather cheery.

The bridge came about because the second Hennepin Avenue Bridge, engineer Thomas Griffith's stone-towered suspension span, was a bust. Most agreed that Griffith's structure was an amazing-looking bridge, but, sadly, it was unable to support a city flourishing much faster than most could have imagined when it was built. In 1885, midway through a decade that would see the city's population increase fourfold,

Horace E. Horton of Rochester, Minnesota, and the Wrought Iron Bridge Company of Canton, Ohio, completed the steel arch over the Mississippi River at Hennepin Avenue. The bridge would last a century. *Photograph by Charles J. Hibbard, 1911; courtesy of the Minnesota Historical Society.*

Minneapolis began construction of a new bridge over the Mississippi River to Nicollet Island, adjacent to the eight-year-old suspension bridge.[1]

Designed as a stone arch bridge with three piers, work commenced on the east abutment in December 1885. It soon stopped. Many never wanted a stone arch bridge, including the thriving milling industry hugging the banks of the Mississippi River downstream of the bridge site. The Minneapolis Milling Company obtained a temporary injunction halting construction, arguing that the three piers would reduce water power to the mills. Work began again in September 1886, after the city substantially modified the bridge plan. Instead of erecting a stone arch with three piers, Minneapolis opted for a steel, two-span, ribbed arch with only a single pier.[2]

The bridge was built in two longitudinal sections. The first forty-foot-wide section was constructed abutting the north side of the suspension bridge, thus creating a structure that almost appeared to be a single bridge with two distinct faces. The superstructure for the steel arch crossing was erected by Horace E. Horton, a bridge builder from Rochester, Minnesota, who later merged his firm with the Kansas City Bridge and Iron Company to form Chicago Bridge and Iron, based in Chicago. Finished about mid-1888, the superstructure was composed of two spans, each formed of three steel arched ribs. Unlike a filled-spandrel arch, such as the Arches or James J. Hill's Stone Arch Bridge, Horton's structure was an open-spandrel arch; a spandrel wall did not exist, so no fill material was necessary to support a deck and roadway. Instead, the bridge's deck was supported at the crown of each arch rib and by the limestone abutments and the single limestone pier. Vertical steel members (also known as spandrel columns) reached upward to the deck from the slope of each rib and added additional support. Large arch bridges have frequently been built in this open-spandrel way.[3]

The odd combination of open-spandrel steel arch and stone-towered suspension bridge continued for nineteen months, and the public readily used either crossing. Finally, in January 1890, the city began removing the suspension bridge. Construction of the south forty-foot-wide section of the ribbed-arch bridge commenced on the site of the former suspension bridge about August 1890. The Wrought Iron Bridge Company,

not Horace E. Horton, was the contractor. Based in Canton, Ohio, the Wrought Iron Bridge Company was incorporated in 1871. Roughly thirty years later it became part of the American Bridge Company, a subsidiary of United States Steel Corporation that was formed through the merger of twenty-six bridge companies.[4]

The Wrought Iron Bridge Company completed the superstructure in late November, although the south half of the ribbed-arch structure would not officially open until about late January 1891, when the approaches were finished. Even though the north and south sections of the bridge looked virtually identical, they were, in fact, slightly different. In totality, the bridge consisted of two spans formed of six ribs each, but while each rib of the north part incorporated three hinges, each rib of the south part had only two hinges. While most arch bridges have no hinges—that is, the bridges are fixed, which makes them rigid—others incorporate hinges, which makes them yielding. The more hinges in an arch bridge, the less rigid it is. After the north longitudinal section of the Hennepin Avenue Bridge was completed, engineers concluded that the three-hinged structure had insufficient rigidity. Eliminating a hinge in each arch rib of the south longitudinal section increased the stiffness of the entire bridge.[5]

The ribbed-arch bridge dramatically altered the look of the late-nineteenth-century riverfront in Minneapolis. More accurately, since the stone towers of the suspension bridge no longer marked the skyline, it made Hennepin Avenue at the river seem rather vacant. Minneapolis had simply traded the aesthetic, however: subtle Victorian in place of unashamed medieval. The refined visual was in keeping with many maturing late-nineteenth-century cities in America. But perhaps a better symbol of Minneapolis's infrastructural maturity was the material employed to build the third Hennepin Avenue Bridge: namely, steel. In truth, steel had supplanted wrought iron as the preferred bridge-building material for most crossings in the state by the 1890s, although southwestern Minnesota remained something of an oddity, erecting a surprising number of stone arches into the early twentieth century.[6]

Perhaps Minnesota's grandest steel bridge is the Soo Line High Bridge, a steel arch that was completed in June 1911, two decades after the steel-arched Hennepin Avenue Bridge. Because of its hiding place within the

St. Croix River Valley five miles above Stillwater, the spectacular crossing is rarely viewed by the public. Bounding across the St. Croix River in a series of leaps, the bridge was raised by the Minneapolis, St. Paul and Sault Ste. Marie Railway, a railroad commonly known as the Soo Line. Although the Soo Line High Bridge has received nary the attention of the Stone Arch Bridge in Minneapolis, it is every bit as monumental as James J. Hill's stone legacy. Whereas the Stone Arch Bridge has a brawny elegance, the Soo Line High Bridge exhibits a lithesome grace. In fact, from a distance, it appears almost fragile.[7]

Specifically, the bridge is a five-span, steel, riveted, three-hinged, open-spandrel arch with several simple approach spans. Costing $500,000, a princely sum for the early 1900s, the nearly 2,700-foot-long bridge was designed by Claude Allen Porter Turner (commonly known as C. A. P. Turner), maybe the most significant engineer to practice in Minnesota. David Plowden goes farther, describing him as "one of America's most brilliant engineers." Turner achieved renown chiefly for his reinforced-concrete, flat-slab framing efforts, a construction method used for multistory buildings that employed supporting columns surmounted with flared capitals, sometimes called mushroom capitals. This type of engineering was also incorporated into some reinforced-concrete bridges, the first of which was Turner's Lafayette Avenue Bridge completed over the Soo Line tracks in St. Paul in 1909. It no longer exists.[8]

The Soo Line High Bridge took the place of another huge structure that was situated a short distance downriver. The earlier bridge was a mix of various truss types and was built by the Wisconsin Central Railway (WC) in 1884. The Soo Line gained controlling interest of the WC in 1909, rerouting the rail line's route from Chippewa Falls, Wisconsin, to St. Paul, which necessitated the new bridge. The original WC bridge was removed a few years after completion of the steel arch.[9]

The Soo Line High Bridge across the St. Croix River north of Stillwater is the most elegant steel arch in Minnesota. *Photograph taken in 2006.*

Like the north half of the steel-arched Hennepin Avenue Bridge, the Soo Line High Bridge incorporates three hinges in each arch. Three-hinged steel arches, although uncommon, are almost always highway bridges. Rarely did railroads build such structures, for the crossing type's uncommon plasticity is largely unsuitable for the heavy weight of a train.[10] Turner's nimble, three-hinged arch bridge is special, however, as noted by Carl W. Condit:

The light traffic of the Soo Line and the smaller axle loading of its locomotives allowed Turner to reduce the arch spans to essentials of remarkable purity and delicacy—slender three-hinged arch ribs identical in span and rise, and an extremely light and open pattern of spandrel bracing. The central hinge is a curious sliding joint designed to lock into a rigid unit under the weight of the train and thus intermittently to transform the rib into a two-hinged arch.[11]

In other words, as a live load passes over the graceful bridge, the structure becomes stiffer, easily supporting the train.

The Soo Line High Bridge replaced the Wisconsin Central Bridge, a large crossing formed of several deck trusses and a through-truss main span. *Photograph by Chester Sawyer Wilson, ca. 1903; courtesy of the Minnesota Historical Society.*

"The most outstanding [multispan railroad arch] and one of the world's most beautiful steel structures," is the label Plowden applies to the Soo Line High Bridge. Worded more subtly, the Soo Line High Bridge, like the Stone Arch Bridge, is a trophy, representing the Soo Line's most remarkable engineering achievement.[12]

Obviously, few railroad crossings match the attractiveness or engineering complexity of the Soo Line High Bridge. Instead, most are modest, such as the plate-girder type. This ubiquitous bridge type is strong, simple to build, and often employed for railroad spans up to about one hundred feet. Plate girders gained popularity in America about the mid-1800s, after metal was introduced as a bridge-building material. More accurately, plate girders became popular with the introduction of iron as a bridge-building material, as steel had not yet become dominant. Usually composed of two load-bearing beams, plate girders are built up. Plate girders are made of beams formed of wide, thin metal plates with flanges riveted to the top and the bottom.

The Soo Line High Bridge was designed by C. A. P. Turner, one of the country's most gifted engineers. *Photograph by John Runk, 1911; courtesy of the Minnesota Historical Society.*

A somewhat ho-hum bridge type, Bridge No. L1393 in Winona County is saved from complete anonymity by its substantial limestone substructure. *Photograph taken in 2005 by Robert W. Gardner Jr.*

Angled members riveted vertically between the flanges stiffen the plates. The load-bearing beams carry floor beams that support the deck. A railroad easily fabricated this type of superstructure in its maintenance shops, placed it on a railroad flatcar, and delivered it to the bridge site, where it was lifted from the train and placed on its abutments. This ease of construction and delivery explains why so many railroad crossings are plate girders. One such bridge is found in Winona County, several hundred feet west of the Arches. A wrought iron plate girder that was completed in the early 1880s by the Winona and St. Peter (W&StP), the superstructure of Bridge No. L1393 was changed to steel by the Chicago and North Western (C&NW) in 1910. Composed of two spans, the bridge escapes the general disinterest in plate-girder structures because of the appeal of its towering limestone abutments and pier.[13]

The Minnesota Highway Commission (MHC) developed specifications for plate-girder highway bridges by the early 1910s. The simplicity and reliability of the bridge type was little advantage to highway depart-

ments that did not have the means to deliver the heavy superstructure to the bridge site, however. As a result, plate girders were never popular as highway bridges in Minnesota. Those that exist are often found near a rail line, implying that the railroad helped the local highway department get the bridge to its site by using a railroad flatcar.[14]

While the appeal of most plate-girder bridges is practical, metal truss bridges often exhibit an attraction that is visual and reflective. Today, there is a romance in truss bridges, an appreciation of their conspicuous geometry that reminds us of a youthful nation flexing its industrial muscle over America's waterways. Of course, truss crossings were not always embraced at the time they were constructed. Many truss bridges erected in the late nineteenth and early twentieth centuries were thought ugly. Plowden notes that the nation seemed almost ashamed of such works. The bland girder bridges of the last half century have mostly elicited groans, however, and many now welcome the novelty of the once-prominent crossing type that wears its skeleton on the outside.[15]

Although truss bridges of wood have been built for centuries, it was the adoption of metal construction that allowed these crossings to achieve their greatest potential as a structural form. Minnesota began building its first truss bridges of wrought iron about the 1870s, roughly two decades after the material was employed for many bridges in the east. In part, wood construction continued in Minnesota because it was cheaper than erecting bridges of wrought iron. Advocates of wrought iron understood that this was only a temporary advantage, however, for wrought iron was stronger and more durable than wood. Bridge builders argued that the increased initial cost for a wrought iron bridge was offset by its increased length of service, a contention that ultimately swayed thrifty governmental administrations. According to Fredric L. Quivik, a historian who completed some of the earliest statewide studies of Minnesota's bridges, Blue Earth County, south of the Twin Cities metropolitan region, was partly an impetus for the state's transition to wrought iron highway bridges. In the early 1870s, believing many, and perhaps most, of the county's wood bridges were subpar, officials in Blue Earth County began a vigorous program of metal bridge construction, first with wrought iron and then with steel. For the next three decades almost every bridge erected by the county was made of metal.[16]

One of the first bridges built under this renewal program was in South Bend Township, a short distance south of Mankato. Spanning the Le Sueur River, the Kern Bridge, erected in 1873, is one of the oldest and rarest bridges still standing in Minnesota. Completed by the Wrought Iron Bridge Company, almost eighteen years before the bridge builder finished the south half of the third Hennepin Avenue Bridge, the crossing was designed as a 189-foot-long, single-span, wrought iron, bowstring-arch through truss. Named for local farmer John Kern, whose property abutted the bridge site, the bridge's most distinctive feature is its arched top chord. The top chord is actually composed of four separate wrought iron members that are riveted together to form a hollow beam. Wrought iron verticals are bolted between the hollow beam top chord and the floor beams supporting the timber deck, with the shortest verticals at the bridge's ends and the highest verticals near the crossing's center. In this way, the top chord is held tautly in a bow.[17]

The bowstring arch through truss was patented in the 1840s by Squire Whipple (Squire was not a title but his name), a renaissance personality born in Hardwick, Massachusetts, in 1804. A graduate of Union College in New York State, Whipple, perhaps America's most famous inventor of bridge trusses, was at various times a schoolteacher, farmer, railroad and canal surveyor, and bridge engineer. His most popular truss design was not the bowstring arch, but rather the double-intersection through truss, commonly known as the Whipple truss, a bridge type that became popular for long railroad spans. The standard length for Whipple's bowstring truss design was usually between 70 feet and 175 feet, which makes the 189-foot-long Kern Bridge somewhat atypical. Although the bowstring truss design was employed for short highway spans into the early 1900s, its heyday had largely passed by the beginning of the 1880s.[18]

The Kern Bridge no longer accommodates traffic, as the roadway over the Le Sueur River at this point closed some years ago. Access to the bridge from the west side is difficult because the former approach is now residential property. The east approach is almost as inaccessible. The gravel roadway to the bridge abruptly terminates in front of large boulders. Beyond the boulders the approach is overgrown with turf. Dense tree growth at the river's edge forces the bridge to peek through leafy branches toward the roadway it once served. The Kern Bridge, so rare that it is the only bridge of its kind in Minnesota, has an uncertain future.

Squire Whipple's bowstring arch bridge type fell from favor because more efficient truss designs gained prominence, especially the pin-connected Pratt through truss. In his study of iron and steel bridges, Quivik observes, "By the 1880s, the wrought iron, pin-connected Pratt through truss had become the standard structural type for long-span bridges in Minnesota." The Pratt was patented in 1844 by Boston architect

The Kern Bridge is a one-of-a-kind crossing in Minnesota. Following a design developed by Squire Whipple, the wrought iron bowstring-arch bridge was completed in 1873, making it one of the first all-metal crossings erected in the state. *Photograph taken in 2005.*

An example of a pinned connection is shown here. *Photograph taken in 2005.*

Caleb Pratt and his son Thomas, an engineer who worked for the Army Corps of Engineers and later for various New England railroads.[19]

The wrought iron Pratt through truss of the mid- and late 1800s is relatively simple, basically resembling a framed rectangle with inclined end posts. Each side of the bridge—the space between the horizontal top and bottom chords, known as the web—consists of wrought iron vertical members and wrought iron diagonal members. The vertical members act in compression while the diagonal members act in tension. As a result, vertical members are heavier and stronger than diagonal members, which are often slender eyebars. Bridge bracing comes from wrought iron members over the deck linking the webs, as well as from wrought iron units between the webs beneath the deck. A unique characteristic of these early Pratt bridges is their pinned connections. At various points on the bridge, the ends of wrought iron members meet. The members are linked together at these joints with wrought iron pins. Broadly, then, early Pratt bridges were raised rather quickly by placing the eyelet end of each wrought iron member in its appropriate joint and installing the pin. Alternatively, these trusses were easily taken down as each pin was removed from its joint, freeing the various wrought iron members and collapsing the bridge.[20]

A fine example of a wrought iron, pin-connected Pratt through-truss bridge in Minnesota is located in Hanover, about twenty miles northwest of Minneapolis. Founded in 1877, Hanover was not incorporated as a city until 1892, seven years after its Pratt truss was erected over the Crow River, linking the Wright County community with Hassan Township in Hennepin County. One of the last wrought iron, pin-connected

The wrought iron, Pratt through-truss Hanover Bridge in Hanover between Wright and Hennepin counties was raised over the Crow River by the Morse Bridge Company of Youngstown, Ohio, in 1885. *Photograph taken in 2005.*

Pratt through trusses in the state, the single-span bridge was constructed by the Morse Bridge Company of Youngstown, Ohio. Morse Bridge Company was founded in 1878 and changed its name to Youngstown Bridge Company sometime between 1888 and 1891. It was one of the many bridge enterprises merged to form the American Bridge Company in 1900. More than 230 feet long, the span of the wood-decked Hanover Bridge is exceptionally longer than that of most Pratt through-truss bridges, which are rarely longer than 150 feet. Built for wagons and carriages, the Hanover Bridge eventually served automobiles. Today it is a pedestrian crossing. In the 1980s, realizing the bridge was a unique city landmark, Hanover citizens rehabilitated the structure. In 2004, the community came together in ceremony to celebrate further rehabilitation of its rare bridge.[21]

A variation on Hanover's Pratt through-truss bridge is found near Silverdale in northern Minnesota's Kooch-iching County. Carrying Minnesota Highway 65, Bridge No. 5721 reaches across the Little Fork River. Erected in 1937, the bridge is composed of seven spans, six stringer (shallow I beam) approach spans, and one 160-foot-long, wrought iron, pin-connected, Camelback through-truss main span. Although a Camelback through truss looks somewhat different from the typical Pratt through truss, it is nonetheless a part of the Pratt truss family. A Camelback's web is similar to a Pratt's, yet it has a polygonal top chord of exactly five slopes. This type of through truss was often employed for spans between one hundred and three hundred feet long.[22]

An interesting characteristic of Bridge No. 5721 is its mix of wrought iron and steel spans. While the approach spans are formed of steel, the Camelback main span is made of wrought iron. Since steel had replaced wrought iron as the principal bridge-building material by the 1890s, it seems odd that a bridge erected over the Little Fork River in 1937 had a main span of wrought iron. As noted, however, it was relatively easy to deconstruct an early truss bridge by removing its pins. And collapsing a truss crossing did not mean that the bridge would never again be used. In fact, it was not uncommon for a truss bridge to be deconstructed at one bridge site and reconstructed at another, which is precisely what happened with the Camelback span of Bridge No. 5721. Unfortunately, the historical record has not revealed where the Camelback initially stood.

Featuring steel approach spans and a wrought iron main span in the form of a Camelback, Bridge No. 5721 was erected over the Little Fork River near Silverdale in 1937. *Photograph taken in 2006.*

At some point, however, this through-truss span, which was clearly fabricated in the late 1800s, was deconstructed at its original bridge site and stored at Sauk Centre in Stearns County. When engineers needed a main span to bridge the Little Fork River near Silverdale in the late 1930s, the wrought iron Camelback through truss sitting in a central Minnesota storage yard was chosen.[23]

Just as wrought iron proved a better bridge-building material than wood, steel was a better bridge-building material than wrought iron. Composed of iron-based alloys, steel contains less carbon than cast iron but more carbon than wrought iron. Its strength in tension and compression surpasses that of wrought iron, which makes it an excellent metal for bridge construction, as well as other types of assembly, such as framing for buildings. For many years, bridge builders understood the benefits of steel, but its cost was prohibitive. With the introduction of the Bessemer converter in the mid-1800s, and subsequent adoption of large-scale open-

One of the most unusual bridges ever built in Minnesota, the Hastings Spiral Bridge is still fondly recalled by many living in and around Hastings. Completed in 1895 and razed in 1951, the bridge, built by the Wisconsin Bridge and Iron Works Company of Milwaukee, Wisconsin, received its moniker from its spiral approach at the Hastings side of the Mississippi River. *Photograph ca. 1895; courtesy of the Minnesota Historical Society.*

hearth steel manufacture, steel became more affordable. By the 1890s, bridge builders stopped using wrought iron.[24]

So, while the circa 1880s main span of Bridge No. 5721 was made of wrought iron, the main span of the Hastings Spiral Bridge was formed of steel. Although the roughly $40,000 bridge no longer stands, the Hastings Spiral Bridge is one of the most unusual crossings ever erected in Minnesota. The bridge was completed in April 1895, with several thousand people attending its dedication, a celebration that included a military band from Fort Snelling, battle reenactments, and a picnic lunch. The structure's main span was a Parker through truss, another variation on the Pratt. A Parker looks much like a Camelback (technically, a Camelback is a form of Parker), but whereas a Camelback has a polygonal top chord of exactly five slopes, a Parker's polygonal top chord is less defined, often forming a shallow arc minus the Camelback's rigid lines. Charles H. Parker, an engineer with the National Bridge and Iron Works in Boston, Massachusetts, patented the bridge type in 1870. This kind of span was often employed to reach distances up to about two hundred feet.[25]

The most interesting aspect of the Hastings Spiral Bridge was not its main span, but rather its south approach spans at the Hastings side of the Mississippi River. The south approach spans were shaped into a spiral, from which the bridge derived its name. Somewhat bizarre looking, the spiral was designed to deposit southbound bridge travelers at Sibley Street in downtown Hastings; if the bridge had been built with a typical approach, vehicles would have exited the crossing a block or two beyond the main part of the commercial district. Unwilling to waste the ground punctuating the center of the spiral, a women's organization turned the small, grassy space into a delightful gathering place known as Meloy Park.[26]

Mystery is part of the roughly 1,900-foot-long Hastings Spiral Bridge, for its engineer is uncertain. The Wisconsin Bridge and Iron Works Company of Milwaukee, Wisconsin erected the bridge, but the company's chief engineer, John Geist, never claimed its design. Additionally, there does not appear to be any known documentation pointing to Oscar Claussen, the supervising engineer for the bridge project. Historian Jack El-Hai notes that there are two other possibilities: "A Hastings machinist named B. D. Caldwell, whose daughter swore that she saw him one day trace the spiral in some sand; and an anonymous but architecturally gifted inmate at Stillwater State Penitentiary." Discovering the bridge's designer is hardly essential, however, for the story benefits from this gap in the record.[27]

The uniqueness of the Hastings Spiral Bridge was not lost on the public. Shortly before the bridge was removed, the local Oldsmobile dealer noted its popularity with visitors: "You'd be surprised how many times a week we are asked in the summer time how and where the travelers may find the Spiral Bridge." A local hotel owner also observed that half the mail her patrons deposited consisted of postcards of the Spiral Bridge. Today, longtime residents of Hastings fondly recall sauntering around its corkscrew and across the river on warm evenings. Some even remember mounting a sled and slip-sliding around the spiral on especially snowy or icy days. The warm feelings for the bridge were not enough to convince most to keep it, however, although the Hastings Chapter of the Fraternal Order of Eagles attempted to save the spiral approaches. The effort failed. As motorized vehicles became the norm and traffic increased, the crossing built for ambling horses and wagons could no longer bear the burden. Further, the bridge suffered poor maintenance. As the bridge's load limit dramatically declined by the late 1920s, much of the community demanded a new structure. In early 1951, that structure came in the form of

The Hastings High Bridge, which replaced the Hastings Spiral Bridge in 1951, is now considered obsolete by some and may soon also be replaced. *Photograph taken in 2006.*

it joins Otter Tail Lake resembled an otter's tail.[29]

The Waterstreet Bridge spans the Otter Tail River at the northwest tip of West Lost Lake, a water body situated about seven miles west of Otter Tail Lake. One of the oldest steel Pratt truss bridges remaining in the state, the pinned crossing was named for Joe Waterstreet, a man who developed an early resort on West Lost Lake. An Otter Tail County history explains that the bridge replaced a wood crossing built on the site in the 1870s or 1880s by a "blind settler" named Hugh Hunter. Presumably, Hunter was not blind when he raised the wood bridge. A local newspaper notes that the eighty-foot-long Waterstreet Bridge was erected by the Milwaukee Bridge Company, but this seems a misprint. Perhaps the paper meant the Milwaukee Bridge and Iron Works, a prominent Milwaukee-based bridge contractor that was founded in 1875 and absorbed into the American Bridge Company five years after the Waterstreet Bridge was constructed.[30]

In the late 1930s, parts of the bridge were rehabilitated under the auspices of the WPA. By the late 1970s, encouraged by a federal program to replace older bridges, Otter Tail County sought to replace the Waterstreet Bridge with a few tedious culverts. Some in the vicinity did not want the culverts, preferring instead to maintain the piece of steel-framed history that has graced the northwest tip of West Lost Lake since 1895. Thankfully, the bridge still exists, but probably not for much longer. Apparently some in the area have again been agitating for the tedious culverts, for they do not obstruct large farm machinery as the truss bridge does. Only recently, the Waterstreet Bridge was damaged when it was hit by a vehicle. The accident may speed the crossing's demise.[31]

a nearly 1,900-foot-long bridge with a deck suspended beneath a steel arch truss, an impressive-looking $2.8 million crossing that is itself now considered historic. Nowadays, Hastings, one of the oldest communities in Minnesota, is much less distinct from the Twin Cities' suburbs than it use to be. Traffic on the current two-lane bridge is so great that some are now calling for another bridge. With the explosive growth in the area, replacement of the current Hastings High Bridge may be inevitable.[28]

Erected in the same year as the Hastings Spiral Bridge, the Waterstreet Bridge is not nearly as large, but it nevertheless occupies a warm place in the hearts of many around West Lost Lake in Otter Tail County in northwestern Minnesota. Featuring one of the state's most peculiar county names, Otter Tail County was christened for the Otter Tail River, which received its moniker from Otter Tail Lake, a water body near the county's center. In truth, both entities trace their appellation to the nomenclature of the Ojibwe, who believed the large sandbar edging the Otter Tail River where

Looking similar to the Waterstreet Bridge, as well as to the Hanover Bridge, which is about thirty-five miles directly east, the Salisbury Bridge carries graveled County Road 190 over the North Fork of the Crow River, about three miles west of the small community of Kingston in Kingston Township, Meeker County. Roughly half as long as the Hanover Bridge, but forty feet longer than the Waterstreet Bridge, the timber-decked Salisbury Bridge adopts the same basic Pratt design as those earlier crossings. It is a pin-connected, Pratt through truss, but unlike the wrought iron Hanover Bridge, the Salisbury Bridge is made from steel, matching the material of the Waterstreet Bridge. Replacing an earlier crossing at the site, the Salisbury Bridge was erected in 1899. Its historic name is derived from local farmer Jonathan Burnett Salisbury, whose farmstead was situated immediately east of the bridge. Salisbury also served in the Minnesota House of Representatives between 1868 and 1870 and later acted as Meeker County surveyor. Even though Salisbury was a leading citizen of Kingston Township, the bridge's historic significance is found chiefly in its age and pin-connected design, as well as its builder, the Hewett Bridge Company of Minneapolis, Minnesota.[32]

The Hewett Bridge Company was formed by Seth M. Hewett, one of Minnesota's pioneering bridge contractors. Before founding the Hewett Bridge Company, Hewett partnered with Commadore P. Jones in the firm Jones and Hewett, of Minneapolis. The partnership lasted for only a year, from 1883 to 1884. Hewett went on to form a few additional bridge firms before establishing the Hewett Bridge Company in 1898, only a year before raising the Salisbury Bridge. In his piece "Montana's Minneapolis Bridge Builders," Fredric Quivik notes that almost all of the early bridge builders based in Minneapolis stemmed from either Hewett or Jones. In fact, the historian views Hewett and Jones as the root of a "family tree" of bridge builders originating in Minneapolis. For instance, descendent firms include the Gillette-Herzog Manufacturing Company, an enterprise that was in part guided by Alexander Y. Bayne, a man who served as an agent for Jones and Hewett but became a prolific bridge builder in his own right. Soon after Gillette-Herzog became part of the goliath known as the American Bridge Company, Bayne established A. Y. Bayne and Company in Minne-

apolis. The pedigree of the Minneapolis Steel and Machinery Company can also be traced to Jones and Hewett. Additionally, Minneapolis contractor William S. Hewett, a man who erected a number of bridges and water towers throughout Minnesota and elsewhere,

Erected in 1899 over the North Fork of the Crow River in rural Meeker County, the Salisbury Bridge is a product of the Hewett Bridge Company of Minneapolis, one of Minnesota's pioneering bridge contractors. *Photograph taken in 2005.*

Bridge No. L5245 in rural Jackson County rests over Okabena Creek. The late-nineteenth-century bridge is the most lightweight pony truss known to exist on a Minnesota roadway. *Photograph taken in 2005.*

and a builder often credited with early development of prestressed concrete construction in this country, was Seth Hewett's nephew. Seth's Hewett Bridge Company lasted a decade or so after completion of the Salisbury Bridge. By 1916, Seth Hewett, the pioneering Minneapolis bridge contractor, had passed away.[33]

As with the Waterstreet Bridge, the Salisbury Bridge is one of the few remaining examples of Minnesota's earliest steel-truss bridges, but it has a cousin—of sorts—in Jackson County. Like the Salisbury Bridge, Bridge No. L5245 is a pin-connected Pratt truss. Unlike the Salisbury Bridge, Bridge No. L5245 is a small pony truss. Pony trusses, like through trusses, are disappearing quickly from Minnesota roadways. Perhaps the only reason Bridge No. L5245 is still standing is because it is off the beaten path. Located on a township road largely given over to nature, Bridge No. L5245 spans Okabena Creek in Alba Township, about two miles east of the small town of Brewster. Almost nothing is known of the history of Bridge No. L5245, except that, like Bridge No. 5721 in Koochiching County, the bridge is not resting on its original site. The bridge was placed amid farmland over Okabena Creek in 1938, but its design is that of a pony-truss bridge fabricated

The upper chord of Bridge No. L5245 exemplifies its light construction. *Photograph taken in 2005.*

at the end of the nineteenth century. Not only is it pin connected, but its upper chord is formed of back-to-back channel members tied together at the top and bottom with V lacing. By the early 1900s, the upper chords of pony trusses were typically formed of back-to-back channel members tied together with a heavy cover plate at the top and V lacing at the bottom. Obviously a preautomotive bridge, this is the most lightweight design of any known pony truss in Minnesota.[34]

Phelps Mill Bridge is not much heavier, but it still features more durable upper chords than are found on Bridge No. L5245. The two-span, 123-foot-long structure with a wood-plank deck is also a pin-connected Pratt pony truss. It reaches over the Otter Tail River in Otter Tail County at the Phelps Mill site, only a few miles east of the Waterstreet Bridge. Both bridges reside in Maine Township, in fact.

Phelps Mill Bridge exists because it served the flourmill and a handful of other commercial interests that grew up around the mill. The flourmill was a hive of industrial activity from 1889, when it began production, until its closing in the 1930s. The mill property was purchased in 1886 by William E. Thomas, a merchant from nearby Fergus Falls. The following year, after moving his family to the mill site, Thomas constructed a timber dam over the Otter Tail River, but other commitments forced him to postpone work on the mill for almost two years. Framed with hand-hewn timbers, the four-story, gambrel-roofed flourmill, located immediately below the dam, was in operation by late 1889. Christened the Maine Roller Mills, the facility ultimately became locally known as Phelps Mill, named for its head miller, Ray Phelps, who functioned in that capacity from 1906 until the mill stopped producing in 1939.[35]

The mill expanded in 1895, with a three-story addition at its north side. Unlike the original component, which held machinery for grinding wheat, the addition housed equipment for grinding feed. By 1908, the timber dam across the river was in such poor condition that it was replaced with one of concrete and rubble rock. Only one year earlier, the current Phelps Mill Bridge was constructed immediately above the dam site.[36]

It is uncertain what type of bridge originally spanned the Otter Tail River above the dam, but it seems likely it was a timber structure in the form of a truss. Timber bridges are like timber dams, rarely lasting for a considerable period. The current Phelps Mill Bridge was

erected by the Security Bridge Company, which was established by Seth Hewett's nephew, William. William S. Hewett was born the son of a cooper in South Hope, Maine, in 1864. His family traced its ancestry to William Hewett, a Revolutionary War soldier who immigrated to this country from England sometime before the mid-1770s, married, and made a home in Maine. As a young man, William S. Hewett moved to Waltham, Maine, working in a watch factory hand-painting watch dials. Heeding Horace Greeley's advice, he moved west in 1887, making his home in Minneapolis, Minnesota, where he joined his uncle's bridge-building business. Ten years later, he founded William S. Hewett and Company; seven years after that, he partnered with his cousin, Arthur Hewett, to form the Security Bridge Company.[37]

The Security Bridge Company erected bridges throughout Minnesota, Montana, and the Dakotas, and William S. Hewett went on to build some of the most fascinating engineering structures in reinforced

Part of the Phelps Mill Historic District, the Phelps Mill Bridge was built over the Otter Tail River in Otter Tail County in 1907. The crossing was completed by the Security Bridge Company of Minneapolis. *Photograph taken in 2006.*

concrete, including the Washburn Park Water Tower in Minneapolis, a roughly 120-foot-high, domed, triple-shelled, poured-concrete edifice designed by renowned architect Harry Wild Jones. The tower features large eagles, wings spread, and medieval-looking knights displaying stern visages while clasping the hilts of genuflected broadswords. Hewett was in his late sixties and well respected when the ornament to the Washburn Park neighborhood was finished in 1932, but a quarter century earlier, while still building that reputation, his Security Bridge Company raised the slender metal bridge over the Otter Tail River at Phelps Mill, one of Minnesota's most picturesque, New England–like settings.[38]

Rock County's Bridge No. 1482 is also nearing the century mark. It is a petite, single-span structure of only twenty-nine feet. Positioned over a narrow channel linking two sides of a small lake in Schoneman Park, immediately south of Luverne, the bridge is an example of a pin-connected, king-post pony truss. Less than a decade ago, Minnesota had four king-post bridges, which obviously qualified the bridge type as rare. But apparently not rare enough: now the state has only two, including the tiny, green-painted structure marking

Schoneman Park. The other is located within a private vacation getaway near Two Harbors. Built in 1908, Bridge No. 1482 in Schoneman Park continues the characteristic unique to many truss crossings: it does not occupy its original site. Formerly, the bridge carried a rural roadway over the Rock River on the boundary line between Luverne and Clinton townships. There it remained until it was replaced by a stronger bridge in 1990. Rather than scrapping Bridge No. 1482, a legacy of the Hewett Bridge Company, it was moved to Schoneman Park as acknowledgement of its historic significance.[39]

The bridge's most distinctive characteristic is its A-shaped truss configuration, a design that has existed for centuries. Indeed, the wooden king-post truss bridge was common to medieval Europe. Bridge builders adapted new materials to the king-post design as the resources became available: wood king posts evolved into wood and iron king posts, which led to king posts made entirely of iron and, finally, king posts of steel, such as Bridge No. 1482. Although Bridge No. 1482 has pinned connections, it is stronger than Bridge No. L5245, evidenced by the sturdy construction of its top chord, which is not unlike that of Phelps Mill Bridge. This is not surprising, for as bridge building moved into the early twentieth century, construction generally became heavier, in part because the Minnesota Highway Commission (MHC) that was formed in 1905 began asserting itself. The MHC continually advocated for stronger bridges, but the government body had limited power. The law that brought it into

One of the last king-post truss bridges remaining in Minnesota, Bridge No. 1482, raised over the Rock River in Rock County by the Hewett Bridge Company in 1908, now resides in Schoneman Park, just south of Luverne. *Photograph taken in 2005.*

Built in 1908 by the Minneapolis Bridge and Iron Company, Bridge No. 6527 is a Warren through truss with verticals. It spans the Watonwan River in the small town of Madelia in Watonwan County. *Photograph taken in 2006.*

the daughter of General Philander Hartshorn, one of the town's founders. The approximate area marked by Bridge No. 6527 has been used as a crossing point for many years. An earthen dam was located near the site at one time and was often used to traverse the river during high-water months, while another nearby location, commonly known as the upper ford, was employed during low-water months. At some point, the community built a ferryboat to transport passengers from one riverbank to the other. This was replaced in the 1870s by a timber bridge, which was removed in 1908 to make way for Bridge No. 6527, a Warren through truss with verticals.[41]

The bridge was built on a county road by the Minneapolis Bridge and Iron Company. The business began in the 1880s as the Minneapolis Bridge Company under the supervision of Commadore Jones. Jones was still a guiding hand when the firm, operating as the Minneapolis Bridge and Iron Company, built Madelia's Warren through truss. Along with the Pratt truss, the Warren truss evolved into one of America's most successful truss bridge types. The Warren truss was patented in England by engineers James Warren and Willoughby Monzani in 1848. Interestingly, Squire Whipple erected the first Warren truss in America only a year later, and yet he was unaware of Warren and Willoughby's patent.[42]

A Warren truss is evident by the sequence of triangles marking either of its sides. Actually, these triangles are composed of a series of diagonal members at alternating angles. Initially, Warrens were constructed with a web formed only of diagonal members—that is, a web that appears to be only a pattern of triangles—but the design was later improved by adding vertical members to the web. So a truss crossing like Bridge No. 6527 exhibits a triangular web pattern interrupted by vertical members—a Warren with verticals. Additionally, Bridge No. 6527 is not pinned. Instead, its intersecting members are riveted together. Pinned connections were falling from favor by the early 1900s, replaced most often by rigid connections like rivets. The relatively sturdy construction of Bridge No. 6527 may indicate

existence allowed it jurisdiction only over bridges built using state funds. This explains why Rock County was able to erect a steel, pin-connected, king-post pony truss over the Rock River in 1908, a design that was not popular with the MHC. Eventually, the commission and its successor, the Minnesota Department of Highways, gained control over much bridge design and construction in the state, and the king post, one of the world's oldest bridge truss forms, began disappearing from Minnesota's roadways.[40]

The same year the Hewett Bridge Company erected Rock County's king-post truss bridge, Bridge No. 6527 was built over the Watonwan River in the southwest section of Madelia. Madelia, a small town tucked into the northeast corner of Watonwan County in south-central Minnesota, was named for Madeline Hartshorn,

the influence of the nascent MHC. Even though the commission had little clout in 1908, being legislatively empowered to impose its will only on construction using state aid funds or to supervise bridge construction on state roads, the agency often advised, and sometimes cajoled, cities, villages, counties, and townships to build stronger and sturdier bridges on roadways not under state control.[43]

Madelia's through-truss bridge was regularly used until 1990, at which time it was replaced by an uninspired concrete bridge immediately to the west. Rather than destroying one of Minnesota's increasingly rare Warren through-truss bridges, however, the city simply

An example of riveted connections is shown here. *Photograph taken in 2007.*

bypassed it with the new bridge, preserving the Warren through truss in place. Realizing the historic nature of the truss, citizens erected a metal placard at the northeast approach that provides some of the bridge's history.[44]

Three truss bridges completed one year after Madelia's crossing continue to demonstrate the varied metal truss types that once marked much of Minnesota. The Prestegard Bridge is a steel, rigid-connected, Pratt pony truss carrying a graveled township road over the Yellow Medicine River in rural Minnesota Falls Township in Yellow Medicine County. The Waterford Bridge is a steel, rigid-connected, Camelback through truss spanning the Cannon River in Waterford Township in Dakota County, almost within sight of Northfield. The Third Street Bridge is a steel, rigid-connected, Pennsylvania through truss in Cannon Falls in Goodhue County. It carries paved Third Street across the Cannon River.

Like Madelia's truss bridge, each of these bridges was built at a time when the MHC did not yet have design control over many of the crossings erected in the state. Still, the infant agency influenced construction of at least one of the bridges, and possibly all three. For instance, each is built heavier and stronger than many truss crossings completed only a short time earlier. Recall, the through-truss Salisbury Bridge was finished only a decade before the through-truss Third Street Bridge in Cannon Falls and the through-truss Waterford Bridge outside Northfield, yet the Salisbury Bridge looks almost frail in comparison.

The Third Street Bridge has a Parker through-truss top chord. More accurately, the Third Street Bridge is a Parker through truss with subdivided web panels. This type of bridge is commonly known as a Pennsylvania through truss, deriving its moniker from its developer, the Pennsylvania Railroad. The 185-foot-long Third Street Bridge is a rather modest version of the type, since these bridges were sometimes employed for spans up to six hundred feet. Even so, Minnesota never featured many Pennsylvania through trusses, making the Third Street Bridge relatively uncommon even at the time it was built.[45]

The Third Street Bridge was engineered by Louis P. Wolff, a partner in the St. Paul firm of Loweth and Wolff. Loweth and Wolff designed a number of bridges, but Wolff went on to engineer two Minnesota structures that emphatically decorate their respective cities, the reinforced-concrete Brainerd and Pipestone water towers. Each tower is reminiscent of a torch handle. The design of the Third Street Bridge was scrutinized by the MHC, because the city of Cannon Falls sought partial funding for the crossing from the state. Wolff's design was not approved until state engineers reviewed his plans and made a few minor changes. The contractor for the project was Alexander Bayne, one of the stems of Seth Hewett and Commadore Jones's bridge-building "family tree." A man who started out as an Iowa school teacher, Bayne became a productive Midwestern bridge builder. Regrettably, there are not many bridges left in Minnesota attributed to Bayne. Actually, there are not many bridges left in Minnesota attributed to a number of the state's early bridge designers and contractors.[46]

It seems that those responsible for the Waterford Bridge near Northfield followed at least some of the design guidelines of the highway commission. The Dakota County Board of Commissioners reviewed the county's bridge-building practices in the summer of 1909, concluding that some officials were spending funds "in a loose and injudicious manner and not … in accordance with the wishes and intentions of the Board." Commissioners must have already formed opinions about the county's thrifty bridge-building habits, though, for in the spring of 1909, the board had Charles A. Forbes, the Dakota County surveyor, design a relatively heavy-duty bridge over the Cannon River in Waterford Township, appropriating $2,500 for roughly half its cost.[47]

The bridge was erected by the Hennepin Bridge Company, a Minneapolis enterprise founded in 1905 by Lawrence H. Johnson, a man who briefly worked for Commadore Jones and his Minneapolis Bridge Company. Johnson also served in the Minnesota legislature from 1901 to 1909. In fact, he was the speaker of the house in 1907. The Waterford Bridge is slightly different from most through trusses erected in Minnesota at the

Engineered by Louis P. Wolff of St. Paul, the Third Street Bridge in Cannon Falls is a Pennsylvania through truss. It was completed over the Cannon River in 1909. *Photograph taken in 2005 by Robert W. Gardner Jr.*

The Waterford Bridge near Northfield spans the Cannon River. It is a Camelback through truss designed by Dakota County surveyor Charles A. Forbes and erected by the Hennepin Bridge Company of Minneapolis in 1909. *Photograph taken in 2005.*

time. As noted, in the early twentieth century, bridge builders were transitioning from pinned construction to rigid construction, usually in the form of riveted connections. But it was not until 1921 that the recently formed Minnesota Department of Highways mandated riveted construction for all through-truss bridges. Thus, in 1909, it was still permissible to build a rigid-connected through-truss bridge using bolts. That is what makes the Waterford Bridge somewhat different. Although much of the crossing is riveted together, part of it is held together with bolts. In fact, the Waterford Bridge is the only remaining Minnesota through-truss highway bridge featuring bolted connections. It is also a span appreciated by the locals. One resident of Waterford Township observed, "Almost every time we passed the Waterford Bridge, [my father] would tell how he helped fill the approach to the bridge in 1909 with a team of horses, and also with a wheelbarrow. It is important that old things like the bridge be kept for the future."[48]

Unlike the Waterford and Third Street bridges, the Prestegard Bridge in rural Yellow Medicine County in western Minnesota is a pony truss. It is obviously more slight than those other crossings, but it was never designed to handle the same traffic loads. But even though the rigid-connected Prestegard Bridge seems slender, it is almost bulky in contrast to the pin-connected Bridge No. L5245 near Brewster in Jackson County. As with through trusses, many early-twentieth-century pony trusses were engineered to be stronger than those completed only a short time earlier. Named for local resident John Prestegard, the Prestegard Bridge has two identical main spans in Pratt configurations. The bridge came about because its forerunner often proved useless in spring. In June 1909, the *Granite Falls Journal* wrote:

A new and much better bridge is to be built over the Yellow Medicine river at the old Sorlien Mill site to take the place of the one carried away by the high water. On May 25th a special election was held in the township of Minnesota Falls to vote on the question of bonding the town for $1,500 for the purpose of building a bridge at the point mentioned, and the proposition was carried. This sum, together with other aid to be received from the county, will enable the town board to build a bridge that will not be washed out every spring.[49]

The bridge was constructed by Milo A. Adams. Adams, like Bayne and Hewett and the others, was one of the early Minneapolis-based bridge contractors. Born in Indiana, Adams moved to Minneapolis in 1882 to work on the Stone Arch Bridge. An expert surface-air diver, he helped construct the bridge's footings beneath the Mississippi River. The following year, he recovered a drowning victim in White Bear Lake, not far from St. Paul. He continued his diving efforts but soon formed his own bridge-building firm. Completing scores of bridges throughout the Midwest, the contractor never retired. In fact, at the time of his death in 1922, when he was seventy years old, he had five bridges under construction in western Minnesota. Clearly, Adams was a favorite with local governments in and around Yellow Medicine County.[50]

Adams's steel legacy over the Yellow Medicine River in Minnesota Falls Township was almost demolished in 1952, when township residents debated whether to repair it or build anew. The fact that the bridge is presently standing provides the conclusion to the debate. Still, pony trusses are disappearing quickly, and it would hardly be surprising to discover this one gone in a short time.[51]

The bridge plate for the Waterford Bridge crowns the crossing's portal and lists many of those involved with the bridge's construction. *Photograph taken in 2005.*

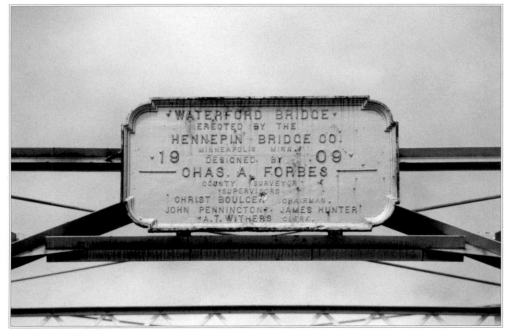

The Prestegard Bridge is a Pratt pony truss reaching across the Yellow Medicine River in rural Yellow Medicine County. It was erected in 1909 by Milo A. Adams, an early bridge builder based in Minneapolis. *Photograph taken in 2005.*

The underside of the Prestegard Bridge shows how floor beams support small I beams (commonly called stringers), which then carry the bridge's deck. *Photograph taken in 2005.*

In 1913, four years after the Waterford, Third Street, and Prestegard bridges were finished, the Minnesota legislature passed a measure that led to MHC control over almost all highway bridge design in the state. The legislation was a highway reform act known as the Dunn Law, named for Robert C. Dunn, a journalist from Princeton, Minnesota, who also was a state legislator and an advocate of the Good Roads Movement. Although the law was concerned chiefly with roadway administration and financing, some provisions addressed bridges. The law required local governments seeking bridges to supply contractors with plans and specifications for any crossing costing over $500. Furthermore, if local governments requested bridge plans and specifications from the state, the highway commission was obligated to provide such. This process soon resulted in state-designed standard plans becoming the norm. With the Dunn Law, the age of the lightly constructed bridge in Minnesota had mostly passed, although, as demonstrated by the Third Street, Waterford,

The Eden Bridge over the Minnesota River between Brown and Renville counties is an early example of the standard Warren pony-truss plan developed by the Minnesota Department of Highways. Erected by Waddell and Hohle of Minneapolis, construction of the bridge began in 1917 and finished the following year. *Photograph taken in 2005.*

and Prestegard bridges, some local governments and bridge contractors had sniffed the changing winds before the winds actually shifted.[52]

Additional change came in 1917, with the formation of the Minnesota Department of Highways (MHD). The MHD replaced the MHC, even though, technically, the highway commission existed through 1921. The MHD was overseen by a full-time administrator who replaced the three part-time highway commissioners. In part, the MHD originated from the Federal Aid Road Act of 1916, which made millions of dollars available to state governments willing to establish highway authorities to manage a national network of principal thoroughfares. Minnesota's trunk highway system sprang from this legislation, but initiation of this roadway network intended to connect all parts of Minnesota would not become reality until the 1920s.[53]

The same year the MHD was born, the commissioners of Brown and Renville counties advertised for a pony-truss bridge over the Minnesota River in southwestern Minnesota, halfway between New Ulm and Redwood Falls. Carrying graveled County State Aid Highway 8, the Eden Bridge serves as a link between the two counties. One of the earliest crossings reflecting a design of the nascent MHD, the Eden Bridge was

christened for Brown County's Eden Township, which hosts the south end of the bridge. In mid-1917, the contract for the nearly $16,000 crossing was awarded to Waddell and Hohle of Minneapolis, a firm including Alan D. Waddell, a man who briefly served as the Minneapolis agent for the Joliet Bridge and Iron Company of Joliet, Illinois. The contractor finished the Eden Bridge about the middle of 1918.[54]

Waddell and Hohle's bridge represents the MHD's standard design for a Warren pony truss with verticals. It was a Warren design that was widely employed between 1917 and 1925. The plan provided bridges that were somewhat stronger than Warren pony designs developed by the MHC, chiefly because the webs were fortified with heavier vertical members. The standard Warren pony truss of the period was between about forty and eighty feet in length. The Eden Bridge features two main spans of eighty-one feet, thus the trusses are at the outermost length approved by the MHD. The MHD altered the standard plan for Warren pony-truss bridges after 1925, making the web even stronger. This new design had little impact, however, for the Great Depression soon squelched almost all bridge construction in the state. By the time large-scale bridge building resumed, the MHD favored deep-section, steel I beams and reinforced-concrete structures, and so Warren pony trusses largely disappeared. The Eden Bridge, nearing the century mark, is perhaps the best remaining example of a Warren pony truss erected employing a standard design created by the MHD.[55]

The MHD adopted a standard through-truss design for another bridge spanning a portion of the Minnesota River well downstream of the Eden Bridge. The Long Meadow Bridge is so far downstream, in fact, that it is at the southeastern edge of Bloomington, almost on the boundary line between Hennepin and Dakota counties. Built by the Illinois Steel Bridge Company, an out-of-state contractor that had a branch office in St. Paul, the Long Meadow Bridge does not actually reach over the main part of the river but across an overflow, a relatively shallow floodplain locally known as Long Meadow Lake, now a component of the Minnesota Valley National Wildlife Refuge. The bridge was completed in 1920 and is formed of five steel Camelbacks, each measuring about 172 feet in length. In Minnesota today it is especially unusual to discover a bridge formed of so many through trusses. Historically, the bridge served as an auxiliary structure, carrying Cedar Avenue to an 1890 steel swing-span bridge that reached across the Minnesota River's navigation channel.[56]

At the time the Long Meadow Bridge was constructed, Bloomington was still a modest farming landscape, as was the area across the Minnesota River, immediately to the south. But Cedar Avenue was a unique roadway, for it traversed this rural setting and delivered travelers directly into the heart of Minneapolis. This direct link to a major urban center proved an impetus to suburban development in southeast Bloomington and in locales south of the Minnesota River. Over the decades, however, as automobiles became wider and traffic became greater, the Long Meadow Bridge clearly became ill suited to continue in its traditional role. Traversing the narrow structure with its timber deck creaking with each turn of the axle made some locals queasy. Timothy Wegscheid remembers journeying over the crossing as a youngster en route to Metropolitan Stadium: "Every time we had to cross that river to get to a Vikings game at the old outdoor stadium (sometimes in a big, one-unit camper/Winnebago thing that barely seemed to fit on the bridge), I was convinced I was going into the drink and would die a horrible, slow, cold death in the deep, scary waters beneath the bridge."[57]

The late 1970s brought a new, much longer and wider bridge just east of the Long Meadow Bridge. A phenomenal population explosion in and around Eagan and Apple Valley south of the river ensued. The swing span over the Minnesota River was razed, but ownership of the Long Meadow Bridge was transferred from the state to the city of Bloomington and continued to be used by motorized vehicles until 1993. For the next several years, the bridge was open only to pedestrians and bicyclists. It became an especially favorite platform for birders. By 2002, however, the structurally suffering bridge was closed to all. Chain-link fencing and concrete barricades now bar the approaches, and conspicuous signage informs visitors to view nature from someplace else. Bloomington is in quandary, for it has little money to rehabilitate the bridge and yet much of the surrounding population is loath to lose this piece of rare structural history that provides a significant link in the trail system winding through parts of

the Minnesota River Valley south of Minneapolis and St. Paul. Hopefully, a financial partnership between Bloomington and other parties will result in the bridge's salvation.[58]

Another large bridge near the University of Minnesota's Minneapolis campus was completed only a few years after the Long Meadow Bridge. It exhibits a nonstandard design. This bridge was not a product of the MHD, however, but of the Northern Pacific Railway (NP). Historically, the railroads have created some of the most intriguing metal truss bridges, and NP Bridge No. 9 is one example. The bridge is a short distance upriver of the Washington Avenue Bridge, which is a double-deck, steel, plate-girder crossing completed in the 1960s that moves automobiles and pedestrians between the University of Minnesota's West Bank and East Bank. A wide, flat stretch of land edging the west side of the river between the two bridges is made uninteresting by a university parking lot. This location, however, was once dominated by Bohemian Flats, one of the most fascinating neighborhoods in either Minneapolis or St. Paul. Begun as a shantytown in the late 1800s, Bohemian Flats was initially a collection of eastern European immigrants who pieced together meek shelters from whatever could be found, including

Designed by the Minnesota Department of Highways and built by the Illinois Steel Bridge Company in 1920, the Long Meadow Bridge spans Long Meadow Lake adjacent to the Minnesota River in Bloomington. Composed of five Camelback spans, the bridge is a rare Minnesota example of a crossing formed of so many through trusses. *Photograph taken in 2007.*

This view shows the original NP Bridge No. 9 looming above Bohemian Flats. Various buildings of the University of Minnesota are in the background and survey the river, bridge, and neighborhood below. *Photograph by Sweet, 1903; courtesy of the Minnesota Historical Society.*

wood deposited on the Flats by the river. Even though the community suffered chronic spring flooding, the appearance of the Flats evolved into something more respectable than what it had been when founded. Still, the neighborhood remained subservient to the bulky metal bridges that passed overhead. To the north, residents peered upward to NP trains belching black clouds above the eaves, while to the south it was horses and buggies that occupied the skyline on the original Washington Avenue Bridge—at least until the automobile arrived and belched as well.[59]

The first NP bridge over the Mississippi River at Bohemian Flats was constructed in 1887, a time when the community below was composed chiefly of humble gable- and shed-roofed houses divided by narrow dirt pathways traversed by hens pecking their way from one crude wood-plank fence to the next. The bridge was a deck truss, an acceptable construction at Bohemian Flats because the lower part of the structure remained well above the Mississippi River. Actually, much of the terrain adjacent to the Mississippi River as it courses through the Twin Cities metropolitan area

Even the steeple of Immanuel Evangelical Slovak Lutheran Church yields to the metal bridges that passed above Bohemian Flats. The original NP Bridge No. 9, completed in 1887, is in the background. *Photograph ca. 1900; courtesy of the Minnesota Historical Society.*

Erected in 1880, the Milwaukee Road's metal, deck-truss bridge across the Mississippi River between Minneapolis and St. Paul continues to mark the waterway just downstream of the Cappelen Memorial Bridge. *Photograph by Sweet, ca. 1904; courtesy of the Minnesota Historical Society.*

is elevated, a geography that practically compelled late-nineteenth-century bridge engineers to raise deck trusses over the waterway. For instance, the Milwaukee Road constructed a deck-truss bridge a short distance downriver, below Franklin Avenue, several years before NP Bridge No. 9 was finished. Completed in 1880, this extant crossing provided a direct link between Minne- apolis and St. Paul, allowing Milwaukee Road trains to avoid the rail line's circuitous route between the cities via the bridge over the Minnesota River at Mendota. Five years later, the Minneapolis Western Railway, a railroad incorporated by several prominent milling industrialists to serve the Minneapolis mills on the west bank of the Mississippi River, erected a wrought

The metal deck-truss Minneapolis Western Railway Bridge spanned the Mississippi River just above NP Bridge No. 9. It was completed in 1885 and razed in 1952. *Photograph taken in 1895; courtesy of the Minnesota Historical Society.*

The original Washington Avenue Bridge, completed in 1885, was not nearly as heavy looking as the crossing carrying Washington Avenue over the river today. Like NP Bridge No. 9, the metal deck-truss Washington Avenue Bridge also peered down on Bohemian Flats. *Photograph by F. M. Laraway, ca. 1885; courtesy of the Minnesota Historical Society.*

iron deck-truss bridge just upriver of the NP bridge site. This was soon followed by the original Washington Avenue Bridge, a deck-truss wagon crossing. However, none of these bridges predate the Tenth Avenue Bridge, a deck-truss wagon and pedestrian structure that joined Tenth Avenue on the Minneapolis side of the Mississippi River with Sixth Avenue on the St. Anthony side. Completed in 1874, the Tenth Avenue Bridge was situated just northwest of the Minneapolis Western bridge site and for several years overlooked the Falls of St. Anthony. By the early 1880s, the view was obscured by James J. Hill's grand arch.[60]

The late 1800s brought two large wrought iron deck trusses to the Mississippi River at St. Paul as well. In fact, both the Wabasha Street Bridge and the Smith Avenue Bridge (commonly recognized as the High Bridge) were built in 1889. Both were incredibly long structures, with the High Bridge reaching almost

2,800 feet. The Wabasha Street Bridge was the fourth incarnation of a river crossing at Wabasha Street. It was also the most visually pleasing of the bunch. The High Bridge was spindly looking with no aesthetic embellishment. Nevertheless, the no-frills crossing upriver of the Wabasha Street Bridge was welcomed as a link between the neighborhoods along West Seventh Street and those across the river at Cherokee Heights. In 1904, an especially nasty windstorm sheared away part of the bridge. The sections lost were subsequently replaced with sections made of steel. Surprisingly, it was these sections that severely deteriorated over the years. The bridge was razed in 1985, with a new bridge taking its place in 1987. The replacement crossing has a curious and attractive main span formed of a steel arch embraced by two half arches. The Wabasha Street Bridge was replaced in the late 1990s with an eye-catching concrete bridge formed of boxed girders.

Designed by St. Paul's chief bridge engineer, Andreas W. Munster, the fourth Wabasha Street Bridge over the Mississippi River was a steel deck-truss bridge with an arched lower chord. The handsome crossing was completed in 1889 and lasted many decades. *Photograph by* St. Paul Pioneer Press and Dispatch, *1955; courtesy of the Minnesota Historical Society.*

Both of the early bridges outlasted the Minneapolis Western Railway Bridge and the Tenth Avenue Bridge in Minneapolis, as well as the original Washington Avenue Bridge. The railroad structure was demolished in 1952, but the Tenth Avenue Bridge was torn down ten years earlier. Its metal was salvaged for use in the war effort against the Axis. A stone pier near the east bank of the river is the most obvious remnant of the old bridge. Unlike the Washington Avenue Bridge, neither the Minneapolis Western Railway Bridge nor the Tenth Avenue Bridge had replacements.[61]

The original NP Bridge No. 9 remained until the early 1920s, when the NP route over the Mississippi River was shifted slightly north. As the NP completed

The wrought iron Smith Avenue Bridge was a deck truss designed by Munster and erected the same year as the fourth Wabasha Street Bridge. Removed in 1985, the Smith Avenue Bridge was longer than the Wabasha Street Bridge but not as attractive. *Photograph ca. 1900; courtesy of the Minnesota Historical Society.*

a new bridge, it incorporated the old truss into the new truss, which explains why a truss bridge completed in 1923 features a number of pinned connections, a construction method that was mostly antiquated by the 1920s. The webs of the original deck truss make up the outside webs of the current deck truss, while a third, much-heavier web fabricated in 1922 and 1923 cuts longitudinally through the bridge's center. This made the bridge better capable of handling the increasing weight of trains. This bridge configuration is different from most deck-truss bridges, although it is quite similar to the first Washington Avenue Bridge, which was fortified with a center web in 1890 so it could support trolley cars. Labeling NP Bridge No. 9 as one truss type or another is problematic, however. A study of the bridge was completed in the mid-1990s, with the author describing the crossing as a "pin and eyebar" truss. Well, it is, but that is broad terminology applicable to other trusses as well. For instance, the Salisbury Bridge in Meeker County is a pin and eyebar

truss, and so is the Hanover Bridge in Wright County, as is Bridge No. L5245 in Jackson County. If a truss bridge is pieced together employing pins and eyebars, then it is a pin and eyebar truss. More accurately, the Salisbury and Hanover bridges are pinned Pratt trusses, as is the lightweight Bridge No. L5245.[62]

The two deck-truss main spans of NP Bridge No. 9, each 245 feet long, resemble Pratts, but that impression is derived from the outside webs. The center web is composed of heavy vertical and diagonal members arranged in an unusual pattern, and so perhaps the best description of NP Bridge No. 9 is that it is a blend of two different truss patterns. In other words, the bridge is a hybrid truss.[63]

Although Bohemian Flats vanished long ago, ultimately replaced with a broad, grassy expanse interrupted by asphalt and parking meters, NP Bridge No. 9 continues to serve traffic, albeit foot traffic; the railroad stopped using the bridge some time ago. Some years back, this unique deck-truss crossing was closed. Now reopened, pedestrians have the opportunity to explore its construction and take in panoramic views of the Mississippi River while strolling from one university bank to the other.

Because they require considerable vertical clearance between the bridge deck and the surface of the water, it is understandable that deck trusses are rarer than either through trusses or pony trusses. For example, a crossing such as NP Bridge No. 9 would never work in the Red River Valley, a lush geographic depression that is home to Grand Forks, North Dakota, and East Grand Forks, Minnesota. The two cities are divided by the Red River of the North, the boundary between northwestern Minnesota and eastern North Dakota. The Red River of the North has a long history of overflowing its banks in springtime, and a deck-truss bridge would exacerbate flooding, acting as a barrier to high water and debris moving downriver. As a result, in 1929, city and highway officials opted for a through-truss bridge on DeMers Avenue to replace the inadequate swing span built in 1889 to link Grand Forks with East Grand Forks over the Red River of the North. At the time that the Sorlie Memorial Bridge replaced the swing span, the movable bridge was no longer necessary because commercial river traffic on the Red River of the North had subsided.[64]

Today NP Bridge No. 9 is heavier and sturdier than it was when assembled in 1887, primarily because of an additional web that runs longitudinally through the center of the old truss. *Photograph taken in 2005.*

The Sorlie Memorial Bridge across the Red River of the North was completed in 1929. Note the solitary stone pier in the foreground, a remnant of NP Bridge No. 95, an intriguing railroad swing bridge built in 1917 (the pier dates from 1887 and the first timber bridge built at the site). NP Bridge No. 95 evolved into a popular pedestrian bridge, but then it became a villain—at least to some, who blamed the bridge for increasing flooding in the area. *Photograph taken in 2006.*

The roller bearings of the Sorlie Memorial Bridge allow the bridge to shift with the plastic river banks. *Photograph taken in 2006.*

The Sorlie Memorial Bridge is situated just south of a lonely remnant of NP Bridge No. 95, a solitary stone pier that appears to be wading the river, perhaps seeking its steel superstructure, which was removed a few years ago after officials concluded the old railroad bridge turned pedestrian bridge contributed to area flooding. It was unnecessary for the MHD to design the Sorlie Memorial Bridge because the North Dakota State Highway Department took up the task. Even so, each state was responsible for $75,000 of the bridge's roughly $316,000 cost. The remaining dollars came from the federal government.[65]

The Minneapolis Bridge Company erected the Sorlie Memorial Bridge, completing a steel, rigid-connected Parker through truss of two spans, each roughly 280 feet long. The builder was not the Minneapolis Bridge Company begun by Commadore Jones that evolved into the Minneapolis Bridge and Iron Company, however. Neither of those firms existed by the 1910s. Instead, a new Minneapolis Bridge Company was established about 1914 by Alexander Bayne, who was, as noted previously, a disciple of Commadore Jones and Seth Hewett. The Sorlie Memorial Bridge is named for Arthur Gustav Sorlie, a former governor of North Dakota who died one year before the bridge was completed. At the time of his death, Governor Sorlie was also a high-ranking official within the highway department and a tireless promoter of well-constructed roads and bridges. In fact, the bronze name plate honoring the governor that is mounted to the Sorlie Memorial Bridge carries the epitaph "A True Friend of Roads and Bridges."[66]

At first glance, the bridge may not seem unusual for a late-1920s Parker through truss. But closer inspection reveals that the bridge is resting on bearings that resemble wheels. Typically, bearings for truss bridges are not wheels, but rockers or some other support that allows slight movement. The Sorlie Memorial Bridge's circular bearings are the result of site conditions. The banks of the Red River of the North are highly plastic under concentrated load, and roller bearings were engineered to help compensate for this instability. An engineering article written during construction explains, "Each truss is provided with a specially devised roller bearing that will roll back on the abutment in case the sliding of the banks moves the abutment toward the river." Engineers for the Sorlie Memorial Bridge also realized that the shifting banks would occasionally force reconstruction of the approaches. This site instability also explains why the bridge was not built entirely of concrete, a building material that had become popular for bridge construction by the time the Sorlie Memorial Bridge was erected. Steel allows some bending and twisting. In a sense, it has more give than concrete. If concrete is torqued, it fractures rather easily.[67]

Officials on both sides of the river welcomed the new bridge. The souvenir program published for the dedication ceremony in mid-September 1929 announced a host of attending dignitaries, including the city commissioner of Grand Forks, the mayor of East Grand Forks, officials of the two highway departments, and the governors of Minnesota and North Dakota. The widow of Governor Sorlie christened the crossing by breaking a bottle of water over a hand railing.[68]

In the past decade, the Sorlie Memorial Bridge, like NP Bridge No. 95, has been a subject of consternation, as some officials believe it contributes to flooding. The anguish and anger of those who suffered the astonishing high water in the Red River Valley in the spring of 1997 was revealed in a letter to the Minnesota State Historic Preservation Office (SHPO) in October of that year. About that time, the SHPO and the Minnesota State Review Board were considering the eligibility of the bridge for the National Register of Historic Places. The timing of the review process was unfortunate, and the letter sent by a commissioner of Polk County chastised the SHPO and the State Review Board. In part, it read:

I find it very upsetting that the State Review Board on Sept. 18 determined the Sorlie Bridge to be a "significant structure." Certainly the board was acting on incomplete information. The Sorlie Bridge is being blamed for having caused a minimum of a one-foot rise in the level of the Red River during the 1997 spring flood … and that one foot may have been the difference in whether our dikes were overtopped or not. Need we remind the board that the flood forced more than 50,000 residents in the two cities to evacuate their homes; that almost 500 homes in East Grand Forks and a similar number in Grand Forks were completely destroyed by flooding; and that all but 8 of the 2,500 homes in East Grand Forks had extensive flood damage.…[69]

An emotional statement, certainly, but the commissioner's anger is misplaced, for the sole objective of the SHPO and the State Review Board was to determine whether the Sorlie Memorial Bridge met the federal definition of a historically significant property, not whether the bridge increased area flooding; that is a task for engineers. The bridge is clearly historic, and it was subsequently added to the National Register of Historic Places. The trauma of the flood likely put many on edge, and the commissioner's letter may have been a means of venting frustrations during a trying period. Ominously, though, the correspondence ends with the county official arguing that the Sorlie Memorial Bridge be razed. Several years have now passed, and the bridge is still standing. Maybe that implies that alternatives to the bridge's demolition have been sought.[70]

Another example of how site conditions influence the design of a bridge is found about 340 miles southeast of the Sorlie Memorial Bridge, in St. Peter in Nicollet County. Like Winona, Red Wing, Pipestone, Stillwater, Northfield, and some other Minnesota cities, St. Peter is a community that has preserved much of its structural heritage. It shows not just in its buildings and residences but also in its most prominent crossing, the Broadway Bridge. Situated near the northeast corner of the commercial district, the Broadway Bridge supports Broadway Avenue (also known as Minnesota Trunk Highway 99, although previously it was Minnesota Trunk Highway 21) as it passes over the Minnesota River into rural Oshawa Township in Le Sueur County. Composed of two riveted spans, the handsome Pennsylvania through truss is made more so by its silver and black color scheme: the webs, top lateral, and sway bracing are painted black, while the top chords, end posts, ornamental railings, and light stanchions are painted silver. As with the Third Street Bridge in Cannon Falls in Goodhue County, the Broadway Bridge's web panels are subdivided, a primary characteristic of the Pennsylvania through-truss design.[71]

Designed by the MHD, the $99,000 Broadway Bridge

was completed by the Minneapolis Bridge Company in June 1931. Its construction came about because one month before citizens of Grand Forks and East Grand Forks celebrated the opening of the Sorlie Memorial Bridge, a grain truck collided with the Broadway Bridge's predecessor, collapsing part of it. Constructed in 1883, the earlier bridge's main span was a swing span, its design similar to the swing span replaced by the Sorlie Memorial Bridge. As with the Red River of the North, in the late 1800s, the Minnesota River was frequented by freight-carrying vessels. Erecting the Broadway Bridge proved challenging because of the quirky nature of the Minnesota River at the bridge site, a difficulty overcome with a somewhat quirky bridge design.[72] Historian Jeffrey A. Hess explains:

The bridge's overall design … is unconventional, largely because the current of the Minnesota River twists in mid-channel at the site. This hydraulic peculiarity dictated the construction of a skewed pier, so as to offer the least resistance to the flow of the water. Because of the oblique placement of the pier, the two truss spans required a skewed configuration at the end supported by the pier. This goal was achieved by designing each span with truss webs of unequal length and slightly different profile. In the west span, the north web is a ten-panel, 195-foot truss with inclined endposts at each end, while the south web is a nine-panel, 176-foot truss with an inclined endpost at the abutment and a vertical endpost at the pier. In the east span, the situation is exactly reversed.[73]

Because the bridge's skewed design imposes asymmetrical end posts where the truss spans meet at the center pier, the Broadway Bridge would have been an ungainly structure if not for a simple, yet creative, solution: MHD engineers inserted a purely ornamental horizontal steel member between the top chords of the trusses as they met at the pier. This small addition softened the effect of the contorted lines while seeming to join the two trusses into a single, visually cohesive unit. The consequence is an aesthetically pleasing truss bridge with a top chord flowing from one truss to the next. Upon its completion, the *St. Peter Herald* noted that the "new St. Peter bridge is the most elaborate and the largest in the locality.… It is a splendid job, a credit to the highway department, the city and its builders."[74]

Adopting the same color scheme as the Broadway Bridge, Bridge No. 5388 carries Minnesota Trunk Highway 24 across the North Fork of the Crow River in Meeker County. The matching coloring is one of the few similarities between the two bridges, however. While both are truss crossings designed by the MHD, Bridge No. 5388 is a pony truss. Specifically, it is a single-span, rigid-connected Warren pony truss with verticals and

The Broadway Bridge across the Minnesota River in St. Peter is a Pennsylvania through truss designed by the Minnesota Department of Highways and erected by the Minneapolis Bridge Company in 1931. Because the bridge is skewed, the truss crossing would have looked awkward if not for a simple aesthetic solution: the insertion of a steel beam between the top chords at either side of the bridge, making the two trusses appear to be a single, cohesive unit. *Photograph taken in 2005.*

Bridge No. 5388 represents the final evolution of the Minnesota Department of Highways' standard Warren pony-truss bridge design. It was completed in 1938 over the North Fork of the Crow River in Meeker County, just upstream of the late-nineteenth-century Salisbury Bridge. *Photograph taken in 2005.*

features a polygonal top chord. Located a short distance upriver of Meeker County's Salisbury Bridge (in fact, if not for a growth of trees, the two structures would be within line of sight), Bridge No. 5388 was built by Teberg and Berg, a St. Paul bridge-building firm that existed from about the early 1930s to the early 1940s.[75]

Constructed in 1935, Bridge No. 5388 is the final evolution of a state-designed Warren pony truss. Whereas the Eden Bridge over the Minnesota River between Brown and Renville Counties reflects the standard MHD plan for Warren pony trusses built between 1917 and 1925, Bridge No. 5388 represents the standard MHD plan for Warren pony trusses erected in the late 1920s and later. As earlier noted, this was a period when the Warren pony truss was made stronger than its predecessor. Bridge No. 5388, for example, is something of a tank. It is heavily built-up and even features outrigger type sway bracing. Arguably, the bridge is overbuilt.[76]

Costing around $22,000, the bridge spans a distance of one hundred feet, roughly twenty feet more than allowed by the earlier Warren pony-truss specifications. The bridge is made economical by its polygonal top chord, a characteristic allowing a web of varying depth. Basically, a polygonal top chord is more economical than

a horizontal top chord because it reduces the amount of steel required to form the web, a fact common also to through trusses. Although this particular Warren pony-truss type was never built in numbers rivaling its predecessors, it nevertheless represents advancement in bridge-building technology. Even so, the MHD soon thought Warren pony trusses antiquated.[77]

That was not yet the dominant view in 1937, however, for that year Koochiching County received $30,000 from the state to help build a three-span bridge over the Big Fork River, and two of the spans were designed by the MHD as Warren pony trusses with verticals and polygonal top chords. Bridge No. 5804 was required because the previous structure washed away in the spring of 1937. Construction of the nearly $60,000 bridge went to Teberg and Berg, the same St. Paul contractor responsible for Bridge No. 5388. The contractor began work in late 1938, and the bridge was finished by summer 1939.[78]

Carrying County State Aid Highway 1, Bridge No. 5804 is located near Lindford, a community about fifty miles northwest of Bridge No. 5721, the wrought iron structure salvaged from storage in Sauk Centre and re-erected over the Little Fork River in Koochiching County in 1937. Tiny Lindford is named for two men, Swedish farmer Andrew L. Lindvall, who lived in the vicinity of the modest settlement, and, curiously, Henry Ford, the automobile industrialist. The Ford Motor Company was established in 1903, the same year Lindvall arrived in the north-central part of Koochiching County where the settlement of Lindford was founded. Presumably, Lindvall, and other locals as well, were so impressed with the efforts of the industrialist that they honored him by including his surname in the community's moniker.[79]

The main span of Bridge No. 5804 is a 180-foot-long, rigid-connected Pennsylvania through truss, while the two 80-foot-long, rigid-connected Warren pony trusses serve as approaches. Sandwiched between the two smaller trusses, the Pennsylvania through truss seems oddly parental. As with the Pennsylvania through trusses in Cannon Falls and St. Peter, the main span of Bridge No. 5804 features subdivided web panels. Interestingly, though, many of the web members are not built-up from smaller steel members but are formed of steel rolled I beams. This was a new way of building truss bridges in the late 1930s and 1940s, a construction method the *Engineering News-Record* praised in 1942: "In both short- and long-span trusses the use of rolled sections instead of built-up members is growing, not only for better appearance but because shop work is reduced, there are fewer pieces to handle and painting is simplified."[80] Presently, the county wants to replace the bridge at Lindford, arguing that it requires considerable repair and that it is not as accommodating to logging trucks as some would like.

That through-truss and pony-truss bridges continued to be erected in the 1930s and 1940s implies that the bridge types were still popular. But steel-truss construction was significantly declining by this time, as builders increasingly turned to reinforced-concrete bridges or crossings made of steel girders. Prefabricated steel I beams were quite large and durable about this period, thus erecting a girder bridge of deep-section steel I beams was often more efficient than piecing together the many smaller metal members required for a truss. Moreover, this period brought the construction of a number of corrugated-iron multiplate arches, a crossing type that frequently replaced pony-truss bridges at sites demanding short spans. Minnesota retains historic examples of both steel I beam bridges and corrugated-iron multiplate arches.[81]

Two early examples of the type of deep-section steel I beam bridge that became ever present on America's highways are Bridge No. 7645 in rural St. Louis County, about twenty-five miles north of Hibbing, and Bridge No. 6679 in rural Houston County, roughly two miles south of the city of Houston. Aesthetically, neither bridge is worth writing to mother about. Still, neither is unsightly.

Costing almost $12,000, seventy-two-foot-long Bridge No. 7645 carries County State Aid Highway 5 across the Bearskin River. It was designed by the St. Louis County Highway Department and built by E. W. Coons of Hibbing, Minnesota. Completed in 1934, Bridge No. 7645 is distinctive because it was one of the first two bridges in Minnesota erected using thirty-six-

A design of the Minnesota Department of Highways, Bridge No. 5804 near Lindford in Koochiching County was raised over the Big Fork River by Teberg and Berg in 1939. The main span is a Pennsylvania through truss edged at either end by Warren pony trusses with polygonal top chords. *Photograph taken in 2006.*

Bridge No. 7645 in rural St. Louis County is an early example of a deep-section, steel I beam. Designed by the St. Louis County Highway Department, it was built over the Bearskin River by E. W. Coons of Hibbing, Minnesota, in 1934. *Photograph taken in 2006.*

inch-deep rolled I beams. The other is Bridge No. 3673, also finished in 1934 in St. Louis County by E. W. Coons. The historic integrity of Bridge No. 3673 is not as impressive as that of Bridge No. 7645, however. Although a bridge erected with thirty-six-inch-deep rolled I beams generates little excitement, its design was nevertheless another step in the evolution of bridge engineering in Minnesota. In the mid-1920s, twenty-four-inch-deep steel I beams were standard. The standard depth later increased to thirty inches and, eventually, to thirty-six inches. This was important because it marked advancement in steel mill manufacture, but it is also significant because it simplified bridge building. Whereas twenty-four-inch-deep I beams allowed for a span roughly forty feet long, thirty-six-inch-deep I beams allowed for spans up to seventy feet or so. Clearly, this type of construction demanded fewer piers to support the bridge superstructure.[82]

Use of thirty-six-inch-deep steel I beams is also part of the construction of Bridge No. 6679, a crossing supporting Minnesota Trunk Highway 76 where it passes over the South Fork of the Root River in Houston County. Designed by the MHD and completed by Leon Joyce of Rochester, Minnesota, the 314-foot-long bridge was finished for about $118,000 in 1949. It is a bit different from Bridge No. 7645 because it features a cantilevered plan. A cantilever is simply a projecting member, or compilation of members,

that is supported only at one end. For instance, a shelf supported by L-shaped brackets mounted to a wall is considered cantilevered. In its most traditional sense, a cantilevered bridge is composed of two opposing cantilevered sections, or cantilevered spans, reaching toward one another. Between the cantilevered sections is often a suspended span; essentially, the two cantilevered sections hold another span between them. Bridge No. 6679 is composed of two sets of cantilevered I beams suspending another set of I beams between them. Significant distances may be achieved using this type of construction.[83]

Examples of corrugated-iron multiplate arches can be found in Kittson, Wabasha, Todd, Crow Wing, and Cook counties, as well as a few other areas of the state. Developed by the Armco Culvert Manufacturers Association in 1931, multiplate arches are formed of curved, corrugated-iron segments. Braced by concrete headwalls and abutments, the curved, galvanized segments are bolted together to form an arch bridge. Fill is placed atop the arch between the bridge's spandrel walls to

Bridge No. 6679 is another example of a deep-section, steel I beam. It was constructed across the South Fork of the Root River in Houston County in 1949 by Leon Joyce of Rochester, Minnesota. *Photograph taken in 2005 by Robert W. Gardner Jr.*

An especially high multiplate arch, Bridge No. 5827 at the edge of Zumbro Falls was erected over a coulee by the Works Progress Administration in 1938. *Photograph taken in 2005 by Robert W. Gardner Jr.*

The Works Progress Administration completed a multiplate arch in Todd County in 1940. Faced with split fieldstone, Bridge No. L7075 crosses Turtle Creek and features three arches. *Photograph taken in 2005.*

carry a roadway, making the construction similar to that of a stone arch bridge. Actually, many multiplate arch bridges resemble stone arch bridges because their facades have been decorated with stone. Unless the corrugated-metal arch beneath the roadway is visible, it is not uncommon for some to assume that a multiplate crossing is a stone arch.[84]

This type of bridge was popular as part of the road-building programs under President Roosevelt's New Deal. Cheaper than stone arch bridges, multiplate crossings clothed in stone appealed to the aesthetic sensibilities inherent in many transportation infrastructure projects of the time; there may never be another period in American history where roadside beautification is so paramount. Many of Minnesota's picturesque multiplate bridges are located in rural places. As a result, few ever see these wonderful masqueraders that represent a time when America believed that even the road less traveled deserved visual enrichment.[85]

One such road is Minnesota Highway 60 in rural Wabasha County. The roadway passes over an outstanding multiplate arch that spans a minor coulee not far from the eastern edge of the small town of

Zumbro Falls. With the exception of locals, most automobile drivers on the highway probably have no idea a bridge exists at the site, for there are no bridge railings to reveal the structure's location. An unusually high multiplate arch, Bridge No. 5827 exhibits finely crafted rough-faced ashlar and stepped and flared wing walls. The bridge must have looked stunning when completed in 1938. Today the structure would benefit from a thorough cleaning, as much of the stone is blemished with the grime of almost sixty years. Costing only about

A small multiplate arch bridge over Grand Portage Creek near Lake Superior appropriately decorates its surroundings. The bridge was likely a federal relief effort. *Photograph taken in 2005.*

$2,000, the bridge was designed by the MHD and erected by the WPA.[86]

The WPA finished another multiplate arch bridge in rural Todd County in central Minnesota two years after Bridge No. 5827 was completed. Bridge No. L7075, although not nearly as high as Bridge No. 5827, is formed of three corrugated-iron arches. The stout-looking structure carries a township road over Turtle Creek amid relatively flat farmland interrupted by stands of deciduous trees. Situated about six miles northeast of Long Prairie, the crossing's impressive masonry face is formed from split fieldstone. Designed by the Todd County Highway Department, Bridge No. L7075 exhibits a crude Classical Revival style, evidenced by the narrow and unrefined pilasters dividing the arches, as well as a simple and slightly protruding stringcourse and coping.[87]

An attractive multiplate arch is found over Grand Portage Creek in Cook County in extreme northeastern Minnesota, almost within shouting distance of the Canadian border. In a scenic setting overlooking Lake Superior near Grand Portage, Bridge No. 7614 is adorned with a stone facing that is not as neatly trimmed as that of Bridge No. 5827 in Wabasha County, but is less raw than the facade of Bridge No. L7075 in Todd County. The petite bridge with a single arch was erected on County State Aid

The Eisenhower Memorial Bridge spanning the Mississippi River at Red Wing is one of the larger truss crossings in Minnesota. Finished in 1960, it was named for Dwight D. Eisenhower. *Photograph taken in 2006.*

Highway 17 one year after the Todd County crossing was completed, but it is uncertain who designed and built it. Given the construction date, it would not be surprising if the bridge resulted from a federal relief effort. As with Bridge No. L7075, the crossing reflects a rudimentary Classical Revival style.[88]

Use of corrugated-iron multiplate arches peaked in the 1930s and 1940s and then largely disappeared. Steel I beam bridges remain popular, however; venturing over the vast highway system provides proof. Truss bridges, although not nearly as common as other bridge types by the middle of the twentieth century, were still

The Eisenhower Memorial Bridge replaced the Red Wing High Bridge, a Parker through truss approached at either end by deck trusses. The crossing was erected in 1895. *Photograph ca. 1896; courtesy of the Goodhue County Historical Society, Red Wing, Minnesota.*

occasionally built. Some of these were exceptionally
large trusses, clearly indicating that the bridge type was
yet necessary for unusually wide rivers. For example,
the Eisenhower Memorial Bridge, originally named the
Hiawatha Bridge, is a huge through truss completed
over the Mississippi River at Red Wing, Minnesota, in
1960. The bridge took the place of the Red Wing High
Bridge, a crossing formed of two deck-truss approaches
and a pinned Parker through-truss main span. The main

span perched atop soaring masonry piers. Completed
in 1895, the High Bridge was a bit more visually interesting than the present structure that eventually was
christened for our thirty-fourth president, who, inci-
dentally, led the bridge's dedicatory celebration.[89]

One of Minnesota's most fascinating trusses was
opened only a year after the Eisenhower Memorial
Bridge. With a total length of almost eight thousand
feet, the Blatnik Bridge over the St. Louis River in

Duluth was the longest crossing in Minnesota until the nearby Bong Memorial Bridge opened in 1984. Joining Duluth with Superior, Wisconsin, the Blatnik Bridge is a rare suspended truss. It features a six-hundred-foot-long trussed main span in the form of an arch towering above the roadway. This arched main span is pinned to the bridge sections at its ends. In other words, it is hung, or suspended, between the adjacent spans. The unusual bridge received its moniker in 1971, when it was named for John A. Blatnik, a congressman from Minnesota who convinced the federal government to pay roughly 90 percent of the structure's $20 million cost. The bridge was rehabilitated in the early 1990s and is likely to remain for many more years.[90]

While both the Eisenhower Memorial Bridge and the Blatnik Bridge are relatively rare examples of steel-truss bridges built in the last half of the twentieth century, neither has a construction date as late as the current bridge over the Mississippi River at Wabasha. A substantial Warren through truss with verticals and a polygonal top chord, the bridge at Wabasha was opened to traffic in late 1988. The bridge replaced an earlier Warren through truss that linked Wabasha on the Minnesota side of the Mississippi River with Nelson on the Wisconsin side. Completed in early 1931, the Wabasha–Nelson Bridge was constructed by the Industrial Contracting Company, a Minneapolis-based bridge builder that was established in 1929. The $550,000 toll bridge took the place of a ferry that began operating between the two communities during the

The Wabasha–Nelson Bridge across the Mississippi River at Wabasha was a Warren through truss constructed by the Industrial Contracting Company in 1931. The crossing began as a toll bridge and featured a winding approach at the Minnesota side of the river. *Photograph ca. 1940; courtesy of the Minnesota Historical Society.*

Civil War. The 420-foot-long main span was an unusually handsome Warren, featuring a polygonal top chord and subdivided web panels. The familiar triangles comprising the web were subdivided by smaller triangles—that is, triangles within triangles—which provided the bridge a pleasing elevation. The bridge was also intriguing because of its odd approach at the Minnesota side of the river. A design that no highway department today would embrace, the approach featured two ninety-degree turns. It was convoluted, certainly, but it served its purpose of carrying travelers into the heart of Wabasha rather than past it. In this way, it was similar to the Hastings Spiral Bridge. The approach for the current bridge at Wabasha is not as compelling as the old one, but the Warren truss primary span is nevertheless reminiscent of the old main span.[91]

In 1942, the city of Winona, downriver of Wabasha, welcomed an enormous through-truss bridge, an attractive crossing that also reaches across the Missis-

The handsome Main Channel Bridge over the Mississippi River at Winona replaced a through-truss wagon bridge that had been built at the site in 1892. The Main Channel Bridge, designed by the Minnesota Department of Highways, was completed in 1942. *Photograph taken in 2005 by Robert W. Gardner Jr.*

sippi River to Wisconsin. With its twin peaks, the Main Channel Bridge is reminiscent of the framing of a colossal carnival tent. The illusion would be complete if the bridge were clad in canvas and pennants fluttered at the pinnacles. The Main Channel Bridge is part of a series of man-made structures joining Winona with Wisconsin's Buffalo County. This assembly includes the Main Channel Bridge, the North Channel Bridge, a number of approach spans, and a few earthen dikes. The entire system measures roughly one and a half miles in length.[92]

The Main Channel Bridge's moniker is derived from its location. As the Mississippi River flows past Winona, it is split into roughly two courses by an oblong-shaped piece of land known as Latsch Island. At the island's north side, near Wisconsin, the river meanders, while at the south side, near Minnesota, the river's flow is swifter and deeper. The north river section is commonly known as the North Channel, and the south river section is recognized as the Main Channel. Since the Main Channel carries most of the river traffic and is highly visible, it is spanned with an elaborate bridge with considerable clearance between it and the river. Measuring more than 930 feet in length, the Main Channel Bridge is a three-span, steel, rigid-connected, cantilevered through truss. The bridge functions similarly to the cantilevered Bridge No. 6679 in Houston County. The chief difference, of course, is that the Main Channel Bridge is a truss crossing functioning at a grander scale. The substantial width of the Mississippi River at Winona explains why a cantilevered truss was chosen to span the watercourse in the early 1940s.[93]

The Main Channel Bridge replaced another cantilevered truss crossing at Winona over the Mississippi River commonly known as the High Wagon Bridge. Built in 1892, the High Wagon Bridge was in no way suitable for the increasing traffic loads of the mid-twentieth century. Moreover, in 1933, as Minnesota expanded its state highway network, the route over the Mississippi River at Winona was designated Minnesota Trunk Highway 43, making it a main transportation artery. Realizing that the nineteenth-century bridge would never do, the MHD designed a newer, stronger crossing linking Minnesota with Wisconsin. Clearly much beefier than the High Wagon Bridge, the new bridge was also more aesthetically pleasing than the old

The High Wagon Bridge at Winona was a through truss with a distressing appearance. *Photograph ca. 1925; courtesy of the Minnesota Historical Society.*

structure, which had the sad fortune of resembling two sperm whales coupled at the tail. Its aesthetic failings were briefly summarized in *Movable and Long-Span Steel Bridges* when the authors observed, "Lacking symmetry and graceful outlines and proportions—disregarding almost every requirement of beauty—[the High Wagon Bridge] is almost fascinating for ugliness."[94]

The MHD was fortunate, for as the agency planned the cantilevered Main Channel Bridge in the late 1930s, the state of Wisconsin was finishing an interstate, cantilevered bridge over the Mississippi River downriver at La Crosse, Wisconsin. Wisconsin's highway department shared the design for its cantilevered bridge with the MHD. Further, Wisconsin agreed to erect the North Channel Bridge, tying the north side of Latsch Island with Wisconsin. Construction of the Main Channel

Bridge began in September 1940 and was completed in November 1942, five months later than planned. The delay came about because of shortages in labor and material as a result of the onset of World War II. Both the Main Channel Bridge and the North Channel Bridge were completed by Industrial Contracting Company, a Minneapolis-based firm established in 1929. The entire project, including bridges and dikes, totaled about $1.3 million, roughly $700,000 below what the MHD had estimated.[95]

Not surprisingly, the Main Channel Bridge looks much like the crossing at La Crosse, but there are slight design differences. For instance, unlike the bridge in La Crosse, the dead load (the weight of the bridge itself) of the Main Channel Bridge is lightened by using perforated plates in the bridge's boxed upper chords. In other words, putting holes in some of the metal plates used to form part of the top chords of the Main Channel Bridge made the chords—and thus the bridge—lighter. Of course, it also decreased costs, for less steel was used in construction. Employing perforated plates was a recently adopted method of truss building in the 1940s. Additionally, as historian Jeffrey A. Hess explains, the Main Channel Bridge features "shortened vertical members ... to give the curvature of the upper chords

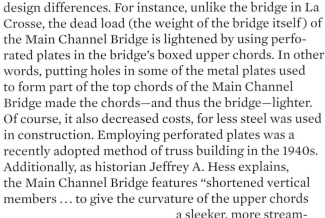

The Kettle River Bridge over the Kettle River at Sandstone resembles an arched truss, but it is a deck truss with an arched lower chord. The bridge was completed in 1948 and replaced an obsolete structure. *Photograph taken in 2005.*

a sleeker, more streamlined appearance. As the Winona press would later note with approval 'the graceful and impressive lines of its cantilever design make it a striking piece of architecture.'"[96]

About the time efforts on the "striking piece of architecture" in Winona were coming to a halt, work was beginning on the Kettle River Bridge in the Pine County community of Sandstone. The bridge straddles the Kettle River at the eastern edge of town, adjacent to the former site of the Kettle River Sandstone Company Quarry, a picturesque wooded and rocky area now on the National Register of Historic Places and serving as a park. A federal prison, largely hidden from the river by bluffs and foliage, is located along the east bank of the waterway, only a short distance from the three-span, rigid-

connected, cantilevered Pratt deck-truss bridge. Superficially, the roughly four-hundred-foot-long crossing appears to be an arch bridge, but only because the lower chord is curved, giving the impression of an arch bridge. Clement P. Kachelmyer, a bridge authority who was the Preliminary Design Engineer for the Minnesota Department of Transportation for more than two decades, explained in a 1983 letter to a state archaeologist:

Inspection [of the bridge] reveals that despite its shape, the curved lower chord does not transmit thrust to the piers or support the remainder of the structure and thus it is not an arch. Rather, the chord and diagonal members are joined to function as a truss.... Thus, this structure should be identified as a Pratt deck truss with curved lower chord.[97]

A curved lower chord serves much the same purpose as a polygonal upper chord: the design is economical because it varies the depth of the truss web and so reduces the amount of steel necessary to build the web. Aesthetically, an arched lower chord is more attractive than a horizontal lower chord.

This deck-truss crossing replaced another deck-truss crossing that was erected over the Kettle River many years earlier. The previous bridge did not have an arched lower chord and, frankly, was a rather frail-looking object. Even so, it was just right for wagons. In other words, the earlier bridge was similar to the predecessor of the Main Channel Bridge in Winona—not in its design but in its inability to handle ever-increasing traffic loads. The traffic issue was compounded when the roadway over the Kettle River was made a state trunk highway in 1933, the same year the roadway over the Mississippi River at Winona received the designation.[98]

While a heavier bridge was needed across the Kettle River by the 1930s, it was several years before it was built. Citizens of Sandstone lobbied for another bridge soon after the route over the river was named a trunk highway, but it did little good. Like many states suffering the privations of the Great Depression, Minnesota was financially strapped and had no money for the bridge project. By 1939, however, federal dollars became available after the federal government opened the prison adjacent to the east end of the bridge. The plans were developed in 1941, and work began the following year. The labor soon stopped, however, as steel was dedicated to the war effort. Material shortages continued immediately after the war, and construction of the bridge did not resume until 1947. The contractor, A. Guthrie and Company, Inc. of St. Paul, finished the $225,000 structure in 1948.[99]

Besides its arched lower chord, the Kettle River Bridge has another design characteristic that makes it unique. As with the Main Channel Bridge, the structure in Sandstone is cantilevered. It also features two suspended spans. But the cantilever is opposite that of the Main Channel Bridge—that is, the Kettle River Bridge features cantilevers near each end that reach toward their respective abutments, not toward the center of the bridge. Further, the suspended spans are located at opposite extremes of the bridge, each hung between one end of the cantilevered section and an abutment. This curious design came about because engineers discovered that the fill at the approaches and abutments had a tendency to shift, moving the abutments.[100] The problem and the solution are probably best explained by civil engineering student Steven R. Brown, writing in the early 1980s:

Experience with continuing subsidence of the bare fills evidently led the designers to accept [the] prediction of "appreciable settlement." Thus the design of the truss itself was modified in such fashion that the expected abutment settlements would cause a minimum of structural distress to the bridge. This was accomplished by placing a pinned-joint hinge in the upper chord of the truss, 50 feet out from each abutment. The corresponding lower chord member was pin-connected at both ends, with one pin riding in a 12-inch-long slot; due to the pin and slot arrangement this actually became a "false member" incapable of transmitting any axial thrust. The net result of these details is that the bridge, while having the elegant arch-like appear-

The 1954 Drayton Bridge spans the Red River of the North between Drayton, North Dakota, and Robbin, Minnesota. The bridge is a substantial Warren through truss designed by consulting engineer Clifford Johnson of Denver, Colorado. *Photograph taken in 2006.*

ance of a continuous curved-chord truss, is in fact composed of three distinct units. The main center span is supported on the river piers and cantilevers toward the abutments; while the two suspended end spans are free to rotate downward about the pin at the cantilever end, in response to abutment settlements.[101]

Shifting abutments were also a concern for one of Minnesota's last large through-truss bridges. Spanning the Red River of the North, about fifty miles north of Grand Forks and East Grand Forks, the Drayton Bridge in Kittson County is a Warren through truss with a polygonal top chord. The bridge opened to traffic in November 1954. Kittson County is a geographically odd county, for it is naturally lakeless, an uncommon characteristic in a state gifted with thousands of lakes. Kittson County remedied this curiosity in the late 1930s, when it erected a dam on the South Branch of Two Rivers, impounding a large water reservoir known as Lake Bronson. The Drayton Bridge is about thirty miles southwest of Lake Bronson, just outside of Robbin, a small town almost immediately across the Red River of the North from the modest North Dakota community of Drayton, from which the bridge gets its name.[102]

As with the Sorlie Memorial Bridge upriver (the

The original Drayton Bridge was a vertical-lift structure erected in 1911, although by that time few steamboats were plying the river and the bridge type was largely unnecessary. *Photograph taken in 1911; courtesy of the Minnesota Historical Society.*

Red River of the North flows to the north, not to the south), the Drayton Bridge is cursed by plastic riverbanks. Under load, the riverbanks of the Red River of the North drift toward the river. Earth fill for bridge approaches moves with the drifting banks. When building the Sorlie Memorial Bridge, engineers solved this problem by supporting the superstructure on roller bearings that moved with the shifting abutments. Additionally, engineers simply accepted that at times it would be necessary to reconstruct the approaches. This was not the plan for the Drayton Bridge, however.[103]

Almost 1,100 feet long, the $650,000 Drayton Bridge is dominated by its Warren through-truss section, although this component comprises only about half the length of the bridge. Nevertheless, it is an uncommonly large truss. The bridge was built as a replacement to another interstate bridge that was erected between Drayton and Robbin in 1911. The earlier bridge was a vertical-lift structure. A vertical-lift bridge is another example of a movable bridge. Unlike a swing bridge, with its main span that pivots atop a central pier, a vertical-lift bridge has a main span suspended between two truss towers. The main span rises between the towers, opening the river channel to large vessels. Since movable bridges were no longer required on the Red River of the North by the 1950s, the current crossing between Drayton and Robbin was designed as a stationary bridge. Truthfully, though, a movable bridge was unnecessary at the site even at the time the vertical-lift bridge was built. In 1954, just before the vertical-lift structure was torn down, a local newspaper stated as much: "[The vertical-lift bridge] is one of the last reminders of the old romantic days of boating on the Red River. According to reminiscences of local persons it was raised three times, but only once for a riverboat to pass." Apparently, in the early 1910s, officials in extreme northwestern Minnesota were not yet convinced that river commerce on the Red River of the North was finished.[104]

Even though North Dakota and Minnesota were responsible for the Drayton Bridge, it fell to Clifford Johnson, a consulting engineer from Denver, Colorado, to design a crossing nullifying the unruly riverbanks. In part, Johnson accomplished this by designing an exceptionally long bridge. In fact, the crossing is more than twice as long as its predecessor. Unlike the rela-

tively steep banks at many bridge sites, the banks at the site of the Drayton Bridge taper for a considerable distance to the river; the site is a saucer-like depression in a somewhat flat landscape. Instead of adding substantial amounts of earth fill to support the approaches, Johnson simply extended the length of the bridge. Less earth fill against the riverbanks meant less movement in the bridge's foundation and, ultimately, less stress to the superstructure. The engineer did not rely solely on a longer bridge to solve foundational movement, however. His steel-stringer approach spans at either end of the truss are hinged to their I beam trestle piers. Further, each approach span is swivel-connected to the next approach span. This construction makes the bridge less rigid and thus more adaptable to shifting foundations.[105]

Johnson's idea of an unusually long bridge over the Red River of the North was validated a decade after it was completed when the *Engineering News-Record* observed, "Designers must keep fills for bridge approaches to a minimum, or the pressures exerted will cause the underlying material to flow to the side and lower the fill. For this reason, engineers lengthen Red River bridges to points where fills will not create excessive loads." Completed primarily by Helseth Engineering Company of St. Paul, a firm overseen by Paul A. Helseth, a Kittson County native, the Drayton Bridge represents a small, yet important, step in the development of bridge building. Surprisingly, the muscular truss bridge that looks as if it could stand for many more decades will soon be replaced.[106]

Although the Eisenhower Memorial Bridge in Red Wing followed six years after the Drayton Bridge was completed, truss bridge construction was well past its prime by then. Certainly, some bridge sites would still beg for trusses, evidenced by the Mississippi River site at Wabasha, but for most sites, the labor- and material-intensive bridge type was unnecessary. Additionally, truss bridges could not be easily widened. As traffic increased and roads were widened in accommodation, truss crossings stubbornly pinched highways. It is probably safe to assume that wider bridges built in response to crowded highways have cost Minnesota more truss bridges than age, decay, or failure.[107]

Railroads never had to widen their thoroughfares as much as highway departments had to widen theirs. As a result, truss bridges on rail lines are still relatively commonplace. Railroad truss bridges are often hidden from travelers because rail lines frequently diverge from highways. A fine example of a railroad truss crossing largely concealed from the public is the Redstone Bridge over the Minnesota River outside of New Ulm, one of Minnesota's most picturesque communities. Impossible to miss, the New Ulm Post Office, now the Brown County Historical Society, is one of the most visually impressive buildings in Minnesota, resembling a gingerbread house that superbly reflects the city's German origins.[108]

The Redstone Bridge receives its name from the long-gone community of Redstone that existed near the bridge site a short distance southeast of New Ulm. In part, the structure is appealing because it is a movable bridge, a crossing type barely addressed up to this point. Most of the state's movable bridges, also called draw-

bridges, are truss crossings. The Redstone Bridge is one of the oldest truss bridges, thus it is one of the state's oldest movable bridges. The bridge was constructed by the Leighton Bridge and Iron Works of Rochester, New York, a company established in 1870 by Thomas Leighton. Leighton's firm completed the Redstone Bridge ten years later. The crossing's main span is a through-truss swing span, by far the most popular type of movable span in the nineteenth and early twentieth centuries. Sadly, Minnesota has replaced virtually all of its highway swing spans, although some railroad swing spans, such as the Redstone Bridge, remain. The wrought iron main span of the Redstone Bridge pivots atop its central pier just like the highway swing span replaced by the Sorlie Memorial Bridge in East Grand Forks and the highway swing span removed for the Broadway Bridge in St. Peter.[109]

The Redstone Bridge across the Minnesota River near New Ulm is a railroad swing span completed by the Leighton Bridge and Iron Works of Rochester, New York. Erected in 1880, the stout structure is one of the oldest bridges still standing in Minnesota. *Photograph taken in 2005.*

iron track mounted to the top of the cylindrical pier. A second, larger-diameter track is also mounted atop the pier. This track is notched around its entire circumference. A vertical driveshaft descends from the bridge's deck to a gearwheel positioned at the bottom of the shaft. The teeth of the gearwheel intersect with the teeth, or notches, of the circular iron track. Positioning a metal key onto the head of the vertical driveshaft and turning it forces the gearwheel to rotate. The teeth of the rotating gearwheel interlock with the notches of the circular iron track, cranking the bridge open. The task was made easier because the Leighton Bridge and Iron Works also constructed a secondary vertical driveshaft. This driveshaft descends but a short distance below the deck to a small gearwheel. This gearwheel intersects with another gearwheel mounted near the top of the main driveshaft. This configuration allows each driveshaft to be turned in opposite directions, increasing energy output to the main driveshaft via the interlocking gearwheels. Relatively uncomplicated, the bridge's gearing system was a resourceful solution for turning a nineteenth-century swing span.

Because it supports train traffic, which is much

Several gearwheels beneath the deck of the Redstone Bridge helped turn the bridge when it needed to open to allow steamboats to pass. *Photograph taken in 2005.*

Understanding that the Redstone Bridge swung open atop its central pier does not explain how the bridge accomplished the task. The bridge opened manually, which was not uncommon for swing-span bridges. For instance, Northern Pacific Bridge No. 95 between Grand Forks and East Grand Forks opened manually. The Redstone Bridge's movable span rests atop a series of iron wheels that are supported on a circular

The Oliver Bridge is a combination railroad-roadway bridge constructed over the St. Louis River between Duluth and Oliver, Wisconsin. It was built by the Spirit Lake Transfer Railway and the Interstate Transfer Railway. *Photograph taken in 2005.*

The main component of the Oliver Bridge was a heavy swing span
that frequently opened to allow vessels to navigate the St. Louis River.
*Photograph courtesy of the Northeast Minnesota Historical Center,
Duluth, S2386b3f2.*

heavier than wagon or automobile traffic, the Redstone Bridge was built stronger than the swing-span predecessors to the Sorlie Memorial Bridge and the Broadway Bridge. With both riveted and pinned components, the movable span of the Redstone Bridge is a Pratt variant that has an extra horizontal member tying together the panels that make up the web, as well as narrowly spaced steel stringers between the floor beams supporting the deck of wood ties and metal rails. The swing span is edged at either end by a wrought iron, riveted, quadruple-intersection Warren, a rare truss type pioneered by Charles Hilton, a man who apprenticed for Howard Carroll, an engineer for the New York Central Railroad. The quadruple-intersection Warren became popular for long railroad spans because its load-carrying capacity is so great. Intersecting Warrens are evident by their intersecting diagonals. Explained differently, the triangles that are formed by the alternating-angle diagonals overlap. The Redstone Bridge also features a modest-sized timber trestle that merges with the quadruple-intersecting Warren at the west side of the river.[110]

Completed by the Winona and St. Peter Railroad, the same company responsible for the Arches in Winona County, the Redstone Bridge took the place of a Howe truss swing span that was built on the site in 1872 as a component of the railroad's march across southern Minnesota to South Dakota. An example of Minnesota's early railroad and riverboat heritage, the Redstone Bridge suffers from the addition of startlingly ugly concrete casts encasing the limestone abutments and piers. But although the modern, unsympathetic repairs to the faltering substructure are shocking, reflection permits some understanding. The crossing has served rail traffic for well over a century and repair is inevitable. Perhaps if the bridge had been more visible, the owners would have adopted a more visually sensitive plan. Still, the concrete casts are an unpleasant distraction on an otherwise fine example of a nineteenth-century swing span.[111]

A cousin to the Redstone Bridge is found in northeast Minnesota on the St. Louis River, just east of beautiful Jay Cooke State Park and a short distance south of the Duluth–Superior Harbor. Linking the southwest section of Duluth with the small community of Oliver, Wisconsin, on the east side of the river, the Oliver Bridge is a hulking composition that appears entirely utilitarian. Indeed, it seems as if the concept of aesthetics was abandoned even before planners gathered to discuss building a bridge. Nevertheless, the Oliver Bridge is one of the most interesting bridges in Minnesota.[112]

Like the Redstone Bridge, the Oliver Bridge is a railroad swing span. The Oliver Bridge offers a twist, however, for it is also an automobile bridge. About 2,100 feet long, the steel superstructure is mostly a collection of plate girders supported by steel-truss piers set on concrete pedestals. The swing span, however, is a ponderous Warren truss with verticals resting atop a central concrete pier. The rail line is carried across the top of the bridge and the automobile roadway is supported below. Functionally, then, the Warren truss simultaneously serves as a deck truss for the rail line and as a through truss for the automobile roadway.[113]

The bridge's appellation is traced to Henry W. Oliver, a Pittsburgh entrepreneur who made his fortune largely in farm machinery. Historian Theodore C. Blegen described Oliver as "a man of decision and vigor, once a messenger boy, later a soldier who fought at Gettysburg, he [rose] to success as an ironmaster by his own abilities. He was a real-life counterpart to Horatio Alger." Oliver entered Minnesota mining in the late nineteenth century, establishing the Oliver Mining Company in 1892 to mine the Mesabi Iron Range, the most productive iron ore field the world has known. In 1901, the properties of the Oliver Mining Company became part of the newly incorporated United States Steel Corporation. U.S. Steel also controlled the principal iron ore railway in the region, the Duluth, Missabe and Northern Railway (DM&N), which later became the Duluth, Missabe and Iron Range Railway. In 1907, acting through its subsidiary, the Minnesota Steel Company, U.S. Steel acquired property in west Duluth near the St. Louis River for a steel plant. The DM&N subsequently formed the Spirit Lake Transfer Railway, a Minnesota corporation, and the Interstate Transfer Railway, a Wisconsin corporation, to serve the new plant. The two rail lines came together at the St. Louis River, necessitating the Oliver Bridge.[114]

Because the Oliver Bridge spanned an interstate navigable waterway, its construction required the approval of the U.S. Congress and the U.S. War Depart-

ment. The War Department demanded that the bridge feature a movable span so as not to obstruct river traffic, while Congress stipulated that the crossing not only hold a rail line but also a roadway for wagons and autos. The Spirit Lake Transfer Railway and the Interstate Transfer Railway, charged with bridge construction, were not keen on Congress's provision, believing that wagon and automobile traffic was the responsibility

of Duluth and of Douglas County, Wisconsin. Building began in 1910, and even though the railroads completed a bridge with two structural levels, the companies did not include a road deck or approaches for the lower highway level. Wisconsin attempted to compel the railroads to finish the bridge in 1913, but it was not until the War Department echoed Wisconsin's demand three years later that the two railways completed the lower

Although the railroads included the supporting framework for the automobile deck at the lower level as construction progressed, the companies did not complete the lower deck until several years later. *Photograph taken in 1910; courtesy of the Northeast Minnesota Historical Center, Duluth, S2386b3f2.*

Steamboat Bridge is a plate-girder swing span that used to open to allow steamboats to guide cut timber downriver. The bridge was built by the Great Northern Railway in 1914 and is situated across Steamboat River adjacent to Steamboat Lake in Cass County. *Photograph taken in 2006.*

highway deck and approaches. The bridge opened to highway traffic in 1917.

As with many swing-span bridges, it is unnecessary to open and close the Oliver Bridge due to lack of river commerce in present-day Minnesota. It is unlikely the bridge could be opened nowadays, anyway, because it appears that the large, heavy swing span was moved via an engine in an operator's house, a component that no longer exists. Northeastern Minnesotans remain quite fond of the crossing, however, for it represents a significant structural component of the region's iron mining heritage, aiding railroad transfer of iron ore from the

mighty Mesabi to processing centers in the east, as well as providing an eastern link for wire products produced at the Minnesota Steel Company's Duluth plant. And for local automobile drivers, using the Oliver Bridge is considerably more convenient than routing over the bridges linking downtown Duluth and downtown Superior to the north.[115]

Puny in contrast to the Oliver Bridge is Steamboat Bridge, a steel railroad structure about twelve miles north of Walker in Cass County, adjacent to State Highway 371. Although it is not formed as a truss, it is a movable bridge worth noting. The bridge was erected in 1914, three years before the Oliver Bridge was officially complete. The fifty-eight-foot-long movable span is a plate-girder structure, that omnipresent workhorse so favored by the railroad. The movable plate girder swings open, rotating on its central pier.[116]

Built by the Great Northern Railway (GN) as a

component of the railroad's forty-nine-mile-long route from Park Rapids in Hubbard County to Cass Lake in Cass County, Steamboat Bridge received its name because it spans Steamboat River, the eastern outlet for Steamboat Lake that funnels flow to Steamboat Bay on Leech Lake. All of these monikers result from a local history of steamboating, once an extensive regional operation for guiding cut timber from north-central Minnesota to sawmills on the Mississippi River via various waterways. Offering little vertical clearance, Steamboat Bridge was opened to allow steamboats and floating logs to pass. By the early 1920s, however, the vast stands of old-growth timber that once dominated north-central Minnesota were mostly gone, so it was no longer necessary to open the bridge. The crossing was turned over to the Burlington Northern Railroad when the GN became part of that railway in 1970. The line over Steamboat Bridge was abandoned two years later, and the state gained control of the structure. The rails have long since been removed from the bridge, and now it is a constituent of a bike trail paralleling the highway. With plentiful traffic on State Highway 371 and numerous sailboats plying Steamboat Lake today, it is difficult to imagine that this rather ordinary-looking crossing was once integral to the commercial enterprise that helped shape northern Cass County during the early 1900s.[117]

Humble Steamboat Bridge is one of the least known movable bridges in Minnesota, a characteristic that does not apply to either the Duluth Aerial Lift Bridge or the Stillwater Bridge. These two bridges are the most documented movable bridges in the state. In fact, with the possible exception of the Stone Arch Bridge in Minneapolis, these crossings may be the best-known bridges of any kind in Minnesota.

Both bridges are composed of steel trusses, and both are vertical-lift structures, just like the bridge replaced by the current Drayton Bridge. A vertical-lift span, as noted earlier, is suspended between two vertical truss towers. The movable span rises between the towers to open the waterway to vessels. Specifically, this is accomplished with heavy-gauge steel cables that are attached to either end of the movable span and ascend to large sheaves, or pulleys, mounted at the tops of the towers. The cables drape over the sheaves and descend to counterweights within the towers. The counterweights counter the weight of the movable span. A vertical-lift bridge opens when a motor initiates upward movement of the movable span. This causes the counterweights to descend, with their tonnage becoming the primary motive force that pulls the movable span upward. It is a straightforward idea, but a bridge built in this way occasionally suffers practical problems. For instance, steel expands when heated and contracts when cooled. So if the main span of a vertical-lift bridge greatly expands because of a particularly hot day, it is possible it will not raise or lower. Simply put, it becomes stuck between its truss towers. This is a rare happening, but it does occur. It has happened to the Duluth Aerial Lift Bridge. The solution is to employ large hoses dispatching copious amounts of cool water. The water sprayed against the expanded bridge forces the metal to contract, allowing the movable span to be raised or lowered.

Minnesota has erected a small number of vertical-lift bridges. One is currently standing over the Mississippi River near the Robert Street Bridge in St. Paul. The northeast approach spans for the Chicago Great Western Railway Aerial Lift Bridge actually lie beneath the Robert Street Bridge. Perhaps the least documented vertical-lift bridge in Minnesota was built over the Mississippi River at Ball Club in northern Minnesota in 1918. Unfortunately, even the structure's engineer seems lost to history. The bridge was demolished in 1939.[118]

The Duluth Aerial Lift Bridge is slightly older than the Stillwater Bridge. The Duluth Aerial Lift Bridge came about because the community of Duluth carved a shipping canal through Minnesota Point, a narrow peninsula that sprouts from Duluth's downtown core and extends about six and one-half miles southeast across the head of Lake Superior. The narrow, sandy mass of Minnesota Point creates a harbor immediately to its south, a fortune of geography that gave rise to one of this country's most prominent inland commercial ports. To the south, the harbor is fed by the St. Louis River, the waterway spanned by the Oliver Bridge, which is only a short distance upriver from the harbor. Although the canal into the natural harbor was completed in the early 1870s, it was not until the early 1900s that a bridge was erected over it. By this time, the canal was owned by the federal government and had been greatly improved.[119]

The Duluth Aerial Lift Bridge over the Duluth Ship Canal began as the Duluth Aerial Ferry Bridge. Here the bridge is under construction. It was erected by the Modern Steel Structural Company of Waukesha, Wisconsin. *Photograph by Fenney and Adams, ca. 1904; courtesy of the Northeast Minnesota Historical Center, Duluth, S2386b1f7.*

The gondola of the Aerial Ferry Bridge courses its way across the Duluth Ship Canal. *Photograph by Charles P. Gibson, ca. 1910; courtesy of the Minnesota Historical Society.*

For many years, officials considered various plans for spanning the canal to connect Minnesota Point with the rest of the city. The federal government mandated that any crossing at the site must offer substantial vertical clearance, while leaving the canal entirely unobstructed. Clearly, such requirements eliminated from consideration any swing-span bridge with a central pier. One design put forth in the early 1890s was a vertical-lift bridge developed by John Alexander Low Waddell, a man who became one of America's most influential bridge engineers, in part because he wrote books on the subject. Perhaps his most popular work is a two-volume treatise simply titled *Bridge Engineering*, a resource frequently referenced by bridge historians and others. Although Duluth was impressed with Waddell's vertical-lift bridge design, it was ultimately rejected. However, his effort came to fruition a few years later, in 1895, with the South Halsted Street Bridge over the Chicago River in Chicago. This was the world's first modern vertical-lift bridge. At this time, Duluth was still shuttling citizens across the Duluth Ship Canal via ferryboat. In 1899, finally, the city adopted a design by city engineer Thomas F. McGilvray. Inspired by a "transporter" crossing in Rouen, France, McGilvray designed the canal bridge on Minnesota Point in a similar fashion. The Duluth Aerial Ferry Bridge consisted of two vertical truss towers surmounted by a horizontal truss that was 135 feet above high water.

This close-up view shows the gondola docked and awaiting additional passengers or vehicles. *Photograph by Hugh McKenzie, ca. 1920; courtesy of the Northeast Minnesota Historical Center, Duluth, S2422n7384.*

The Aerial Ferry Bridge was modified into the current Aerial Lift Bridge in 1929 by the Kansas City-based engineering firm of Harrington, Howard, and Ash. *Photograph taken in 2005.*

Vertical supports suspended a large gondola from the horizontal truss. The gondola coursed along trackage inside the lower chord of the horizontal truss. Carrying passengers, streetcars, and wagon teams between Minnesota Point and the main part of the city, the gondola was easily shifted out of the path of any ship traversing the canal.[120] In 1910, a writer colorfully explained the bridge's operation for confused visitors to Duluth:

About the first question asked by every stranger who arrives at Duluth, no matter whether they come by the water route or by rail, is: "What is That?" "That" refers to a colossal erection of steel work which rears itself on Minnesota Point, and which is silhouetted against the skyline in majestic proportions. It looks like a bridge, but the bridge is at the top of the soaring steel columns that rise from either bank of the waterway which the structure spans. Speculation immediately arises in the mind as to how the people get on to the bridge. Do they go up in elevators? Or maybe the bridge lowers itself to the earth level and re-ascends to its elevated position after being used? While the spectator is looking and forming all sorts of theories he notices something moving like a great spider across the waterway under the bridge. It is suspended to the overhead spanning framework by a long, slender web of steel and is a moving platform on a level with the land approaches. The platform slowly moves

The Stillwater Bridge is shown here in early spring. The crossing over the St. Croix River at Stillwater was opened to traffic in 1931. *Photograph taken in 2005.*

The early bridge across the St. Croix River was a dubious-looking crossing, although it featured a unique pontoon section that swung open like a door to allow ships to pass. Here the pontoon section is left open during the winter months. *Photograph by John Runk, 1926; courtesy of the Minnesota Historical Society.*

across the stretch of water that intervenes between the great columns, only after a short time to retrace its journey to the side from which it started.[121]

Work on the ferry bridge began in 1901, but troubled financing stalled the structure's completion until 1905. Constructed by Modern Steel Structural Company of Waukesha, Wisconsin, the $100,000 steel structure was one of the most unusual bridges ever erected in

America. By the late 1920s, however, the imaginative crossing was obsolete, as it could not support the vastly increasing traffic. In 1929, the transporter crossing was converted to the current Aerial Lift Bridge, a vertical-lift structure modified by the Kansas City–based firm of Harrington, Howard, and Ash, successor to Waddell and Harrington, an enterprise established by J. A. L. Waddell and John Lyle Harrington. Harrington was a talented civil and mechanical engineer who helped turn Waddell's vertical-lift plan into a cogent and successful design. The horizontal truss atop the truss towers of the Duluth crossing remained, but the engineering firm extended the height of the towers and raised the horizontal truss to accommodate the highest elevated position of the new movable roadway span. Another steel-truss tower was erected inside each of the original towers; this peculiar tower within a tower configuration makes for an attention-grabbing visual. The interior towers support the movable through-truss roadway span, or lift span, that replaced the gondola, while the exterior towers support the original horizontal truss at the top of the bridge. Interestingly, the $400,000 alteration makes the horizontal truss unnecessary as a supporting component of the bridge; its only purpose is to carry utilities across the canal to Minnesota Point. Raised and lowered about 5,500 times per year, the Aerial Lift Bridge has been in operation for more than seventy-five years now. During that time it has become the symbol of

Duluth, the city's structural signature to the world.[122]

The vertical-lift Stillwater Bridge followed only two years after modification of the crossing over the Duluth Ship Canal. The contract for construction of the Stillwater Bridge was actually awarded the same year the Duluth Aerial Lift Bridge was completed. The firm of Ash, Howard, Needles, and Tammen, the successor to the company that altered the Aerial Lift Bridge, engineered the lift span for the Stillwater Bridge. Just as the Aerial Lift Bridge is the symbol of Duluth, the Stillwater Bridge is the symbol of Stillwater, one of Minnesota's oldest and most visually appealing communities. It is almost impossible to imagine Stillwater without the lift bridge.[123]

Spanning the St. Croix River, the waterway marking the boundary between Minnesota and Wisconsin east of the Twin Cities metropolitan area, the bridge carries Minnesota Highway 36 to merge with Wisconsin State Route 64 on the east side of the waterway at the town of Houlton. The roughly 1,100 foot-long bridge is composed of a few concrete-slab approach spans and six steel Parker through-truss spans, all designed by the MHD. A seventh steel Parker through truss serves as the lift span. The lift span's sheaves at the tops of its

Although the Minnesota Department of Highways designed the Parker through-truss fixed spans of the Stillwater Bridge, the engineering firm of Ash, Howard, Needles, and Tammen, the successor to the company that modified the Duluth Aerial Ferry Bridge into the Duluth Aerial Lift Bridge, designed the lift span. *Photograph taken in 2005.*

D. R. L. AND W. R. R. ROLLING LIFT BRIDGE, RANIER, MINN.

towers are more visible than those of the Aerial Lift Bridge in Duluth, chiefly because the towers of the Still-water Bridge are not surmounted by a horizontal truss. The cost for the $500,000 Stillwater Bridge, built by the Minneapolis contracting firm of Peppard and Fulton, was shared by Minnesota and Wisconsin.

The Stillwater Bridge was sorely needed, for its predecessor was a long and rickety timber crossing that many likely felt uncomfortable trundling over. The bridge was formed of several timber pony-truss spans, stringer spans, and one swing span. The swing span was fascinating, for it was a pontoon, and so floated upon the river. In a way, it resembled a long, low houseboat hinged at its east end to a fixed section of the bridge. A bridge tender motored it out of the way—swinging it like a door—when a ship needed to pass. Despite the appeal of the bridge, it was in sorry shape by the 1920s, a fact recognized at least by 1926 when E. J. Miller, a bridge engineer for the MHD, penned a letter to Charles M. Babcock, the commissioner of highways: "This structure is fast deteriorating so as to be a source of apprehension for the safety of both the bridge and loads it is obliged to carry.... Routine maintenance on the [bridge] amounts to over $3,000 per year and the

The Duluth, Rainy Lake and Winnipeg Rolling Lift Bridge is one of the most unusual cross-ings in the state. It is a type of movable bridge that was devel-oped by the Scherzer Rolling Lift Bridge Company of Chicago, Illinois. The railroad erected the unique bridge over the Rainy River on the Canadian border in 1908. *Photograph ca. 1910; cour-tesy of the Minnesota Historical Society.*

The Lyndale Avenue Bridge was a double-leaf bascule that spanned the Minnesota River at Lyndale Avenue in Bloomington. Designed by the Minnesota Department of Highways, the bridge was constructed by William S. Hewett of Minneapolis in 1920. It was removed about four decades later. *Photograph courtesy of Mn/DOT.*

Constructed in 1927, the Arrowhead Bridge was a substantial double-leaf bascule over the St. Louis River joining West Duluth with Superior, Wisconsin. It often opened to allow freighters passage. The bridge was replaced by the Bong Memorial Bridge in the 1980s. *Photograph courtesy of the Northeast Minnesota Historical Center, Duluth, S2386b1f11.*

structure may become so unsafe next year as to necessitate closing to traffic."[124]

It does not appear that the timber bridge was closed the following year, but a flurry of correspondence between highway officials in the late 1920s indicates that the MHD wanted the crossing quickly replaced. And so it was. In 1931, trepidation was replaced by confidence as travelers ventured onto the bulky, steel vertical-lift bridge, the antithesis of its forerunner that became Stillwater personified. As the twentieth century drew to a close, however, traffic over the crossing was often very great, as some older towns near the St. Croix River continued to evolve into bedroom communities of St. Paul. Many parties pushed for a new bridge. In the mid-1990s, the Federal Highway Administration and the Minnesota and Wisconsin departments of transportation proposed a new crossing at a location downriver from the lift bridge, while agreeing to retain the lift bridge to serve local traffic needs.[125]

The National Park Service (NPS), after reviewing the project under the Wild and Scenic Rivers Act, determined that the scenic and recreational qualities of the St. Croix National Scenic Riverway would be harmed by the addition of the proposed bridge, citing "proliferation of crossings" as a concern. The NPS concluded that the historic lift bridge must be removed if a new crossing was constructed. This confounded many preservationists, as the NPS was the very agency that had listed the lift bridge in the National Register of Historic Places in 1989.[126]

The situation caused the project to be suspended until the Federal Highway Administration, working with the United States Institute for Environmental Conflict Resolution, convened a group of agencies, local governments, and organizations in Stillwater. This stakeholder group met over the course of three years. Ultimately, the discussions have produced a new crossing proposal. This plan modifies the location and design of the new bridge to better address river and historic impacts. It also includes construction of a loop trail, which augments the recreational amenities of the river with a pedestrian and bicycle route on each side of the river, connecting over the lift bridge and over the new bridge. The environmental Record of Decision for this project, issued in November 2006, includes an agreement to rehabilitate the historic lift bridge as part of this trail system.[127]

There is little discussion concerning the future of a movable bridge in Koochiching County in northern Minnesota, but it is uncertain how long that may remain so. It is a bridge that has stood for a century and, hopefully, will stand much longer. As with Steamboat Bridge in Cass County, the movable crossing in Ranier on the Minnesota–Ontario border is not well known. It should be, for the Duluth, Rainy Lake and Winnipeg Rolling Lift Bridge is a marvelous trussed crossing that rears on its haunches when opened. The bridge is a bascule, a movable crossing type that rotates in a vertical plane about a horizontal axis: the leaf, or arm (movable section), elevates at one end until it is roughly perpendicular to the river, opening the channel to vessels.

Few bascule bridges have been built on Minnesota roadways (it is uncertain how many railroad bascules have been built, but it is unlikely that there are many). One of Minnesota's bascules included the double-leaf bascule over the Minnesota River on Lyndale Avenue in Bloomington. Designed by the MHD and erected

The Minnesota Slip Bridge is a small pedestrian bascule completed in Duluth's Canal Park in 1991. *Photograph taken in 2006.*

The Duluth, Rainy Lake and Winnipeg Rolling Lift Bridge opens by rocking on its rockers, not unlike rocking backward in a rocking chair. *Photograph taken in 2006.*

distance to the west. Another bascule spanned the Mississippi River about six miles southwest of Cohasset in north-central Minnesota. Consisting of three pony-truss approaches and a single-leaf bascule main span, the Collinge Bridge was cranked open only a few times. Erected in 1923, it was cut up in 1983 after a new reinforced-concrete crossing was constructed as a replacement. A third bascule was built across the St. Louis River, a short distance above Duluth–Superior Harbor. Completed in 1927, the Arrowhead Bridge was a toll bridge linking West Duluth with Superior, Wisconsin. The double-leaf bascule featured timber trestle approaches of more than two thousand feet. The most prominent bascule operating in Minnesota, the Arrowhead Bridge was replaced in the mid-1980s by a fixed crossing, the Bong Memorial Bridge. A bascule constructed relatively recently is located in Duluth's Canal Park, only a short distance from the Aerial Lift Bridge. The Minnesota Slip Bridge is a petite, double-leaf pedestrian bascule finished in 1991. Virtually identical to a bascule erected in Venice, Italy, around 1922, the Minnesota Slip Bridge is a Dutch-style bascule, a moniker derived from the type's popularity in the lowlands of Europe.[128]

The Duluth, Rainy Lake and Winnipeg Rolling Lift Bridge is a 134-foot-long bascule developed by the Scherzer Rolling Lift Bridge Company of Chicago. The bridge type differs from most bascule crossings because it is not supported upon a trunnion; the leaf does not rotate upward from a hinged end. Rather, a Scherzer relies on rockers, not unlike the rockers of a rocking chair. Because of this rocking design, the bridge is subject to two kinds of movement: as the arm rocks upward to vertical, it also moves backward to the degree permitted by the rockers. Movement of the span is initiated by a motor, but a counterweight

by William S. Hewett in 1920, the bridge was removed roughly four decades later when the interstate highway was completed over the Minnesota River a short

mounted at the rear (shore end) of the bridge provides the principal lifting force, rocking downward and shifting the leaf upward.[129]

The Scherzer at Ranier was erected over the Rainy River at the point where the waterway receives the output of Rainy Lake. But one lyrical local history notes it is often difficult to determine precisely where the lake ends and the river begins; maybe the rolling lift bridge is not always the demarcation:

All winter long … an argument [goes] on here between Rainy Lake and the Rainy River as to where the lake relinquishes and the river takes on the job of getting all this water to Hudson Bay. The argument keeps a patch of water open far out from the Ranier drawbridge, which is where the map-makers say the lake ends and the river begins. The map-makers haven't watched the game this lake and this river play. When winter is tending to business and the cold rolls in as though it were the only weather we would ever see again, the lake advances on that drawbridge, staking its claim with a cover of ice. And on days when winter relaxes even slightly, the river sneaks lakeward again, opening first a narrow channel in the ice, then sweeping that little corner of the lake.[130]

The rolling lift bridge created a link between Ranier and the community of Fort Frances in Ontario. It was built as part of the route of the Duluth, Rainy Lake and Winnipeg Railway (DRL&W), a line incorporated in 1901 as the Duluth, Virginia and Rainy Lake Railway. By early 1913, the DRL&W was part of the Duluth, Winnipeg and Pacific Railway. The DRL&W completed its movable structure across the Rainy River five years before the merger, the same year Ranier was incorporated. When the rolling lift bridge was finished in 1908, the popularity of the crossing type was growing, not just in America but worldwide: Scherzer rolling lifts had already been erected across the Swale River in England (1904), over the Sparne River at Haarlem, Holland (1906), across the Suir River in Waterford, Ireland (1906), over the harbor at Port Soudan, Egypt (1907), and across the Ngawun River in Burma (1908).[131]

Even so, Scherzer rolling lifts never were common as automobile bridges; the type was most often used for railroad crossings demanding a movable bridge capable of withstanding heavy loads while opening quickly, although its popularity eventually waned. Today, most bascules incorporate trunnions, but the majority of these are likely highway bridges. It is unclear how frequently railroads today need to erect a new bascule—or any new movable bridge. The need seems rare, however, because many navigable sites in Minnesota are seldom navigated by large watercraft. The Duluth, Rainy Lake and Winnipeg Rolling Lift Bridge, for example, is operated remotely by Canadian National North American, which now owns the bridge. However, that may be less novel than it sounds, for the structure operates infrequently. Nevertheless, the bridge remains one of the state's most interesting movable bridges, a type that was seldom built in Minnesota. The bridge is antiquated, however, like other metal crossings that still grace the North Star state. Yet, *antiquated* means out of style, not worthless or ineffectual. If properly maintained, these bridges can still serve their original purpose for many more years: we simply need to get past our often-erroneous notions of age.

Metal bridges are not as common as they used to be, but they are still built. The new ones are usually deep-section, beam-span structures. Concrete now dominates as the bridge-building material of choice in the modern world. In fact, not long after steel usurped iron as the preeminent material for building bridges, concrete usurped steel. Still, steel will remain a popular construction material for a very long time because it is so durable. Moreover, ironically, early concrete bridge builders and engineers realized that most concrete crossings would quickly falter if not for steel.

CONCRETE

BRIDGES

The big push to make the new Hennepin Avenue Suspension Bridge into something special is looking successful—but it may be for all the wrong reasons. As the six-lane bridge over the Mississippi River in downtown Minneapolis moves toward completion, it has raised questions …

—Mike Kaszuba, "It's a Beauty of a Bridge, with a Beauty of a Price," *Minneapolis Star Tribune*, September 19, 1989

IN THE LATE TWENTIETH CENTURY, Minneapolis built a new bridge across the Mississippi River at Hennepin Avenue. For a century, the steel ribbed arch completed by Horace E. Horton of Rochester, Minnesota, and the Wrought Iron Bridge Company of Canton, Ohio, faithfully carried citizens of Minneapolis across America's grandest river. By the 1980s, some in city government believed the bridge had outlived its usefulness and pushed hard for a new crossing. Others pushed back. Some politicians and engineers argued that the bridge was in such poor shape that even rehabilitation would not allow it to support modern traffic loads. Not so, claimed one engineer and others desiring to preserve the bridge. Opponents believed the arch bridge could be rehabilitated to handle traffic loads common to downtown at a cost substantially less than building a new suspension bridge. Perhaps, but

when political powers demanded that a bridge over the Mississippi River at Hennepin Avenue must accommodate six lanes—a stipulation that made some eyes roll—the four-lane, ribbed arch bridge was doomed.[1]

Whether the steel ribbed arch needed to go is debatable, but at least the city erected a handsome replacement. Since the site had hosted two previous suspension bridges, Minneapolis thought it appropriate to honor that heritage with another suspension structure. Although the site did not require a modern-day suspension span, city leaders understood—as city leaders before them understood—that this was a gateway site: a location compelling a special bridge because it would shepherd citizens into the city's core. Of all the bridge designs submitted for Hennepin Avenue at the Mississippi River, the city chose, in the words of one local journalist, the "Cadillac version."

Dedicated in 1990, the fourth bridge at Hennepin Avenue in Minneapolis was a pricey crossing, but city leaders wanted a structure reminiscent of the city's early suspension bridges. *Photograph taken in 2006 by Robert W. Gardner Jr.*

The cost for the Cadillac version shocked some, who argued that a girder crossing like that on Broadway Avenue just upriver could be erected for a third of the cost of a suspension span. Probably, but if the fourth bridge raised over the Mississippi River at Hennepin Avenue had resembled that on Broadway Avenue, city officials would still be hearing the howls.[2]

Costing more than $28 million, the new suspension bridge was a product of Howard, Needles, Tammen, and Bergendoff (now known as HNTB). HNTB is the most recent manifestation of the engineering company formed by Waddell and Harrington a century ago. Dedicated on September 12, 1990, the suspension structure was officially christened the Father Louis Hennepin Bridge. In 1680, as a kind of roving prisoner of the Dakota, Belgian friar Louis Hennepin named the falls downriver of the Hennepin Avenue Bridge for his patron saint, Saint Anthony. The roughly thousand-foot-long suspension bridge honoring the friar was built by Johnson Brothers, a contracting company from Little Falls, Minnesota. While the girders below the bridge's deck are steel, the 150-foot-high, obelisk-like towers with an Art Deco nuance are formed of reinforced concrete, as are parts of the substructure and railings. This is not surprising, for reinforced concrete had become the primary bridge construction material by the early part of the twentieth century.[3]

Concrete is composed of sand and aggregate combined with cement and water. The mixture solidifies into a stonelike mass. The benefit of concrete is that it can be formed into virtually any shape and yet remain rigid and durable. The practicality of the material was known by the Romans, who used it to build walls, breakwaters, domes, and other structures. After Rome collapsed, much of their concrete-building knowledge was lost for centuries. However, by the eighteenth century, concrete was again evolving into a significant building material in parts of Europe, but its regular use in America did not come about until the second half of the nineteenth century.[4]

The first concrete bridge in America was the Cleft Ridge Park Bridge, a pedestrian crossing erected in Brooklyn's Prospect Park in 1871. The bridge was an arch—it had to be. While concrete is exceptionally strong in compression, it is especially weak in tension, thus early concrete bridges were arches, a compres-sive form. The tensile problem was solved when metal bars were introduced into the concrete to take up the tensile stresses and so significantly increase the tensile strength of a concrete bridge. The first engineer to do this in America was an Englishman, Ernest L. Ransome. Ransome's reinforced-concrete Alvord Lake Bridge in Golden Gate Park in San Francisco was completed in 1889. Other reinforced-concrete crossings followed, many adopting the designs of Viennese engineer Josef Melan. Melan's reinforced-concrete bridge design incorporated parallel steel I beams bent into the shape of an arch. This was conservative reinforced-concrete construction, as Melan's bridges were essentially steel ribbed-arch structures encased in concrete. Even though Ransome had demonstrated that metal bars were all that were necessary to substantially strengthen a concrete bridge, it took time to convince some engineers and contractors of that fact. The first Melan bridge in America was raised at Rock Rapids, Iowa, in 1894. It was designed by Fritz von Emperger, an Austrian engineer, and built by William S. Hewett three years before the contractor founded the Security Bridge Company and about a dozen years before he constructed the Phelps Mill Bridge in Otter Tail County, Minnesota. Besides the bridge in Iowa, Hewett also erected a number of Melan arches in the Twin Cities, including the Interlachen Bridge on William Berry Parkway in Minneapolis.[5]

Costing almost $7,000, the Interlachen Bridge spans the former Como-Interurban-Harriet trolley line, an electrical streetcar route completed by the Twin City Rapid Transit Company that tied together the Lake Harriet area with Como Park in St. Paul. Today the Minnesota Streetcar Museum operates renovated streetcars on the tracks passing beneath the bridge, a service reminiscent of a bygone age that carries modern-day passengers on a short and pleasurable jaunt between Lake Calhoun and Lake Harriet. The Interlachen Bridge was erected in 1900, which makes it possibly the oldest reinforced-concrete bridge still standing in Minnesota. It receives its name because it links William Berry Parkway (formerly Interlachen Drive) with the roadways that encircle Lake Calhoun and Lake Harriet within the Chain of Lakes District of Minneapolis; in other words, the bridge has an inter-lake location. Like Bridge No. 5827 near Zumbro Falls

Adopting the construction method developed by Viennese engineer Josef Melan, the Interlachen Bridge between Lake Calhoun and Lake Harriet in Minneapolis was completed in 1900, perhaps making the structure the oldest reinforced-concrete bridge in Minnesota. *Photograph taken in 2006.*

metropolitan area. Before that happened, though, the state welcomed many smaller, yet appealing, reinforced-concrete crossings.

The vast majority of reinforced-concrete bridges in Minnesota and elsewhere have been built on highways. Of course, rail companies built reinforced-concrete bridges as well. For example, in the early 1900s, the Florida East Coast Railway built a line through the Everglades and to the Florida Keys, a remarkable engineering achievement requiring thirteen years and the completion of many reinforced-concrete bridges. Additionally, the Delaware, Lackawanna and Western Railroad revamped its rail line about the same time, a huge task that included the construction of reinforced-concrete crossings, counting the incredible Tunkhannock Viaduct at Nicholson, Pennsylvania, a bridge formed of ten reinforced-concrete arches and measuring almost 2,400 feet in length. Still, in Minnesota, reinforced-concrete railroad bridges have been uncommon.[7]

In large part, reinforced-concrete railroad bridges are scarce because the railroad hardly needed to build many. By the early 1900s, rail lines and the necessary bridges to support them webbed across America. It was unnecessary to build new reinforced-concrete bridges since suitable metal bridges already existed.[8] Moreover, as noted earlier, railroads often did not need to adapt the bridge infrastructure of rail thoroughfares to increasing traffic loads. This contrasts sharply with highways, which have supported a perpetually increasing flow of vehicles, frequently forcing highway departments to upgrade roads and bridges. Recall that the Redstone Bridge over the Minnesota River has existed for more than 125 years, yet there appears little need to remove the railroad crossing and build anew. The same holds for the attractive and innovative Soo Line High Bridge across the St. Croix River, and the heavy Oliver Bridge spanning the St. Louis River, as well as the plain-looking Bridge No. L1393 in Winona County.

Some of the earliest reinforced-concrete roadway bridges in Minnesota were Gillham arches built in Rock County in southwestern Minnesota. Named for their designer and contractor Perley N. Gillham, the small, elliptical arch bridges are mostly reserved and yet suggest classicism. Classical Revival style was popular in the first part of the twentieth century, as is evidenced by many public buildings, banks, and houses of the time.

in Wabasha County and Bridge No. L7075 in rural Todd County, as well as Bridge No. 7614 near Grand Portage in Cook County, the Interlachen Bridge masquerades as a stone arch crossing. The forty-foot-long, single-span, stone-faced Interlachen Bridge is an exceptionally early masquerader, however, the outcome of the foresight of the Minneapolis Board of Park Commissioners, the governmental entity charged with enhancing parkland throughout the city. The segmental-arched Interlachen Bridge is clearly a landscape asset, its attractiveness derived in part from the blue-gray, randomly coursed ashlar spandrel walls contrasting with the yellow stone of the arch rings and abutment faces.[6]

The Melan arch Interlachen Bridge reflects conservative construction, and is perhaps the earliest reinforced-concrete bridge still standing in Minnesota. Although the crossing is one of the state's most historically significant bridges, it is not the most impressive Melan arch. That honor goes to the huge Third Avenue Bridge over the Mississippi River, just downriver of the Hennepin Avenue Bridge. The story of the Third Avenue Bridge is larger than its placement within the evolution of Melan arches, however, for the crossing represents the initiation of monumental reinforced-concrete-arch bridge construction in the Twin Cities

Bridges, too, sometimes evoked the style, but these crossings were mainly in urban areas. That fact makes Gillham's bridges somewhat more remarkable, since most were built in rural locations. His arch bridges typically featured solid concrete railings topped with a concrete coping and marked at the ends by simple, cylindrical classical posts. The architectural detailing was not much, but it certainly harkened to antiquity. For many of these arch bridges, Gillham inscribed his name, as well as the names of local officials involved with the bridge project, into the top of the railing coping. The contractor completed concrete beam-span bridges as well, but it was the arched crossings that carried his signature, each looking virtually identical to the next. In a way, Gillham was a Henry Ford of bridge building.[9]

Born in Wisconsin in 1855, Gillham ultimately found his way to Luverne, the county seat of Rock County, home to one of the state's most beautiful county court-houses and, coincidently, a Sioux quartzite structure the contractor helped build in the late 1880s. He also erected the Beaux-Arts-style Luverne Carnegie Library, which was finished in 1904. Gillham was doing bridge work in Rock County at least by the early 1880s, when he repaired a bridge over Rock County's Ash Creek. It appears, however, that many of his reinforced-concrete arches were erected just after the turn of the twen-tieth century, a time when bridge contractors were just beginning to experiment with reinforced concrete and the state had yet to gain control over much bridge building.[10] It is unclear exactly how Gillham came up with his basic plan for small, reinforced-concrete arch bridges, but his design became a structural tradition in Rock County. It is surprising that a man so far removed from a major metropolitan center completed so much bridge work in reinforced concrete, especially at a time when many were just learning how best to employ the material. Robert M. Frame III, a Minnesota historian who has completed some of the earliest study of the state's bridges, addressed this curiosity and the possible foundation for Gillham's arch bridges:

Where did such an obscure ... contractor, living and working in what is among the state's most remote counties even today, learn to design and build reinforced-concrete arch bridges during the earliest years of reinforced-concrete bridge construction? Other early Minnesota reinforced-concrete arch bridges, such as

those built around 1900–1905 for the Twin Cities Rapid Transit Company, are clearly different from Gillham's designs. The only hint of an outside influence on Gillham is found in the Fritz von Emperger–designed Melan-arch concrete bridge, which was built near Rock Rapids, Iowa, in 1894. [Rock Rapids is literally just down the road from Luverne]. The only published photo-graph shows a bridge whose proportions are almost identical to Gillham's designs, and even the reported dimensions are similar to Gillham's. Adding to the possible connection is the reported name of the contractor [for the Rock Rapids bridge], Minne-apolis bridge builder William S. Hewett.... It is known that, at the time, William was the agent and a joint proprietor with his uncle Seth in S. M. Hewett and Company, bridge builders.... Seth Hewett received the 1884 contract to replace the same Ash Creek bridge that Gillham had repaired a year earlier, suggesting that there were opportunities for Gillham to meet the Hewetts and, perhaps, establish a relationship that later led to an exchange of information about reinforced-concrete and the Iowa bridge.[11]

Not long ago, Rock County featured several Gillham arches, but not anymore. A couple of remaining Gillham arches are now on the National Register of Historic Places, one carrying automobile traffic and the other, depressingly, supporting grass. Gillham's single-span Bridge No. L4646 was completed in 1911 and spans Spring Brook in the small town of Beaver Creek, only

Gillham erected Bridge No. L4646 across Spring Brook in the tiny Rock County community of Beaver Creek in 1911. *Photograph taken in 2005.*

a short distance west of Luverne, near Minnesota's intersection with the South Dakota–Iowa border. Like Gillham's other arched crossings, the thirty-eight-foot-long Bridge No. L4646 is a barrel arch: an arch roughly resembling half a cylinder. The Interlachen Bridge, for instance, is a barrel arch, even though it has steel I beam ribs embedded within it. Bridge No. L2162 is located to the northwest of Beaver Creek and Bridge No. L4646. Situated in Rose Dell Township amid rolling farm fields, even closer to the South Dakota border than Bridge No. L4646, the single-span Bridge No. L2162 extends over a tributary of Split Rock Creek, the same waterway spanned by the stone arch Split Rock Bridge, located to the north in Pipestone County. Erected about

Reflecting the modest classicism common to many Gillham arches, Bridge No. L2162 no longer carries traffic. The bridge raised over a tributary of Split Rock Creek was completed in Rock County's Rose Dell Township about 1907. *Photograph taken in 2005.*

1907, the sixty-four-foot-long Bridge No. L2162 is no longer used, as the gravel roadway that once passed over it has been shifted slightly to the east. The new thoroughfare goes over a new bridge, a concrete-girder crossing that deserves little attention.[12]

Bridge No. L2162 no longer carries vehicles; it has been allowed to drift back to nature. While the sod and grass sprouting across the deck make for an interesting visual, it also spurs disenchantment and an obvious question, Will this be the fate of many historic bridges? The answer to that question continues to be debated among those who work within the preservation field, as well as those governmental agencies responsible for the various historic crossings marking Minnesota. The public has a voice in this debate as well, although that voice is often silent.

At the same time Gillham was finishing his modest-sized reinforced-concrete arch structure in Beaver Creek, the Marsh Engineering Company was erecting the Marsh Concrete Rainbow Arch Bridge in Cambria Township in Blue Earth County, the same county hosting the Kern Bridge. Alas, the Marsh Concrete Rainbow Arch Bridge is reminiscent of Gillham's Bridge No. L2162—not in design, but in fate. Again, the roadway has been shifted to the east slightly, requiring a new, undistinguished bridge. The small Marsh Concrete Rainbow Arch Bridge decays, and its deck sprouts turf.

The Marsh Engineering Company of Des Moines, Iowa, was founded by James Barney Marsh as the Marsh Bridge Company in 1904. Marsh was a native of Wisconsin who moved to Iowa in 1877 to attend the Iowa State College of Agriculture and Mechanic Arts (now Iowa State University). He remained in Des Moines for the rest of his life, working as an agent for a few bridge companies before establishing his own. The Marsh Bridge Company was renamed the Marsh Engineering Company in 1909, two years before Marsh filed a patent for a reinforced-concrete rainbow arch design. The same year he received the patent for the unique bridge type, he completed the sixty-foot-long crossing in Cambria Township over the Little Cottonwood River in northwest Blue Earth County. Clearly, then, this is one of the oldest Marsh rainbow arches in the country, and it is definitely the oldest Marsh rainbow arch remaining in Minnesota.[13]

A Marsh rainbow arch is formed of two arched ribs.

The Marsh Concrete Rainbow Arch Bridge in Cambria Township in Blue Earth County was erected across the Little Cottonwood River in 1911; it no longer serves traffic. Designed by the Marsh Engineering Company of Des Moines, Iowa, the bridge is one of the oldest Marsh arch crossings still in existence. *Photograph taken in 2005.*

The bridge type differs from most arched crossings because the arches carrying the deck are not below the roadway but rise above it; verticals descending from the arches hold the floor beams that support the deck. This type of arch bridge is sometimes called a through arch, because drivers pass through the arches. Travelers negotiating a Marsh rainbow arch see the arch crowns at either side. This is similar to passing over a pony-truss bridge and viewing the trusses to left and right. Marsh rainbow arches ultimately suffered the same lot as many truss bridges, since they could not be easily widened to support greater traffic flow or the ever-increasing size of farm machinery. When Blue Earth County's Marsh Concrete Rainbow Arch Bridge was added to the National Register of Historic Places in 1980, Minnesota had but a half dozen of these modest-sized structures. Some of these have now been lost, including Bridge No. 944, which was constructed in Blue Earth County's Danville Township in 1914 and spanned the Big Cobb River. It was replaced in the early 1980s. The Alvarado Bridge was erected across the Snake River immediately west of Alvarado in Marshall County in 1925. Removed in 1969, this crossing may have been the most striking Marsh Arch ever raised on a Minnesota roadway.[14]

As Blue Earth County officials accepted the intriguing design of the Marsh Engineering Company for its crossing in Cambria Township and officials in Rock County welcomed Gillham's arched signature bridge in Beaver Creek, the city of Duluth embraced the completion of several reinforced-concrete arch bridges on one of the port community's most attractive passageways, Seven Bridges Road.

Seven Bridges Road is but a piece of Skyline Parkway, a pleasing roadway coursing generally northeast–southwest for about 25 miles, riding the crest of the hills above much of Duluth and providing stunning views of the city, harbor, and Lake Superior. The thoroughfare is so attractive that one recent study of the parkway gushes, "Few roads in North America combine the concepts of 'urban' and 'wilderness' as dramatically as Duluth's Skyline Parkway, or offer such radical contrasts of experience." Although Duluth hosts most of the parkway, the roadway's southwestern end carries into

the city of Proctor, as well as Midway Township. Seven Bridges Road, which comprises the northeastern end of the parkway, actually has a north–south alignment.[15]

Work on Skyline Parkway began in 1889 and continued for decades, finally finishing about 1940. The designation Skyline Parkway was not officially adopted until 1929. The first section of the roadway completed was named Terrace Parkway, which soon became Rogers Parkway, in honor of William K. Rogers, the first president of the Duluth Park Board. This portion of parkway was finished in the 1890s and reached from Chester Park in the northeast to Lincoln Park in the southwest. By the turn of the twentieth century, Samuel Frisby Snively, a renaissance personality who made a fortune in Duluth real estate, lost it, then ventured to the gold fields of Alaska before returning to Duluth to again work in real estate, began building a roadway near his farmland just above the northeastern Duluth neighborhood of Lester Park. This roadway soon joined

The Alvarado Bridge near Alvarado in Marshall County was perhaps the most attractive Marsh Arch ever built on a Minnesota roadway. Completed over the Snake River in 1925, it was razed in 1969. *Photograph taken in 1933; courtesy of Mn/DOT.*

Rogers Parkway as a constituent of Skyline Parkway. Eventually, a portion of Snively's Road evolved into what is now known as Seven Bridges Road.[16]

Seven Bridges Road was one of the many park legacies of Snively, Duluth's longest-serving mayor and a man enamored with nature's offerings. Historian Mark Ryan explained the origins of the mayor's environmental values: "Snively had inherited his appreciation for the outdoors from his mother, Margaret H. Snively. 'My mother,' he once wrote, 'was a woman of restless energy, a lover of all that was grand and beautiful in nature, and an influential representative of that which was most ennobling and uplifting in life.'"[17]

Seven Bridges Road reaches southward and downward toward Lake Superior from that section of Skyline Parkway running the crest above the city. At the bottom of the hill, it intersects with Superior Street, a principal transportation artery, near where Superior Street crosses the Lester River at the northeastern end of town. Seven Bridges Road follows Amity Creek, a

Duluth's Seven Bridges Road receives its name from seven handsome concrete arches marking the thoroughfare. Designed by the Minneapolis firm of Morrell and Nichols, the bridges were constructed along the two-mile stretch of roadway in 1910 and 1911. Three of the seven bridges are shown here. *Photographs taken in 2006.*

waterway that works its way downward from the crest, from near the former Snively farmstead, until it merges with the Lester River, which carries onward a short distance to Lake Superior. Lester Park is mostly to the northeast of the roadway, as is the striking rocky and wooded gorge through which the Lester River travels.

Initially, the roughly two-mile-long Seven Bridges Road section of Skyline Parkway crossed Amity Creek in several locations with wood bridges. These crossings did not last, however; each rapidly deteriorated, as did the roadway. Between 1910 and 1911, the city of Duluth improved the roadway and hired the Minneapolis firm of Morell and Nichols to design new crossings to replace the dilapidated bridges. Anthony Morell and Arthur Nichols were well-known in Duluth, since the duo helped create the landscaping at the Chester and Clara Congdon Estate, a Duluth residence commonly known as Glensheen, featuring considerable grounds and a Jacobean Revival mansion, all belonging to a prominent legal counsel and his wife. In fact, Glensheen is only a short distance from Seven Bridges Road. Morell and Nichols designed nine reinforced-concrete barrel-arch bridges of various lengths for Seven Bridges Road. Only seven of the bridges inspire the name for the roadway, however, apparently because that is the number of crossings on the thoroughfare that are still in use. Each of the bridges is faced with local stone—again, handsome structures pretending to be stone arches.[18]

By the mid-1990s, these wonderful bridges were suffering their years. One crossing was rehabilitated in 1996, and another in 1999. In 2002, another bridge was rehabilitated and the second crossing up from Superior Street was completely rebuilt. The rebuilt structure retains much of its original look because citizens of Duluth understand the importance of the crossing's architectural character and how it reflects the city's heritage. Moreover, Duluth continues to maintain Skyline Parkway, a roadway showcasing not only the attractive crossings on Seven Bridges Road, but other rustic public appurtenances as well, including the raw-looking Stewart Creek Stone Arch Bridge, one of the few park stone arches in Minnesota.[19]

The 165-foot-long, single-span Lester River Bridge is only about a stone's throw from Seven Bridges Road, nearer the shore of Lake Superior. Like the crossings that give the name to the picturesque roadway coursing up from Superior Street, the Lester River Bridge is a reinforced-concrete arch. It is not, however, a barrel arch like those on the parkway. Peering beneath the bridge reveals that the crossing is made of six reinforced-concrete ribs, generally elliptical in form. This bridge also was designed by Morell and Nichols, but with assistance from the engineering department in Duluth and additional aid from the Minneapolis architectural firm of Tyrie and Chapman.[20]

The Lester River Bridge was built between 1924 and 1925, about the same time as the Stewart Creek Stone Arch Bridge, but well after the structures on Seven Bridges Road. As with the crossings on Seven Bridges Road, native stone was employed as a facing for the Lester River Bridge, yet the bridge has a more sophisticated appearance than those earlier bridges. Surely, all of the crossings are handsome structures with Classical Revival detailing, but those on Seven Bridges Road are slightly more rustic than the Lester River Bridge. The stone for the bridge over the Lester River is randomly coursed ashlar. In other words, the gabbro stone is dressed, with each stone exhibiting sharp lines to top and bottom and left and right; the facing is a series of carved rectangles of various dimensions that offers a clean appearance. This is not the case with the structures on Seven Bridges Road. Additionally, the Lester River Bridge features vivid accents unmatched by Morell and Nichols's earlier effort, most notably the archivolt, which is the decorative band tracing the curve of the arch at either side of the bridge. The archivolt is reminiscent of elaborate ring stones for a stone arch bridge. This detail is made of Cold Spring granite from Rockville, a town near St. Cloud in central Minnesota.[21]

The roughly $50,000 Lester River Bridge exists because in the early 1920s Minnesota began building its trunk highway system, the previously mentioned state-owned roadway network that cohesively linked different parts of Minnesota. Surprisingly, at that time, Minnesota did not have a principal, well-maintained roadway leading from Duluth up the North Shore. The construction of Minnesota Trunk Highway 1 changed that. Minnesota Trunk Highway 1, also called North Shore Drive, as well as Lake Superior International Highway, presumably because it stretched from Iowa to the Canadian border, took advantage of the natural scenic beauty found on the North Shore, paralleling the edge of the largest freshwater lake in the world. Construction of the roadway north of Duluth to Canada was finished in 1925. In 1934, Minnesota Trunk Highway 1 was renamed Minnesota Trunk Highway 61.[22]

For many, the Lester River Bridge, situated where the Lester River empties into Lake Superior, just down from Superior Street and Seven Bridges Road, represents the gateway to the stunning North Shore. Travel writer Shawn Perich explained, "… the North Shore begins at Twelfth Avenue East in Duluth—the starting point for State Highway 61. However, not until you cross the Lester River Bridge do you first see the lake up close and leave the city behind. For most of us, this marks the real beginning of the North Shore Drive."[23] Perich penned those words in the early 1990s, but certainly many in the 1920s also viewed the Lester River Bridge as the doorway to the beautiful highway, a roadway praised by one travel writer from the period:

Beyond argument, the drive on this northern shore of Lake Superior between Duluth and Port Arthur [Canada] is a natural classic. This is the land of the sky-blue water and the cathedral red rocks, where the prophetic Indian voice of Gitchie Manitou booms to the joyous loneliness amid the million sea gulls flying like snow. A most satisfying road clings to the shore, now streaming with light, now cut through somber jungle of blue-black trees.[24]

For those responsible for the Lester River Bridge, a plain-looking crossing as a gateway to such inspirational vistas would have been obscene.

Up the road from the Lester River Bridge, the MHD completed another handsome crossing as part of North Shore Drive construction. Bridge No. 3589 was finished in 1924, just before the Lester River Bridge. Decorated with Classical Revival detailing, barrel-arched Bridge No. 3589 is situated over the Stewart River, a short distance northeast of downtown Two Harbors, a community born of the iron ore trade and named for its two bays on Lake Superior, Agate Bay and Burlington Bay. Ornamental pilasters embrace Bridge No. 3589's seventy-foot-long elliptical arch. Unlike the Lester River Bridge, Bridge No. 3589 is not faced in stone. Instead, its walls are faced in concrete. The concrete finish is both coarse and smooth. It is coarse on the abutment walls, recessed panels of the pilasters, and spandrel walls, yet smooth on the pilaster surrounds

The Lester River Bridge over the Lester River in Duluth is an exceptionally handsome concrete arch, chiefly because it features a facing of neatly cut stone. Built between 1924 and 1925, the bridge was designed by Morell and Nichols. Unlike most concrete arches of its size, the Lester River Bridge is supported on arched ribs. *Photograph taken in 2006.*

and the pronounced archivolt. With an overall length less than that of the Lester River Bridge, and adorned with a fascia lacking stone, Bridge No. 3589 cost considerably less than the structure over the Lester River, coming in at just over $9,000.[25]

Originally, the roadway over the bridge was nineteen feet wide, but in 1939 the MHD widened the road to thirty feet to accommodate increasing traffic loads, a task costing more than the initial construction, about $12,000. The width of the bridge was extended when an additional concrete arched section was poured at the east side. While the bridge's footprint is wider than its original design, its detailing largely remains the same as when it was built. One architectural difference between the bridge's original and current forms, however, is found in the railings, which were modified during the 1939 construction. The current open balustrade railings are somewhat less ornamented than the original railings. Nevertheless, they continue to blend well with the overall design of the bridge.[26]

The Nymore Bridge is similar to Bridge No. 3589, for it also is a reinforced-concrete arch exhibiting a Classical Revival facade entirely of concrete. Finished

The Minnesota Department of
Highways designed an attractive
Classical Revival–style concrete
arch just northeast of Two
Harbors. Like the Lester River
Bridge at Duluth, Bridge No.
3589 edges Lake Superior. The
crossing was completed in 1924.
Photograph taken in 2005.

almost a decade before
Bridge No. 3589, the
Nymore Bridge was
built on First Street (Old
Highway 2) in Bemidji in
north-central Minnesota's
Beltrami County. Span-
ning the short Mississippi
River channel between
Lake Bemidji to the north
and Lake Irving to the
south, the bridge is less than a minute away from one
of Minnesota's most famous roadside attractions, the
statues of Paul Bunyan and Babe the Blue Ox, which
punctuate the shore of Lake Bemidji. The bridge
received its name because it connected Bemidji with
the village of Nymore, a community that was annexed
by Bemidji about the time the bridge was finished.[27]

Because the Nymore Bridge was completed in 1917, it
is a relatively early example of a Classical Revival–style
crossing in Minnesota. Not as early as some of Gillham's
modest arches, of course, but it nevertheless is a size-
able, well-proportioned, urban crossing reflecting the
style. Nowadays, such characteristics make the bridge
rare. With three segmental barrel arches, the bridge
is almost 170 feet long. The piers are adorned with
prominent pilasters and round starlings, and the solid
concrete railings feature classical posts. Raised panels
mark the pilasters, spandrel walls, railings, and abutments. At one time, several ornamental light standards
rose from the railings, but only a few of the standards
remain and the lamps are absent.[28]

Technologically, the attractive bridge is intriguing
because it is similar to a Melan arch. But where a
Melan arch's metal reinforcement is formed of bent
I beams, this bridge has an arched, metal truss. The
pieces making up the truss are basically a series of
panels made of metal members. All of the panels are
pinned or wired together. When the Nymore Bridge
was constructed, forms were placed against the finished
truss and concrete poured over the framework. As a
result, the framework—the truss—became the concrete
bridge's reinforcement. Like a Melan arch bridge, the
Nymore Bridge is essentially a metal bridge clad in
concrete.[29] This type of reinforced-concrete bridge
construction was developed by George M. Cheney of
Indianapolis, Indiana. Cheney's 1906 patent explains
his reasoning for this reinforcing process:

The object of my present invention is to produce a reinforcing
structure adapted to be embedded within the concrete, the
construction and arrangement of said reinforcing structure
being such as to eliminate or nearly eliminate the probability
of cracking, but also being such that if there be cracking it will
occur along predetermined lines, the concrete structure being so
formed as to render less apparent any such cracks.[30]

Cheney assigned his patent to the Standard Reinforced Concrete Company of Indianapolis, Indiana,
the same enterprise responsible for the plans and
specifications for the Nymore Bridge. The nearly
$23,000 crossing was built by the Illinois Steel Bridge

Company, whose Minnesota agents, John Zelch and P. T. Walton, operated from a St. Paul office from 1912 to 1921, implying that this duo oversaw construction of the Nymore Bridge.[31]

Today, the Nymore Bridge is relegated to a secondary road. More accurately, the principal roadway once carried by the Nymore Bridge is no longer principal. Instead, a main transportation artery is positioned a short distance to the north, edging Lake Bemidji. In truth, the Nymore Bridge could not support the substantial traffic that presently moves into and out of downtown Bemidji, but, thankfully, like the Nymore Bridge, the relatively new concrete-girder bridge currently carrying mainline traffic over the Mississippi River channel between Lake Bemidji and Lake Irving is a landscape asset rather than a landscape blight.

A relatively large, attractive, and impressively built concrete arch, the Nymore Bridge simply cannot compare to a concrete-arch bridge that was erected in the Twin Cities about the time Cheney's patent was put to use in Bemidji. The Third Avenue Bridge over the Mississippi River in Minneapolis is a huge reinforced-concrete, open-spandrel arch. It was the beginning of a fantastic concrete-arch bridge-building program

that made the Twin Cities metropolitan area the envy of almost every major municipality across the country. The Third Avenue Bridge spans the Mississippi River just below the Hennepin Avenue Bridge and immediately above the Falls of St. Anthony and the Stone Arch Bridge, the location where James J. Hill purposely avoided placing his splendid railroad structure for fear of destroying the falls. But more than three decades after the Stone Arch Bridge was built, bridge engineering had clearly advanced, and thanks to the innovative mind of Minneapolis's chief engineer in the early twentieth century, Frederick William Cappelen, the city was able to erect an enormous bridge on a site previously believed unsuitable for such a structure.

Cappelen is a celebrated Minnesota engineer. In fact, one of the state's grandest bridges is named for him, although most Minnesotans probably do not realize that. Cappelen is one of four influential Norwegian American engineers who helped create the infrastructure of Minneapolis and St. Paul in the late nineteenth and early twentieth centuries. The others are Kristoffer Olsen Oustad, Martin Sigvart Grytbak, and Andreas W. Munster. Educated in Sweden and Germany, Cappelen came to the United States in 1880 and soon was working for the Northern Pacific Railway. He arrived in Minneapolis in 1886, and by 1893 he was serving as city engineer. He began consulting work in 1898, but by 1913 he again was working as city engineer for Minneapolis, and so oversaw construction of the Third Avenue Bridge.[32]

The Classical Revival–style Nymore Bridge in Bemidji spans a short channel between Lake Bemidji and Lake Irving. Erected in 1917, the bridge follows the construction method developed by George M. Cheney of Indianapolis, Indiana. *Photograph taken in 2006.*

The Third Avenue Bridge over the Mississippi River in Minneapolis is a huge concrete arch employing the Melan construction method. It is the last major example of this type of construction in Minnesota. The bridge was designed by one of Minnesota's most prominent engineers, Frederick William Cappelen, and completed in 1916. *Photograph taken in 2006 by Robert W. Gardner Jr.*

Public advocacy for a bridge at Third Avenue in Minneapolis began in 1912, one year before Cappelen returned to the prominent municipal engineering position. A bridge was necessary for the same reason each Hennepin Avenue Bridge was erected: the population continued to flourish. Minneapolis asked the Concrete Steel Engineering Company of New York to complete a design for a concrete-arch bridge, but power and milling businesses along the river that were dependent on the Falls of St. Anthony were not enthused, fearing that a heavy bridge above the falls might destroy the natural resource. As Hill realized so many years earlier when seeking a location for his stone crossing, much of the river foundation at this point is weak. After some of the enterprises that used the power of the falls threatened a lawsuit against Minneapolis, Cappelen opted for an unusually long-span parabolic through-truss

bridge erected on a slightly different line from what was planned for the concrete arch, thus avoiding the delicate stratum. This time the public was unhappy, for its growing aesthetic sophistication demanded that an artistic-looking crossing span the greatest of all American rivers inside the Twin Cities metropolitan area. Despite the public criticism, the city council endorsed Cappelen's truss bridge design. Interestingly, Cappelen did not.[33]

Even as he was planning the large truss bridge, Cappelen was reworking the problem of building an aesthetically pleasing concrete arch just above the falls. He concluded that such a bridge could be built by curving it around weaker stratum areas and creating a number of spans of more than two hundred feet to leap over other weak foundation sites. After laying his plan before city officials and others, Cappelen's concept was

The arches of the Third Avenue Bridge are taking shape across the Mississippi River. *Photograph by C. J. Hibbard & Company, ca. 1915; courtesy of the Minnesota Historical Society.*

accepted. Work on the structure began in 1914 and was largely complete by 1916. Consisting of a few girder approaches, two 134-foot-long, open-spandrel barrel arches, and five 211-foot-long, open-spandrel ribbed arches, Cappelen's refined, gently sweeping, 2,200-foot-long bridge was a welcome addition to the Minneapolis waterfront. Although the $860,000 bridge's classical-looking railings were replaced with Art Deco–style railings in 1939, and even though the late 1970s brought additional modification, the bridge nevertheless retains much of its original appearance and today continues to ornament the river.[34]

The Third Avenue Bridge was a departure from the commonplace designs of the early decades of the 1900s. This partly came about because engineers were moving beyond truss bridge construction, but also because they were moving beyond the early experimental years of reinforced-concrete bridge building. By the time the Third Avenue Bridge was erected, engineers had largely perfected small and modest-sized reinforced-concrete arch bridges, mostly of the barrel variety. They had also developed the fundamental designs of reinforced-concrete girder and slab bridges that would become prevalent on Minnesota's roadways in the ensuing decades, thanks in large measure to increased bridge-building standards put forth by the MHC and then the MHD. The Third Avenue Bridge clearly was different, however, as it was a concrete arch of monumental proportions and it was primarily formed of ribs, providing it a kind of airy elegance. The bridge was demonstration of growing engineering confidence in what could be built in concrete, but, oddly perhaps, it still was somewhat conservative, for it was a Melan arch, and so formed of substantial quantities of steel. The bridge was the last major use of Melan-type construction in the Twin Cities metropolitan area, and as such, it was, according to historian Robert M. Frame III, the preamble to what followed.[35]

As reinforced concrete continued to be embraced as a bridge-building material in the early twentieth century, it was only natural that officials in a maturing Twin Cities metropolitan area would seek to erect beautiful concrete arches between the bluffs over the Mississippi River. The landscape was ideal for such bridges and the need for major river crossings at this time was becoming paramount, as Minnesota highways increasingly converged on the Twin Cities. Smitten with the automobile, Minnesotans eagerly filled those highways. While the Third Avenue Bridge represented the first go at monumental concrete-arch construction, it soon was followed by the Cappelen Memorial Bridge, the Robert Street Bridge, the Fort Snelling–Mendota Bridge, the Intercity Bridge, the Anoka–Champlin Mississippi River Bridge, and the Cedar Avenue Bridge. Each crossing was necessary to support increasing traffic in the region, and each was intended as an artistic engineering statement. Bridge historian David Plowden noted this effort: "The first really sophisticated American program of concrete highway bridge construction evolved around Minnesota's Twin Cities. Their ambitious highway-improvement plan, which included a large number of large, well-designed bridges, started in

[1914] and continued until the mid-twenties."[36]

Only a few years after the Third Avenue Bridge was finished, Minneapolis was erecting the Cappelen Memorial Bridge, the handsome reinforced-concrete arch crossing named for the longtime city engineer. The bridge carries Franklin Avenue over the Mississippi River in Minneapolis, immediately downriver from the newer Interstate Highway 94 Bridge, a multi-span steel girder that offers nothing to brag about. Because of its location, the Cappelen Memorial Bridge is often referenced as the Franklin Avenue Bridge, but in reality it was dedicated to the prominent engineer, who died while the open-spandrel crossing was under construction.

The Cappelen Memorial Bridge was designed by Cappelen with aid from Kristoffer Olsen Oustad. Oustad worked as Minneapolis's chief bridge engineer for many years in the early part of the twentieth century. Actually, when Cappelen became city engineer in 1893, Oustad became the city's principal bridge engineer, a position he would hold until 1929.[37]

The Cappelen Memorial Bridge replaced a combination through truss–deck truss that was located on the site and could no longer support the growing traffic of a major urban center. Indeed, as historian Kenneth Bjork explains:

The need for a new crossing at [Franklin Avenue] was so great that Cappelen, after completion of the Third Avenue Bridge, immediately put his mind to the problem; it was he who made the general plans, though he did not live to see them completed. Oustad was immediately responsible for the design of the structure that was to become a memorial to Cappelen's long municipal service.[38]

Construction of the roughly 1,100-foot-long, five-span, ribbed structure began in 1919 and was finished in 1923. The bridge's main span is four hundred feet long and is the chief reason the structure is unique. At the time it was built, the main, or center, span was the longest reinforced-concrete arch in the world. The main span is so long because it had to allow for navigation of the river, but even more, the span needed to encompass the old bridge. In the planning phase, Cappelen decided that the existing bridge would prove invaluable as a means of moving building material from one part of the construction site to the next, thus the new bridge was raised up around the old metal-truss bridge, with the center concrete arch essentially leaping over the piers supporting the main span of the truss bridge. Today, the crumbling remains of these stone piers can be seen inside the concrete arch of the main span, near the springing line at either end of the arch. During construction, the scene must have looked somewhat bizarre to passersby, as a graceful arch rose from the river to seemingly swallow a metal truss and its stone piers.[39]

As the bridge neared completion, the *Engineering News-Record* remarked that the $900,000 Cappelen Memorial Bridge "is one of the most important and interesting works of structural engineering now in progress." The technical journal continued, noting the bridge's unfussy, yet pleasing, appearance, "[The bridge] is unusually simple in its architectural features, making use of almost no ornament … the result is a demonstration of what can be achieved with plain details provided the structural proportioning is good." Many years later, Plowden's praise went farther: "The bridge … remains a classic work, drawing from the past yet anticipating the future. The utter simplicity of its flattened arches and its refined design make it one of America's most beautiful concrete bridges."[40]

Certainly it is, but some in St. Paul may argue that their city's monumental concrete-arch highway bridge is every bit as attractive as the Cappelen Memorial Bridge, and perhaps more so. St. Paul without the Robert Street Bridge is like Stillwater without the Stillwater Bridge, or Duluth without the Duluth Aerial Lift Bridge, or Minneapolis without the Stone Arch Bridge. Linking downtown with South St. Paul across the Mississippi River at Robert Street, the bridge, along with other notable structures in the capital city, puts a face on St. Paul. And it is an appealing face. The Robert Street Bridge is made more attractive because it nestles the Chicago Great Western Railway Aerial Lift Bridge. Although the railroad structure is a visually intriguing utilitarian crossing, sidling the Robert Street Bridge, it is reminiscent of an ugly duckling snuggling a swan.

Completed in 1885 to support horse-drawn vehicles, the previous Robert Street Bridge was in no way a swan. Instead, the long-span, wrought iron truss crossing was thought functional, which was about as much praise as most truss crossings could expect in the late nineteenth century. Specifically, the earlier Robert Street Bridge

was composed of several deck trusses and a through-truss main span that passed over the river's navigation channel near the waterway's northwest bank. The main line of the Chicago Great Western Railway crossed the Mississippi River on a generally north–south axis and beneath the main span of the Robert Street Bridge. The intersection of the two bridges cluttered the area beneath the roadway crossing's main span. The navigation channel remained unobstructed, however, because the railroad bridge section beneath the Robert Street Bridge's main span was a swing span, and so could easily swing open to allow vessels to pass. Nevertheless, the merger of the two bridges over the navigation channel looked clumsy.[41]

The wrought iron truss was designed by St. Paul

The Cappelen Memorial Bridge across the Mississippi River is a fitting tribute to the Minneapolis engineer who helped complete so much of the city's infrastructure. This graceful bridge was designed by Cappelen and Kristoffer Olsen Oustad and completed in 1923. *Photograph taken in 2006.*

chief bridge engineer Andreas W. Munster, who was also responsible for the design of the Smith Avenue Bridge (High Bridge) and the fourth Wabasha Street Bridge. Traffic over the Robert Street Bridge dramatically increased after Robert Street was widened between 1912 and 1914. By 1920 the bridge was supporting almost three thousand motorized vehicles and about four hundred streetcars every twelve hours, clearly impressive for a bridge originally built for horses and wagons. Two years later, traffic on the roadway and over the bridge had about doubled. Construction of the current highway bridge at Robert Street began in 1924 and finished in 1926. It was engineered by Toltz, King, and Day of St. Paul. The firm was founded in 1919 when Max Toltz of Toltz Engineering Company partnered with Wesley Eugene King and Beaver Wade Day. Besides the Robert Street Bridge, the company

also helped design Bridge No. 6009, a steel movable crossing erected over the St. Croix River in 1922. King ran the company after both Toltz and Day died in the early 1930s. The firm became Toltz, King, Duval, and Anderson in the mid-1950s.[42]

Toltz, King, and Day designed the most structurally diverse of the grand reinforced-concrete arches in the Twin Cities region. Roughly 1,500 feet long, the Robert Street Bridge is formed of three separate arch types: barrel, ribbed, and through. This curious combination results from site conditions. Since the banks of the Mississippi River are not very high at Robert Street, engineers concluded the different arch types were necessary if St. Paul and Ramsey County insisted on a concrete arch at the site. While the four spans reaching from the southeast bank are formed of ribs, each measuring 112 feet long, the main span over the

navigation channel is a 264-foot-long through arch,
also called a rainbow arch. It is similar to the Marsh
Concrete Rainbow Arch Bridge in Cambria Township
in Blue Earth County, except it reflects a much larger
scale. The three arch spans at the northwest side of the
river are barrels and together total about 291 feet. These
spans resemble concrete slabs that have been bent into
arches.[43]

The engineering firm designed a through-arch main
span because it allowed considerable vertical clearance
between the navigation channel and the deck of the
bridge. A through arch is essentially a ribbed arch, but
it is a nontraditional ribbed arch because a single rib
passes through either side of the bridge deck, each rib
crowning well above the roadway. If the arches of the
Robert Street Bridge's main span had been traditional
ribs peaking beneath the deck, plying the navigation

channel with large vessels would be impossible because
the ribs would obstruct the watercourse. It appears that
barrel arches rather than ribbed arches were employed
at the northwest end of the bridge because extra
headroom was required at that point as well; the barrel
arches have a higher springing line than the ribbed
arches. With the construction of the new Robert Street
Bridge, the line of the Chicago Great Western Railway
was rerouted beneath one of the barrel arches rather
than below the main span. This made the intersection of the bridges less convoluted looking than previously, although the junction of the two still appears a
bit odd. By the time the railroad line over the river had
been rerouted, the Chicago Great Western Railway
had replaced its original swing span with the current
vertical-lift span. The Robert Street Bridge's other
barrel arches were designed to span additional railroad

tracks that paralleled the Mississippi River, but only a
few of these tracks remain today.[44]

Although mostly hidden from view, the $1.75 million
Robert Street Bridge also features a 311-foot-long
concrete trestle approaching the ribbed-arch sections at
the southeast end of the crossing, while three concrete
trestles totaling 89 feet in length and a steel, deck girder
span roughly 53 feet long merge with the barrel-arch
spans at the northwest end of the bridge.[45]

Besides comeliness derived from its disparate arches,
the Robert Street Bridge's attractiveness is augmented
with various embellishments. The bridge has ornate
railings and posts, while the edges of the concrete piers
are accented with narrow, vertical incisions. Horizontal,
incised lines decorate the broad side of each pier. The
ribs of the rainbow arch are traced with incised lines
as well. These ribs also feature wedge-shaped indentations. The various lines and indentations add texture
to the bridge, breaking up otherwise flat surfaces. Piers
are further festooned with medallions. The overall

appearance of the crossing can perhaps be thought Art Moderne or Art Deco. Pleased with the look of the new bridge, the *St. Paul Pioneer Press* exuberantly remarked, "Combining artistry and utility, the new Robert Street Bridge presents a type of bridge architecture that, in its artistic effects, is different from any other bridge structure in the United States. It represents the very latest word in bridge construction engineering...."[46]

While the Robert Street Bridge is perhaps the most handsome of the monumental Twin Cities arches, the grandest arch remains the Fort Snelling–Mendota Bridge tying together Hennepin County and Dakota County. Completed only months after the Robert Street Bridge, this magnificent reinforced-concrete arch was erected at Mendota. The bridge actually spans the Minnesota River, near its junction with the Mississippi River. It is an immense crossing formed of thirteen parabolic ribbed arches, most about three hundred feet long. Bounding over Fort Snelling State Park, a picturesque wooded expanse that divides the western metropolitan area from the eastern metropolitan area, near the Minneapolis–St. Paul International Airport, the crossing is more than 4,100 feet long. It was designed by Walter H. Wheeler with assistance from C. A. P. Turner, the engineer responsible for the Soo Line High Bridge above Stillwater in the St. Croix River Valley. Plowden believes that the Fort Snelling–Mendota Bridge is a Turner "masterpiece," noting that "apart from some of the West Coast bridges, [the Fort Snelling–Mendota Bridge] is usually considered to be the most sophisticated design for a concrete arch built in the 1920s, equaling Turner's other great work, the steel-arch viaduct over the St. Croix River."[47]

Although he did not achieve the acclaim of Turner, Wheeler was still a nationally recognized Minnesota engineer. Based in Minneapolis in the early twentieth century, Wheeler engineered a number of prominent structures, including the Cream of Wheat Building in Minneapolis, which was begun soon after completion of the Fort Snelling–Mendota Bridge. He also was responsible for Pioneer Hall at the University of Minnesota. One of his most significant works was finished in 1936. Completed by the Public Works Administration, the Minneapolis Armory is widely considered the most important building erected in the Twin Cities during the Great Depression. The Art Moderne–style quarters for the Minnesota National Guard is the first Minnesota use of the Wheeler Shear Head. The Wheeler Shear Head is a structural-steel column-head assembly embedded within a reinforced-concrete floor/ceiling slab. Employing this assembly for some reinforced-concrete construction eliminates the need for column capitals or beams beneath a concrete floor/ceiling, thus increasing headroom and decreasing costs. This building process was first employed for the U.S. Appraisers Building in Baltimore, a structure erected in 1934. Wheeler's personal papers and various engineering drawings have been preserved at the Northwest Architectural Archives at the University of Minnesota.[48]

The through arch is an especially fetching feature of the large Robert Street Bridge. *Photograph taken in 2007.*

Measuring more than 4,100 feet long, the Fort Snelling–Mendota Bridge is by far the largest of the grand arches marking the Twin Cities. It was designed by prominent engineers Walter H. Wheeler and C. A. P. Turner. *Photograph ca. 1927; courtesy of the Minnesota Historical Society.*

Before the Fort Snelling–Mendota Bridge was erected, travelers from the south and east of the metropolitan area either traveled into St. Paul and then on to Minneapolis or shuttled across the Minnesota River at Mendota by ferry. A ferry had served at Mendota for about a century, but by the 1920s, powers in Minneapolis demanded a bridge to provide greater access to the city. Hennepin County funded the $1.87 million crossing. The cost irked some because the county could have funded a cheaper bridge. In fact, Wheeler presented four separate bridge designs for review by the Hennepin County Board of Commissioners. The first was an open-spandrel, reinforced-concrete ribbed arch on concrete piers, while the second was a steel arch supported on concrete piers. A steel deck truss on concrete piers was the third option, and a steel deck

truss on steel piers was the fourth choice. Wheeler recommended option three, but Hennepin County insisted on the most expensive crossing, the open-spandrel, reinforced-concrete ribbed arch. For many, surely, this was not surprising, since reinforced-concrete ribbed-arch highway bridges had clearly become fashionable at major crossing points in the Minneapolis–St. Paul region.[49]

Begun in early 1924 and completed in late 1926, the bridge hosted a huge dedicatory gathering, although it was a day late due to a November snowstorm. The throng of roughly four thousand included Governor Theodore Christianson, Miss Hennepin County (Marguerite B. Johnson), Miss Dakota County (Maxine Paulson), three bands, and Battery C of the 9th Field Artillery stationed at Fort Snelling, a unit that fired a canon salute in celebration. The bridge was dedicated to members of the 151st Field Artillery from Minnesota who died in the First World War. President Calvin Coolidge sent a telegram noting the tribute: "It is fitting that the memory of the men of the 151st field artillery who died in the WW should be honored by so fine and useful a monument."[50]

The mammoth bridge remained largely unchanged until the early 1990s, when the original deck was removed. It was a strange sight: arches and spandrel columns reaching upward to support ... nothing. This soon changed, however, as a new, much-wider deck was put in place atop the columns and arch crowns. Thankfully, the renovation retained the original railings and posts, which were removed from the original deck, refurbished, and reinstalled with the replacement deck. Several hundred people gathered for the grand reopening in mid-October 1994. And just as when the bridge first opened, there was canon fire, as rounds from a pre–Civil War canon and a modern-day howitzer exploded in salutes. An Apache attack helicopter even

A ferry across the Minnesota River at Mendota had served for about a century before the mammoth Fort Snelling–Mendota Bridge was erected. Note the timber swing-span bridge in the background: this is the railroad bridge that the Milwaukee and St. Paul Railway completed a few years before the Minneapolis and St. Louis Railway erected a similar crossing at Carver. *Photograph ca. 1890; courtesy of the Minnesota Historical Society.*

Construction of the Fort Snelling–Mendota Bridge began in 1924 and finished in 1926. *Photograph taken in 1925; courtesy of the Minnesota Historical Society.*

swirled overhead, as two surviving members of the 151st Field Artillery peered skyward. The *St. Paul Pioneer Press,* demonstrating that romanticism in journalism had not yet entirely vanished, noted the setting on this rededication day: "It was a gorgeous, sunny autumn day to dedicate a bridge. The Minnesota and Mississippi River Valleys stretching off to the horizon on both sides were painted with Mother Earth's finest colors for the occasion."[51]

In his classic work *American Building,* Carl W. Condit acknowledges the uniqueness of the Fort Snelling–Mendota Bridge: "The whole complex of ribs, spandrel posts, and long deck has a finely articulated quality that has seldom been matched in American bridge design."

No concrete arch built in the Minneapolis–St. Paul region after the Fort Snelling–Mendota Bridge equaled its "articulated quality," but then none had a similar site demanding such an extraordinarily long crossing.[52]

The next large reinforced-concrete arch was raised over the Mississippi River at Ford Parkway, connecting the southern neighborhoods of Minneapolis and St. Paul. The Intercity Bridge, also known as the Ford Bridge, is only a spirited hike northwest from the Fort Snelling–Mendota Bridge. The Intercity Bridge was built because civic leaders in Minneapolis and St. Paul desired residential development near the Ford Motor Company plant, a complex completed in 1924 on the east side of the Mississippi River, adjacent to Edsel Avenue (renamed Ford Parkway in 1928). The plant's construction included a hydroelectric facility, which was erected at the east end of Upper Mississippi River Lock and Dam No. 1, a structure situated immediately downriver of the bridge site.[53]

A joint committee of public officials and engineers from Minneapolis and St. Paul was created to bring the bridge to fruition. The committee was chaired by none other than Charles Merritt Babcock, an official so important to Minnesota's transportation heritage that he is deserving of a comprehensive biography. Minnesota's first commissioner of highways when the MHD replaced the MHC, Babcock merits much credit for bringing about the state's trunk highway system. In fact, the legislation inaugurating the roadway network is titled the Babcock Amendment. Born in Minnesota's Sher-

burne County and educated at the University of Minnesota, Babcock became so well-known in the 1920s and early 1930s for his Babcock Plan for major transportation arterials that Minnesotans could scarcely peruse their local newspapers and not read his name. Interestingly, the constitutional amendment named for Babcock and adopted by public vote in 1920 is so detailed that its length is greater than all previous amendments combined. Minneapolis and St. Paul could not have chosen a more qualified individual to chair the Joint Bridge Committee.[54]

Construction of the 1,500-foot-long Intercity Bridge began in August 1925. It finished in June 1927. Costing Minneapolis and St. Paul roughly $1.4 million, the bridge is formed of five ribbed arches, two that are 139 feet long and three measuring 300 feet in length. Of all the grand open-spandrel, reinforced-concrete

The deck has been widened to accommodate modern traffic loads, but the Fort Snelling–Mendota Bridge still features that "articulated quality" that brought it national renown. *Photograph taken in 2006.*

arches decorating the Twin Cities area, the Intercity Bridge is the most classical in appearance, although the Anoka–Champlin Mississippi River Bridge evokes the style as well. The classicism of the Intercity Bridge is derived from the paired spandrel columns with defined pedestals and capitals rising from the ribbed arches to support the deck. Additionally, the structure bridging the space between each set of paired columns is semi-circular in form, a pleasing aesthetic for a monumental bridge that received no artistic recommendations from architects, a fact that angered some local architects.[55] The bridge's principal designer, Martin Sigvart Grytbak, an engineer who emigrated from Norway about 1905, voiced displeasure with other design professionals who felt spurned because they were not consulted on the bridge's final appearance:

Certain factions in St. Paul were anxious to postpone the project indefinitely, and for awhile had the newspapers and a number of city organizations attacking the committee and engineers which had the bridge in charge, and the architects especially were incensed over not having been consulted in the design of the structure. The plans when completed were severely criticized by the architects....[56]

It appears, however, that once this bridge designed by committee was finished, criticism faded and accolades began, clearly a credit to the efforts of Grytbak and the others on the team. Grytbak, who worked for the Northern Pacific Railway before becoming the bridge engineer for St. Paul in 1913, designed other notable structures as well, including the Kellogg Boulevard Viaduct, which was erected in 1930. He remained in his municipal engineering position until after the Second World War. Eventually, his 2,100-foot-long viaduct was demolished.[57]

Regrettably, the Intercity Bridge did not have the desired effect on development around the Ford plant, at least initially. Not long after St. Paul built and paved new roadways near the complex, the stock market tumbled, taking livelihoods with it. As occurred just about everywhere, the Great Depression tempered residential and commercial development around the Ford plant. Further, growth increased somewhat in already developed areas across the river in Minneapolis, since many who worked at the Ford facility now had easy access across the river via the Intercity Bridge. Not

until after World War II did robust construction begin near the automobile plant.[58]

Like the other huge reinforced-concrete arches, the Intercity Bridge has endured time's toll well. Not surprisingly, its deck has been rebuilt and widened, a rehabilitation project that is largely inevitable in a region with a continually expanding population. When the deck was rebuilt in the early 1970s, the original railings were replaced with bland horizontal, metal pipe railings that were common at the time, replacement railings similar to those currently detracting from the otherwise splendid profile of the Cappelen Memorial Bridge. Thankfully, when the deck of the Intercity Bridge again was rehabilitated at the turn of the twenty-first century, aesthetic notions had rebooted and attractive new railings appropriate to the bridge's period of construction were installed.[59]

The Intercity Bridge was followed by the Cedar Avenue Bridge and the Anoka–Champlin Mississippi River Bridge, the last two monumental arches in the Twin Cities region built during this prolific era of reinforced-concrete arches. The Cedar Avenue Bridge spans the Mississippi River at Cedar Avenue, near the west bank campus of the University of Minnesota, and immediately downriver of the site of the former Interstate Highway 35W Bridge, the interesting-looking steel deck truss with a curved lower chord that collapsed on August 1, 2007, killing thirteen people and injuring dozens of others. In the northwest metropolitan area, the arch bridge over the Mississippi River that links Anoka in Anoka County with Champlin in Hennepin County carries U.S. Highway 169. Both open-spandrel, ribbed-arch bridges were completed in 1929. Even though some of the I beam approaches for the Cedar Avenue Bridge were built beginning in 1923, work on the arches did not start until 1926. Erection of the Anoka–Champlin Mississippi River Bridge started in 1928.[60]

The Cedar Avenue Bridge, which was especially welcomed by those living in South Minneapolis yet working in the industrial areas of Northeast Minneapolis, is the most reserved of all the grand arches, implying that it too was a construction project with little architectural input. As with the other arch bridges, its visual appeal is derived chiefly from the arches themselves, and with the exception of simple, narrow, vertical recessions in the piers, detailing is mostly

absent. The bridge was the major engineering achievement of Kristoffer Olsen Oustad, the same municipal engineer who finished the Cappelen Memorial Bridge after Frederick William Cappelen died. It also was Oustad's last bridge, as he retired soon after it was finished. When completed, Oustad's $1.1 million Cedar Avenue Bridge was the second-longest monumental arch in the Minneapolis–St. Paul area. Nearly 3,000 feet long, it was shorter than only the Fort Snelling–Mendota Bridge. Eventually, the approach spans were rebuilt and redirected, reducing the length of the bridge to about 2,200 feet. Besides the approaches, the structure is formed of seven arch spans, with the two main arches each about 265 feet in length and the five flanking arches each measuring 93 feet in length. Although not as pronounced as the curvature of the Third Avenue Bridge, the footprint for the Cedar Avenue Bridge has a subtle sweep at either end.[61]

The deck of the Cedar Avenue Bridge was rehabilitated in the early 1970s, about the time the I beam approaches were replaced with concrete girders. The original railings were probably replaced about this time as well. The current railings at either side of the roadway and the single line of railing edging the

sidewalk at the east side of the bridge are exceedingly ugly. It is unfortunate that the handsome bridge is crowned in such a fashion, but this unsightliness often has come with modern railing safety standards. This is not the case with the Anoka–Champlin Mississippi River Bridge, however. That bridge was rehabilitated in the late 1990s. The effort included replacement of the deteriorating classical-looking railings with similarly designed railings with higher safety standards. Mercifully, by the late 1990s, the starkness common to much of what we built in the recent past, including bridge railings, was slowly giving way to concepts learned long ago and then seemingly forgotten—that is, embellishment counts.[62]

The Anoka–Champlin Mississippi River Bridge was not the first at its site. In 1884, Horace E. Horton, the bridge builder and designer who completed the north half of the steel-arch Hennepin Avenue Bridge in 1888, erected an iron-truss swing span that replaced a ferry joining Anoka and Champlin across the Mississippi River. In January 1885, the *Anoka Herald* described the four-span, nine-hundred-foot-long structure as "one of the finest bridges that spans the Father of Waters." Four decades later, the bridge, unable to support the growing traffic, was no longer as fine as it once was. In addition, a substantial crack had developed in the bridge's pivot pier. Initially, the MHD designed another truss as a replacement crossing, but this plan was forfeited in favor of a reinforced-concrete ribbed arch. Why the

The Cedar Avenue Bridge was built across the Mississippi River just upstream of Northern Pacific Bridge No. 9 in 1929. The product of municipal engineer Kristoffer Olsen Oustad, the bridge became an important link between the residential areas of South Minneapolis and the industrial areas of Northeast Minneapolis. *Photograph taken in 2005.*

MHD changed its design is unclear, but perhaps the agency felt it should continue the precedent of building concrete arches at major roadway-river junctions in the Twin Cities area.[63]

Almost a thousand feet long, the $500,000 Anoka–Champlin Mississippi River Bridge is formed of eight main spans and two approaches. The main spans are open-spandrel ribbed arches, each measuring a little more than one hundred feet in length, while the approaches are thirty-nine-foot-long, closed-spandrel arches. Abutments and piers are ornamented with either recessed panels or fluting, and the railings exhibit a subtle classicism, all of which augment the bridge's attractiveness. Noticeably, the Anoka–Champlin Mississippi River Bridge is not nearly as high as the other arches, a result of relatively low riverbanks at this point on the Mississippi River. In August 1998, after the Anoka–Champlin Mississippi River Bridge was rehabilitated with a new deck, patching, strengthened arches, and new railings matching the look of the old, Anoka and Champlin came together in celebration of their landmark. The gathering included city and state officials, with entertainment by the Anoka Senior High School Brass Quintet.[64]

With the completion of the Cedar Avenue Bridge and the Anoka–Champlin Mississippi River Bridge in 1929, the age of building grand reinforced-concrete arch bridges in the Minneapolis–St. Paul region came to a close—well, mostly. Six decades after the bridges were built, the Twin Cities reflected on its past monumental concrete-arches when planning a new bridge over the Mississippi River linking Lake Street in Minneapolis with Marshall Avenue in St. Paul. Designed by HNTB, the same engineering enterprise responsible for the Father Louis Hennepin Bridge, the open-spandrel, reinforced-concrete ribbed arch structure completed in the early 1990s replaced an elegant, yet faltering, wrought iron arch bridge that was erected in 1888. Losing the wrought iron arch, one of the oldest bridges to span any part of the Mississippi River, was regrettable, but its successor is nevertheless impressive. In part, the present crossing is so fine because its two main arches are each 555 feet long, by far the longest concrete arch spans of any bridge in Minnesota. As with the wrought iron crossing, the current bridge vaults the river in but two leaps. With a total length of nearly 1,500 feet, the bridge is a rare build in modern America and clearly contributes to its geographic and built surroundings.[65]

Other Minnesota examples of open-spandrel, reinforced-concrete ribbed arches similar to those in the Twin Cities Metropolitan Area have been built. For example, both Brainerd in central Minnesota and Faribault in southeastern Minnesota erected substantial open-spandrel concrete arches in the first half of the twentieth century. The city of Oronoco in southeastern Minnesota also completed an impressive open-spandrel concrete arch. While its length of 275 feet is large compared with many nearby bridges, it is small in contrast to the Cedar Avenue Bridge in Minneapolis, and it is tiny when measured against the Fort Snelling–Mendota Bridge in Mendota.[66] Still, relatively large open-spandrel ribbed arches are almost always eye-catching. One that is especially fetching is Bridge No. 5557 on picturesque Minnesota Trunk Highway 11 in Lake of the Woods County in northern Minnesota. Completed in 1950, the bridge leaps the Rapid River flowing through the small community of Clementson. At this point, the Rapid River drains into the Rainy River, the waterway linking Lake of the Woods and Rainy Lake and serving as a natural boundary between

Minnesota and Ontario. The striking bridge within its striking setting of lush greenery and rocky outcrops—the kind of scene for which postcards are made—is described by historian Jeffrey A. Hess:

Bridge No. 5557 seem[s] an almost ethereal ornament for its wilderness-like setting. Airiness and lightness rule the design, from the double-ribbed, open-spandrel configuration of the 126-foot concrete arch, to the graceful scalloping of the arch curtain wall, to the elegant cambering of the concrete, deck-girder approach spans.[67]

An appropriate description, surely, but before the bridge's original railings were altered to the current metal pipe railings in the 1980s, the crossing was even more handsome. In fairness, these metal pipe railings

on a low concrete base, similar to those on the Cappelen Memorial Bridge, almost always look worse from the roadway than they do from the side. But although it is difficult to wreck the appearance of an arch, it has been tried. It seemed as though it might happen with Bridge No. 5557, when the highway department planned to erect a heavy, solid-concrete parapet as replacement to the original balustrade railings. This raised the ire of local citizens who demanded something better. While the current railings deserve little praise, they are more acceptable than plain, cumbersome-looking concrete parapets.[68]

Bridge No. 5557 replaced a through-truss with a pony-truss approach that was placed over the Rapid River at Clementson in 1915. The new bridge did not

Completed in 1884 by Horace E. Horton, the first bridge linking Anoka and Champlin across the Mississippi River consisted of four wrought iron through trusses. The main span was a swing span supported atop a circular stone pier. *Photograph ca. 1905; courtesy of the Minnesota Historical Society.*

come soon enough for some, including Leonard R. Dickinson, a state legislator from the Clementson district who sought an explanation from the MHD, noting that "[the] bridge at Clementson apparently is one of the worst from a traffic angle. There have been some very serious accidents and some deaths." The Second World War had stalled bridge construction in the state, as well as other civil works projects, but the MHD had continued to develop plans for future crossings during this period, including plans for a new bridge spanning the Rapid River at Clementson. By 1948, however, Dickinson wanted to know what was taking so long, Why had construction not started on a new bridge? The highway department responded that it was having difficulty acquiring materials and placing "bridge work under contract ... at

Although not as high as the other large concrete arches in the Twin Cities region, the Anoka–Champlin Mississippi River Bridge is nevertheless a handsome structure. Designed by the Minnesota Department of Highways, the bridge was completed in 1929, replacing Horton's wrought iron structure. *Photograph taken in 2007.*

The Lake Street–Marshall Avenue Bridge is the most recent large concrete arch completed over the Mississippi River between Minneapolis and St. Paul. The bridge was erected in the early 1990s and designed by HNTB, the same engineering firm responsible for the current Hennepin Avenue Bridge. *Photograph taken in 2006.*

reasonable prices or with any assurances that the work could be completed without considerable delay." By spring 1949, the state had found a contractor to erect the bridge at a reasonable price. L. M. Feller Company of Rochester, Minnesota, finished the delightful bridge in 1950 for about $114,000.[69]

By the time Bridge No. 5557 was constructed, the most common types of bridges being built in Minnesota were reinforced-concrete slabs, reinforced-concrete culverts, reinforced-concrete girders, and steel girders. Truthfully, by World War II the age of the reinforced-concrete arch, like the age of the truss bridge, had largely passed. With exploding highway construction after the war, most evident in the creation of the Interstate Highway System, the demand for roadway bridges was so great that the country moved away from costly arches, instead building simpler, almost mass-produced, crossings. The result was roadways strewn mostly with cost-effective, yawn-inducing bridges, almost all of which followed a standard design.[70]

Yet, some of Minnesota's early examples of concrete girders, slabs, and culverts deserve attention. In Princeton, in the east-central part of the state, the MHD designed a reinforced-concrete deck girder on County State Aid Highway 29 spanning the West Branch of the Rum River near the city's downtown. A deck girder is simply a bridge with its deck resting atop girders. Erected in 1931, the nearly 165-foot-long Dunn Memorial Bridge was named in honor of Robert C. Dunn, the state legislator and Good Roads Movement advocate from Princeton who pushed forward the 1913 law that made almost all highway bridge design in Minnesota

The original Lake Street–Marshall Avenue Bridge was an elegant wrought iron arch erected in 1888. It lasted a century. *Photograph ca. 1888; courtesy of the Minnesota Historical Society.*

the purview of the state. Replacing a truss bridge at the location, the three-span Dunn Memorial Bridge appears to be a striking, classical-looking concrete arch. Its elevation is deceptive, however, because the decorated spandrel walls are but curtain walls hiding the girders supporting the bridge's deck. There is merit in this kind of construction, for it demonstrates that even a simple concrete-girder bridge can be made visually appealing and contribute to the structural and geographic context that frames it. Besides, a slavish concrete girder would have been an unfitting tribute to Robert C. Dunn.[71]

About the time the MHD completed its homage to Dunn, it also finished two agreeable concrete deck girders over the Redwood River in Marshall, a community in southwestern Minnesota's Lyon County named for former governor William R. Marshall. Bridges Nos. 5083 and 5151 are virtually identical. At the time of construction, the *Marshall News-Messenger* referred to them as "twin brothers." Both are located on Minnesota Trunk Highway 19 (originally Minnesota Trunk

Highway 14), a roadway that was formally aligned through Marshall in 1931. Bridge No. 5083 is located near the city's core, while Bridge No. 5151 is situated near its western edge. Since the trunk highway passed through the city's heart, including its main park on the banks of the Redwood River, some citizens had misgivings. But the highway department promised that few trees would be removed from the park for road alignment. Further, the agency guaranteed that Bridge No. 5083 over the Redwood River in the park would be a pleasant addition to its groomed setting. Civic leaders were so impressed with the ornamental bridge design that they convinced the MHD to apply the design to Bridge No. 5151 at the less prominent site at the west side of town.[72]

Neither bridge resembles the Dunn Memorial Bridge, as there is no curtain wall disguising the concrete girders carrying the deck. Nevertheless, both bridges, each roughly one hundred feet long, are again evidence that lowly concrete-girder crossings can be made engaging with modest effort. The two-span structures built by Guaranty Construction Company of Minneapolis are garnished with decorative, metal balustrade railings set between rectilinear concrete posts with recessed panels. Classical Revival–style metal light standards, accented with fluting, acanthus leaves, and scrolls, spring from concrete posts. The outside edges of the piers resemble simple, classical columns, and even the concrete brackets supporting the sidewalks exhibit a limited classicism.

Completion of each bridge and the alignment and paving of the trunk highway was big news in Marshall, so big that the city sponsored a parade and speeches by various state and local officials. A throng of about ten thousand people gathered along the roadway and at the site of the new bridge in the city park, where Charles M. Babcock offered congratulations to a rural community with two beautiful new bridges and a newly aligned and paved trunk highway stretching all the way to the Twin Cities.[73]

After nearly eight decades, the historic integrity of the Marshall bridges remains exceptional. This is some-

what surprising since time has ravaged so many ornamental concrete-girder bridges developed by the MHD. Historian Jeffrey A. Hess provides details:

Although the state highway department applied its ornamental urban bridge design to numerous trunk highway crossings before World War II, it is now rare to find good surviving examples of the type. In the post-war decades, road-widening projects eliminated sidewalks and railings, obsolescence (and vandalism) claimed lighting fixtures, and bridge-replacement projects did away with entire crossings. Bridge No. 5083 and Bridge No. 5151 in Marshall are among the few surviving, intact examples of the design.[74]

Concrete deck girders are built virtually everywhere today. We hardly notice them because most are not worth noticing. Recently, however, the Minnesota Department of Transportation, the successor to the MHD, has drawn from its past, building many ornamental concrete deck girders in urban areas. Minneapolis has number of them. For example, when the highway department removed some federal relief

crossings over State Highway 100 in the northwest metro as part of a road-widening project, it replaced the attractive bridges with attractive bridges. These new structures are concrete deck girders decorated with ornamental railings and lighting. Additionally, the piers have an Art Deco flair, while the abutments appear to be made of stone. The abutments are concrete, of course, since stone is an expensive proposition in modern times, but the flourishes once more prove that it does not take much to create a smart-looking bridge.

Smart looking is an inappropriate description for Bridge No. 1238. Perhaps unassuming is apt. While the crossing attracts little attention, in part because of its rather remote setting, the concrete girder is still a rare bridge type. Completed in 1918, the four-span, 142-foot-long structure is located on a gravel road at the outskirts of Sanborn, a tiny community cradled into the southeast corner of Redwood County in southwestern Minnesota, less than an hour's drive southeast of Marshall. The bridge was built as part of a roadway project connecting

Sanborn with Redwood Falls. It was erected by Milo A. Adams, the same contractor who built the pony-truss Prestegard Bridge in nearby Yellow Medicine County in 1909, before the state assumed authority over most bridge building. With Bridge No. 1238, Adams followed a standard plan developed by the state for a concrete through girder. Whereas a concrete deck girder is composed of a deck resting on top of girders, a concrete through girder is formed of two concrete girders holding the bridge deck between them. As a result, the heavy girders also serve as parapet railings. The girders, or railings, for Bridge No. 1238 are embellished with recessed panels, a characteristic that gives the bridge a needed bit of texture.[75]

Where vertical clearance between a waterway and a bridge is limited, a through girder offers clear advantage over a deck girder. The bridge type's major disadvantage, however, is that it cannot be easily widened. Not surprisingly, then, the crossing type has all but disappeared from modern roadways.[76]

Bridge No. 1238 was one of two crossings erected in Sanborn as part of the roadway project reaching to Redwood Falls. The other is located only about 450 feet to the north. Bridge No. 1238A looks much like Bridge No. 1238. Actually, its initial impression is that of a virtually identical concrete through girder. But closer examination reveals that Bridge No. 1238A's concrete parapet railings with recessed panels only resemble the girders of Bridge No. 1238. In fact, they are too narrow to be load-bearing girders. Instead, they are merely concrete parapet railings resting atop either edge of a concrete-slab bridge. It appears the bridge designers wanted to maintain a consistent visual context even though the two crossings are structurally different.[77]

A concrete-slab bridge is composed of a thick slab of concrete that makes up the crossing's deck yet carries the weight of a live load, such as an automobile. A bridge of almost any length can be erected using a concrete slab, but the bridge type quickly reaches a point of diminishing return. Since the deck of the bridge—the slab—carries the load passing over it, as well as the load of the slab itself, it must be exceptionally strong. Its strength is determined in large measure by its depth. The longer the distance between supporting piers, the thicker the slab must be to support the loads. Therefore, at a certain point, it is less troublesome and more cost effective to simply build a girder bridge.[78]

Bridge No. 1238A was also completed by Adams. It is nearly seventy feet long and is formed of three thick, concrete-slab spans. The bridge's most interesting component is its deck, but not because it is so thick. The deck is cavitated, a characteristic evident only by peering beneath the bridge. The series of cells, or cavities, punctuating the deck's underside makes the bridge a cellular slab, a concrete-slab bridge type that is scarce. Interestingly, this curious cellular deck construction is repeated for Bridge No. 1238, making that crossing an especially rare type of concrete through girder.[79]

Cellular construction became popular during the First World War. The construction method came about because reinforced-concrete bridges were being erected in place of steel crossings, bridge types that had become prohibitively expensive due to soaring steel prices. Further, the Minnesota Highway Commission (the predecessor to the MHD) discovered that

Bridge No. 5151 is one of two concrete girders spanning the Redwood River in Marshall in Lyon County. Both are attractive girders, a rarity for this bridge type. Both bridges were erected in 1931 and designed by the Minnesota Department of Highways. *Photograph taken in 2005.*

Bridge No. 1238 is located at the southern edge of the small town of Sanborn in Redwood County. It is a concrete through girder, an early concrete bridge type that is becoming increasingly rare because these bridges cannot be easily widened. Bridge No. 1238 was erected in 1918 by Milo A. Adams, a bridge builder based in Minneapolis. *Photograph taken in 2005.*

decade after the standard plans for cellular concrete through girders and concrete slabs were developed by the MHC, the MHD abandoned the designs, apparently because of declining steel prices that again made steel bridges cost effective. The fact that these two uncommon concrete bridges at the edge of Sanborn are extant eight decades after their construction is probably a result of low traffic and limited development in the area.[81]

Intriguing from a technological viewpoint, Bridge No. 1238A is hardly the most attractive concrete-slab bridge in Minnesota. Still, it remains more pleasing than other concrete-slab bridges, many of which are dreadfully plain. As with other bridge types, some of the state's most striking concrete-slab crossings were built as federal relief projects instituted during the Depression, which lasted from the late 1920s through the early 1940s. One such bridge was erected in 1938 in Ramsey Park in Redwood Falls in Redwood County, roughly 25 miles due north of Sanborn.

Since a belch is inappropriate at nature's table, the WPA ensured that its crossing over the agitated Redwood River as it passes through the Redwood River Gorge was a toast to the leafy reveling that is Ramsey Park. Christened for former governor Alexander Ramsey, Ramsey Park began as a state park in 1912. The city of Redwood Falls, named for a nearby cascading section of the Redwood River, gained ownership of the picturesque parcel in 1957.[82]

Like many federal relief bridges, such as Split Rock Bridge in Pipestone County, as well as the multiplate arches in Wabasha and Todd Counties, the WPA incorporated local stone into the Ramsey Park Swayback Bridge. This was especially important given the bridge's

it could conserve construction material and reduce bridge-building costs by forming semicylindrical cells in the concrete decks of slab bridges. In 1916, the MHC explained that it had "developed a new standard design of reinforced-concrete bridge … in which the volume of concrete is reduced by cells in the underside of the slab…. The cells are made of arched iron with wood bulkheads which may be taken out, nested, moved to another bridge site and used again…. This design saves about one-third of the volume of concrete required in the flat-slab type for the same load and using the same unit stresses." About the same time, the MHC noted that it was employing the building method for the decks of concrete through girders as well.[80]

Minnesota never built a slew of concrete through girders or concrete slabs with cellular decks, but the state did complete at least a few dozen during and immediately after World War I. In 1922, less than a

park locale. Albert H. Good, an architectural consultant writing for the National Park Service in the 1930s, lectured bridge engineers on this subject: "Only those [materials] which are native to the area and predominate near the bridge site will constitute a convincingly appropriate and harmonious medium of structural interpretation."[83]

Good's comment was not original thought, as demonstrated by the stone-faced structures gracing Seven Bridges Road, crossings completed in a parklike environment well before the consultant wrote *Park and Recreation Structures*. Nevertheless, his observations continued to remind society of its aesthetic obligations when building in parks:

After wise choice of a native material, used in a sufficiency pleasing to the eye, the next demand to be made upon [park] bridges would be for variety within reason, avoiding the commonplace at one extreme, and the fantastic at the other. The ranges of use, span, and height, and the broad fields of materials … promise endless combinations and cross-combinations making for much individuality among [park] bridges.[84]

The 183-foot-long Ramsey Park Swayback Bridge is certainly distinct. It is composed of a concrete-slab deck carried by nine extremely short piers made of native granite. Oddly, the roadbed declines toward the middle of the bridge. In a sense, it is as if the roadway over the bridge is sagging between the abutments. The bridge is swaybacked, a term frequently applied to aging equines with drooping backs. Because site conditions welcomed the form, the Ramsey Park Swayback Bridge was purposely designed with a swayback. Swayback bridges, sometimes noted as low-water bridges, are ideal at crossing sites that inevitably will be overrun by high water during the flood season.[85] A low-water crossing like the Ramsey Park Swayback Bridge is a

sturdy, yet modest, obstruction to spring flows. Good enlightens:

Where terrain and other afflicting conditions are such that the approach roads to the bridge and nearby streamside use areas are unusable during flood periods, it is purposeless to elevate the bridge above flood stage to a resulting awkward relationship with the terrain. In such locations the low water bridge has proper place. Predicated on frequent submersions by flood, this type of bridge calls for a rugged, "weighted" scale that gives unmistakable assurance of permanence.[86]

The aesthetic appeal of the Ramsey Park Swayback Bridge is enhanced by its stone sidewalls tracing the arc of the roadbed and ending in square abutments capped with stepped parapets. The rough-faced, native granite that makes up the sidewalls and parapets is neatly trimmed and randomly coursed, giving the bridge an air of rugged sophistication.

That rugged sophistication is also displayed on U.S. Highway 169 near central Minnesota, between Onamia and Garrison in Mille Lacs County. Nuzzling Mille Lacs Lake, one of the most popular water bodies in the state, Bridge No. 3355 is another example of a concrete-slab crossing adorned in rough-faced granite. Completed one year after the Ramsey Park Swayback Bridge, Bridge No. 3355 was also a federal relief project. This bridge, however, was not built by the WPA but by the Civilian Conservation Corps, commonly known as the CCC. Like the WPA, the CCC was a federal relief program instituted to counter the financial and emotional bludgeoning of the Great Depression. The program was established in 1933, soon after Franklin Roosevelt became the country's chief executive. Although it was immediately referred to as the Civilian Conservation Corps, the designation did not become official until 1937. The primary purpose of the CCC was to employ relatively young, unemployed men in conservation projects such as forestry, soil erosion, and flood control efforts. Roadside improvement projects also were part of the CCC mandate. Planting, seeding, and grading all made the roadsides

more appealing, as did construction of wayside rests, which, like many federal relief bridges, were often formed using native stone. For instance, only a short distance north of Bridge No. 3355, the CCC finished a native-stone concourse overlooking Mille Lacs Lake in Garrison, a wonderful appurtenance framing a replica of a humongous walleye that is eyeing pedestrians as if eyeing bait.[87]

Bridge No. 3355 was built over Whitefish Creek by the same CCC unit that erected the wayside in Garrison. In fact, between 1935 and 1940, this unit completed a number of roadside beautification projects adjacent to Mille Lacs Lake. The bridge was designed by the National Park Service, which frequently completed drawings for structures built by the CCC.[88]

Technically, Bridge No. 3355 is a remodeling of an existing bridge, but the remodeling is so extensive that the finished product seemed more like an entirely new bridge. Built by the MHD in 1921, the original structure was a sixteen-foot-long concrete slab carrying a twenty-foot-wide roadway embraced by solid-parapet

The Ramsey Park Swayback Bridge in Ramsey Park in Redwood Falls is a swayback bridge, a crossing type common to areas that frequently flood. Completed across the Redwood River by the Works Progress Administration in 1938, the bridge is so low that floodwaters typically rush over it without doing substantial harm to the structure. *Photograph taken in 2005.*

concrete railings. To support the roadway's increasing volume, the CCC tripled the width of the original bridge by pouring an additional concrete slab adjacent to the old slab. Stone formed the new, wider abutments, however, and rough-faced granite railings replaced the boring concrete parapet railings. The bridge is designed in such a way that the randomly coursed railings are merely an extension of the bridge's randomly coursed face, as are the retaining walls extending from the abutments. The CCC also laid granite sidewalks at either side of the roadway, but traffic on U.S. Highway 169 today is so heavy it is doubtful the walkways are frequently used.[89]

In Fergus Falls, the county seat of Otter Tail County, the MHD and the Great Northern Railway raised a concrete-slab bridge over the railroad's trackage at Union Avenue, near the central part of the city. Built the same year as Bridge No. 3355, Bridge No. 5453 looks almost nothing like the bucolic crossing peering out at Mille Lacs Lake. It looks almost nothing like Bridges Nos. 5083 and 5151 either, but it nevertheless mirrors

the same aesthetic notion. As with the concrete girders in Marshall, the concrete slab over Union Avenue adhered to MHD design concepts applied to many city bridges erected in the late 1920s and 1930s: while the core of the structure is rather ordinary, its outward appearance is enhanced with modest decoration. The five slabs of concrete making up the superstructure of the 125-foot-long bridge are topped with mildly classical concrete balustrade railings set between concrete posts with recessed panels. At one time, ornamental light standards rose from the railings. Bridge No. 5453 is another fine example of how a simple bridge is made pleasing through simple means.[90]

Visual overachieving is evident on an unpaved roadway bisecting cropland in western Minnesota's Yellow Medicine County, not far from the South Dakota border. Two remarkably simple bridges on Township Road 27, only a quarter mile apart, are made charming by the addition of classical railings. The appeal of these tiny bridges results from the contrast between their high-style accoutrements and their pastoral location,

Bridge No. 3355, spanning Whitefish Creek and edging Mille Lacs Lake near Garrison, is a concrete slab, but here the lowly bridge type has been decorated in dressed stone. The crossing was built in 1939 by the Civilian Conservation Corps. *Photograph taken in 2005.*

an emerald green agricultural expanse punctuated by deciduous clusters. In the distance, an abandoned farmhouse scrutinizes the quiet road and the two bridges, apparently still puzzled by the stylish structures that have marked the gravelly lane for decades.

Finished in 1925, the bridges are culverts, specifically reinforced-concrete box culverts. A culvert is a covered water channel. It allows water to flow beneath a roadway or some other form of construction, such as an embankment. Culverts are often metal or reinforced-concrete pipes, but occasionally square or rectangular concrete box culverts are employed, mainly at sites where the flow is too great for a pipe culvert. Even so, many box culverts are small. Bridges Nos. L7897 and L7898 are each only about ten feet long, which barely qualifies them as bridges.[91]

Culverts are ubiquitous in the south and west sections of Minnesota because of the many ditches serving the growing

fields. Bridges Nos. L7897 and L7898 cross Ditch No. 53. The bridges are identical, both following a standard box-culvert plan developed by the MHD. It appears the fanciful railings were the inspiration of the Yellow Medicine County Highway Department, however. Why this agency designed and added handsome railings made of urn-shaped balusters to many of its early rural box culverts is uncertain, especially since only a few locals would ever see them. Even though the reasoning for the refreshing addition to a ho-hum bridge type appears lost, it is likely that the county highway department simply desired to add a little classical panache to western Minnesota's agricultural expanse. Today, these delightful bridges appear to be the only box culverts in the county that have retained their urn-shaped head-pieces. Frankly, it is surprising that they have, for farm machinery has become an enemy of bridge railings.[92]

Bridge No. 5699 in Austin in southern Minnesota will be less fortunate than the tiny gems over Ditch No. 53. The sixty-two-foot-long, single-span structure is a reinforced-concrete rigid-frame bridge. Historian Robert M. Frame III briefly describes the type as follows: "If a solid, horizontal slab is rigidly connected

with vertical walls, a simple rigid-frame bridge has been created. The critical point is that the three sides are rigidly connected at the two 'knees' or corners, and all work together in carrying a load." Put another way, as a load moves over a rigid-frame bridge, the vertical walls flex slightly under the weight because they are performing useful work in supporting the load. Perhaps this is more easily understood if we think of a rigid frame as an inverted U. As the live load passes over the top of the inverted U, the legs bow slightly because they help carry the moving weight. Frame offers further explanation of the type: "In the conventional slab arrangement, its abutments are heaviest at the bottom and lighter at the top where the bridge seat is located. In the rigid frame, the reverse tends to be true: the transverse vertical walls, which replace traditional abutments, are wedge-shaped, tapering downward to the footing."[93]

The concept of the rigid-frame bridge was imported from Europe in the early 1920s. Arthur G. Hayden, the designing engineer for the park commission in Westchester County, New York, was the first to employ it, completing numerous rigid-frame crossings before the 1930s. More economical than many bridge types, the rigid frame garnered wide popularity among highway departments in less than two decades. Curiously, the bridge type was never popular in Minnesota.[94] The city of Robbinsdale, a suburb of Minneapolis, featured

a rigid-frame bridge for many decades. The structure, which carried County Road 9 over State Highway 100, was one of the federal relief crossings recently razed to allow widening of the state highway in the northwest metro.

Bridge No. 5699 is also the result of a federal relief undertaking. In 1937, the MHD rebuilt Minnesota Trunk Highway 16 (Oakland Avenue) at the east side of downtown Austin, a community roughly fifteen miles north of the Iowa border that serves as county seat of Mower County. The primary purpose of the project was to eliminate a dangerous railway-highway intersection. The MHD solved the problem by depressing the four-lane roadway and erecting three bridges over the depression, which, technically, makes the crossings underpasses. One bridge carried the line of the Chicago Great Western Railway, the same railroad that completed the vertical-lift bridge adjacent to the Robert Street Bridge in St. Paul, while the other two bridges supported automobile traffic. Single-span Bridge No. 5374, the railroad bridge, and single-span Bridge No. 5700, one of the automobile crossings, were constructed side by side, thus forming what appears to be a single exceptionally wide bridge. Viewed from below, however, it is obvious that these are two separate bridges. The superstructure of Bridge No. 5700 is made of several steel I beams. The superstructure of Bridge No. 5374 is also made of steel I beams, except that its steel members are much deeper than those of Bridge No. 5700 and there are considerably more of them, clearly demonstrating that this bridge supported the massive weight of a train.[95]

The most interesting crossing remains Bridge No. 5699, the other automobile bridge and the only rigid-frame bridge completed as part of the project. But it was not suppose to be the only rigid frame. The original plan for the corridor also included a rigid-framed

Bridge No. 5700 and a rigid-framed Bridge No. 5374. Since the two structures were to be contiguous, the MHD asked the Chicago Great Western Railway to design the bridges. The railroad company discovered that the foundations at the bridge sites were inappropriate for rigid-frame structures and so opted for steel-girder bridges instead. Even so, at roadway level, Bridge No. 5700 and Bridge No. 5374 were made to look like Bridge No. 5699. This was accomplished by providing the bridges with a shallow, arched curtain wall, an aesthetic matching the shallow curve of the slab that makes up the deck of Bridge No. 5699. Further, all of the bridges were lavished with Art Deco detailing, announcing that each was akin to the next.[96]

Cohesiveness and visual appeal were important because the depressed roadway represented the eastern gateway into downtown Austin. As the corridor was being constructed, the local newspaper excitedly proclaimed that the approach to the city would be "without equal in the Northwest." The excitement eventually waned, however, and in time trains stopped using the rail line over Oakland Avenue. The tracks were removed some years ago. Today, with the main reason for the depressed thoroughfare no longer in existence, the city has concluded that maintenance of the physically suffering corridor is too costly. It will be filled with earth and the handsome bridges razed, including Bridge No. 5699, one of Minnesota's few examples of a concrete rigid-frame bridge. A new roadway will be laid atop the fill.

The concrete rigid-frame bridge was one of the last bridge types introduced to America's roadways. By the time the rigid frame gained adherents, the reinforced-concrete girder was quickly becoming the crossing of choice at many bridge sites. Concrete slabs and concrete culverts also had their place. All of these bridge types became favorites of the MHC and then the MHD because each had proven its practical worth in the first couple of decades of the twentieth century. In truth, many of the major advances in basic reinforced-concrete bridge design came about during this period. The ensuing decades have been marked largely by technological improvements to the existing designs.[97]

Some of the concrete bridges built today are a nod to the past; the new bridges over State Highway 100, for instance. Making concrete abutments look like

stone and decorating piers and railings with Art Deco accents is aesthetically pleasing. Nevertheless, creating faux stone for a traditional concrete girder bridge does not demand much imagination on the part of the designer. Some creativity was employed in developing the current concrete bridge design for the new Interstate Highway 35W Bridge. The design is modern and features a slightly arched concrete superstructure carried by elegantly curved piers embracing either side of the river. But although it is an attractive design for a major bridge over a storied river, innovation is largely absent. The bridge is a precast concrete box girder with embellishment. That is better than a precast concrete box girder without embellishment, but the design explains much about our approach to bridges: we rarely create edifices that truly stand out. When some of our older bridges were constructed, they did not exactly stand out either, but now they do, chiefly because so many of their brethren have been lost.

Part of a depressed roadway system that historically served as the eastern gateway into the city of Austin, Bridge No. 5699 is a concrete rigid-frame bridge, a type not often found on Minnesota roadways. *Photograph taken in 2005 by Robert W. Gardner Jr.*

BRIDGE

PRESERVATION

A century old is a long time we're told;
It's the life of most things, and of man.
Though built just as true as any man knew
It gives way to a modern span.

—Matthew Lowth Carrigan, "The Old Covered Bridge," *Covered Bridges of New England*

A NUMBER OF YEARS ago, I was in leafy northern Wisconsin researching and surveying the Taylor Bridge, a tiny crossing named for a local man who helped build it. The bridge was a timber queen post, an especially rare type of truss bridge. The Taylor Bridge was so rare that it was the only known example of its type on Wisconsin's roadways (Minnesota has none). I spent an hour photographing the delightful structure, taking notes on its construction and admiring its prodigious hornet's nest, a magnificent goiter of humming activity drooping like

The Taylor Bridge in northern Wisconsin was so rare that it was the only known automobile bridge of its type in the state. The timber queen-post bridge was removed in favor of a new crossing. *Photograph taken in 1998; courtesy of Hess, Roise and Company.*

a teardrop from a floor beam. During that time, perhaps two cars passed over the bridge. This was not surprising, for the crossing was on a low-volume gravel road somewhat removed from the area's principal thoroughfare. But even though the bridge received light traffic, its days were numbered, which was why I was there: I was completing a Historic American Engineering Record (HAER) documentation for the bridge. In preservation parlance, a HAER is a mitigation effort, a study undertaken on an engineering-related work (such as a mill, dam, or bridge) that has been determined historic under National Register of Historic Places (NRHP) standards but slated for removal or significant alteration nonetheless. Containing historical information, photographs, and measured drawings, a HAER study is viewed by some as an elaborate obituary.[1] After talking with a local township official, as well as a county highway official, I learned that the Taylor Bridge was to be replaced because it had a faltering deck, which certainly was true. Peering at the deck, I realized that an engineering degree was unnecessary to conclude that the timber platform was suffering. Still, it seemed so wasteful, financially and culturally, to

replace the entire bridge rather than replace only the deck. I have not journeyed to the bridge site since that visit a decade ago, although I have passed near. In truth, I do not wish to see what has taken the place of the Taylor Bridge.

About the time I was completing the HAER for the Taylor Bridge, I was also part of a statewide bridge study in Minnesota, the latest in a handful of Minnesota bridge studies.[2] The first study began in the mid-1980s, and the next culminated in the completion of three historic bridge contexts covering masonry bridges, iron and steel bridges, and reinforced-concrete bridges. These three contextual pieces proved immensely valuable, for they provided an analytical framework for assessing the historic merit of most highway bridges in Minnesota. A few additional studies followed these earliest efforts, but all of the studies inexorably led to the state's most substantial bridge study to that time, the "Minnesota Historic Highway Bridge Inventory," a project that began in the mid-1990s. This study was more in-depth than previous projects and required considerable time on the road researching and surveying 856 bridges believed to have potential for listing on the NRHP. The study was funded by the Minnesota Department of Transportation (Mn/DOT), which wanted to discover which potentially historic roadway bridges in the survey sample were indeed historic. Mn/DOT needed to know which bridges in the study met the criteria for a historic structure as defined by the National Park Service (NPS), the federal agency within the Department of the Interior that administrators the NRHP. This was important, because the results of the survey provided Mn/DOT a trans-portation planning tool. Instead of commissioning a historic bridge study every time Mn/DOT wished to replace or alter a particular bridge, the agency could now consult the conclusions of the "Minnesota Historic Highway Bridge Inventory" to learn whether the bridge in question met the federal definition of a historic structure. The agency could then plan accordingly.

During one six-month period, I spent every other week on the road researching bridges throughout Minne-sota. I visited so many municipal libraries, college libraries, regional libraries, county historical societies, county courthouses, city halls, and Mn/DOT district offices that much of this mad, wonderful experience is a blur. One repository I always visited was the local county highway department, as most roadway bridges are not maintained by Mn/DOT, but by counties and cities. Often this visit was a unique experience, for those at the county highway departments, while always civil and helpful, were not always pleased I was there. Indeed,

Erected in 1883 over the Le Sueur River in Blue Earth County, the Kennedy Bridge is one of the oldest crossings in Minnesota. Recently it was removed from its abutments and plopped down on one of its gravel approaches. *Photograph taken in 2006.*

sometimes irritation stewed just beneath the smile. This annoyance seemed to grow from a fear that a historic designation for any bridge was a potential headache for local government, for it could prove an obstacle to the replacement or removal of the bridge. But as preser-vationists understand, the designation is rarely the obstacle some envision and governments frequently get their way. For example, at the time of this writing, the historic Kennedy Bridge, a pin-connected Pratt through truss erected over the Le Sueur River in Blue Earth County in 1883, not far from the bowstring-arched Kern Bridge, has been sold by the Mankato Township Board. Apparently believing the 140-foot-long, wrought iron crossing a liability, the township passed ownership of one of the oldest bridges in Minnesota to a contractor who has lifted the structure from its stone abutments and plopped it down on the approach to the Le Sueur River. What will become of the crossing is uncertain, but even if it survives, it will almost certainly be removed from the National Register.[3]

The memory of a visit I made to one central Minnesota county highway department is rather vivid. As I sat at a table perusing a stack of bridge files, a perfectly social gentleman perched just over my right shoulder, perusing what I was perusing. About every third file I opened, he proceeded to tell me what was wrong with the bridge represented by the file. In other words, he would tell me why the bridge needed to go. I suppose he believed I had more influence than I actually had and with persistence he would win me to his view. But after several files of this, the irritation began stewing behind my own smile. Finally, upon opening a file and being told that this bridge had to be replaced because the abutments were crumbling, I turned in my seat, looked up, and, in an exasperated tone, asked, "Can't you just repair the abutments?" "Well," he said, "some beams beneath the bridge are rusting badly." "Can't you replace the beams?" I asked. "The railings are also in poor shape," he responded. I quickly realized the circular pattern to the conversation and resumed my perusing. My attendant resumed his task as well.

This occurrence is representative of a flaw in our thinking regarding bridge infrastructure. Although I am not an engineer, I am puzzled by our seeming propensity to allow bridges to become faulty to the point that replacement becomes the chief—and perhaps only—option. Instead of waiting for a bridge to become substandard to a degree that it must be replaced, why could we not continually maintain and occasionally rehabilitate the bridge? Would that not be more cost efficient than tearing down the bridge and building an entirely new one every few decades? It certainly would

have been more cost efficient to replace the deck of the Taylor Bridge rather than replace the whole bridge. Of course, we must not forget that substantial traffic increases are often a primary reason why an old bridge needs to be replaced by a new one. This is a very legitimate argument, but it is hardly an argument that is true in every instance.

Soon after the Interstate Highway 35W Bridge collapsed, Samuel I. Schwartz wrote an opinion piece for the *New York Times* titled "Catch Me, I'm Falling."[4] The article highlighted some failings in how we think about our transportation infrastructure. Schwartz's thoughts should be taken to heart because of his background. A longtime engineer with the New York City Department of Transportation, Schwartz argues that we have a peculiar penchant for stifling common sense when it comes to our bridge infrastructure. For example, Schwartz observes, "The typical federal and state response to a bridge collapse is to throw a bucket of money at the problem but then attach strings. Usually, the money can primarily be used on expensive capital improvements or new bridges but not for the 'mop and pail' work the bridges really need. It's like not doing basic maintenance on your car, letting the oil run out, waiting for the engine to seize up and then replacing the car. The cure of routine maintenance would have cost much less."

As a Minnesota historian, I do not mean to imply that this curious approach to our bridge infrastructure is more rampant in Minnesota than anywhere else. No, it appears endemic to the nation as a whole. Frankly, it is simply our accepted practice, even though to the layman it does not always make sense. For the bridge historian and preservationist, it is especially perplexing, for we have the fortune (some may argue misfortune) to frequently contemplate the cultural value of older structures. Perhaps it is a kind of arrogance, but bridge historians and preservationists have difficulty understanding why more people do not think as we do. If a structure can be safely maintained at reasonable costs and yet continue to contribute cultural value to society, is that not a good thing?

In the late 1990s, at the completion of the "Minnesota Historic Highway Bridge Inventory," 84 highway bridges were determined eligible for listing on the NRHP. Of these 84, only 15 were in fact placed on the

Bridge No. L8471 was an exceptionally rare combination king-post bridge over railroad tracks in Crookston. The railroad tore the bridge down a few years ago. *Photograph by Cynthia de Miranda, 1995; courtesy of Hess, Roise and Company.*

National Register. More specifically, 15 bridges out of a survey sample of 856 highway bridges were placed on the National Register. But even more specifically, 15 bridges within a state containing roughly 19,500 highway bridges were added to the National Register, or about 0.0008 percent of the state's total highway bridges. Interestingly, 14 of the 15 bridges are main-

tained by Mn/DOT. The remaining bridge was owned by one of the counties; it has subsequently been razed. With the exception of that one county, no other local governments (county or city) responsible for bridges determined eligible for the NRHP through the "Minnesota Historic Highway Bridge Inventory" sought formal listing.[5]

Historic or not, preserving bridges is not common to our mindset, but then, preservation of other structure types does not seem common either. We so regularly replace old things with new things that even rarity rarely triggers second thoughts. Only a few years ago, Bridge No. L8471 carried a city road over railroad tracks in a residential area of Crookston in northwestern Minnesota. The bridge was a king-post truss made of wood and metal, commonly known as a combination truss. Like the Taylor Bridge, Bridge No. L8471 was so rare it was the only one of its kind in the state. Singularity was not a special enough quality, however, and it was razed by the Burlington Northern Railroad.[6]

To an extent, our affinity for the new is understandable. Architects and engineers attend school primarily to learn how to design and build new things, not to preserve old things, although, thankfully, courses in historic preservation are more common than they used to be. Moreover, historically, we have been a forward-looking people, fixed on the promises of tomorrow. There is nobility in this because each generation must consider its contribution to those that follow. Regrettably, however, all too often that contribution ignores heritage that has already been inherited. While each generation longs to leave its imprint on society—and should leave its imprint on society—we often act as if history begins anew with each new generation. This is silly, naturally, for we are but links in a chain, and while today we build heritage for tomorrow, we shoulder responsibility for passing on heritage that was passed to us.

Nevertheless, we cannot rely on moral obligation alone to ensure preservation of structural components of our past. Sometimes we need a bit of nudging, which is why the National Historic Preservation Act of 1966 came about. It was this law that gave us the NRHP, as well as Section 106. Under Section 106 of the National Historic Preservation Act, federal agencies are compelled to consider impacts to historic properties due to federal undertakings or federally assisted undertakings. Since highway-improvement projects in Minnesota often receive federal assistance, provi-

sions of Section 106 apply to some bridges in the state. Section 4(f) of the U.S. Department of Transportation Act of 1966 also affects some of the state's bridges, because it requires highway projects to avoid historic sites unless there is no "prudent or feasible alternative." Section 144(o) of the Surface Transportation and Uniform Relocation Assistance Act of 1987 encourages preservation and reuse of historic bridges since it is in the country's national interest. The Act prompted many statewide bridge inventories, permitting states to discover their historically significant bridges. It also has allowed the federal government to aid states for costs incurred for preserving historic crossings or mitigating damage to them. Additionally, the Intermodal Surface Transportation Efficiency Act of 1991 features provisions encouraging historic preservation of bridges.[7]

Despite these laws, over the past two decades it is estimated that the nation has lost roughly half of its historic bridges. In part, this results from conflicting legislation, such as the Federal-Aid Highway Act of 1987, which brought about the Highway Bridge Replacement and Rehabilitation Program (HBRRP). The HBRRP requires that each bridge receive a sufficiency rating based on various criteria, including safety and serviceability. Safety will always be a primary concern, certainly, but by applying modern standards to historic bridges it is not surprising that many of the crossings receive a low sufficiency rating. The low score pushes them to the front of the line for replacement. Still, we are forced to admit that the legislation designed to encourage bridge preservation simply has not encouraged as hoped.[8]

In 2005, the National Trust for Historic Preservation (NTHP), a prominent nonprofit preservation organization that was chartered by Congress in 1949, presented a National Preservation Honor Award to the Oregon Department of Transportation (ODOT). This prestigious award was recognition of the state agency's commitment to historic bridge preservation. As with the Vermont Agency for Transportation, which received a similar award in 1997, ODOT discovered that embracing its bridging heritage rather than rapidly whittling it away was the right thing to do. Writing of ODOT's honor, Eric DeLony, the longtime Chief of HAER, observed, "It was time to recognize the other state transportation agency that has demonstrated exemplary, sustained, national leadership in protecting historic bridges and, by extension, the scenic roads and highways of which bridges are the most visible icon."[9]

ODOT's path to well-deserved recognition by the National Trust began in the early 1990s after Oregon lost the large and handsome Alsea Bay Bridge in Waldport to corrosion. With public support, ODOT developed preservation techniques for the remaining Depression-era bridges on the Oregon Coast Highway that were designed by state bridge engineer Conde B. McCullough. This preservation effort has convinced many Oregonians of the worthiness of such tasks. Here is DeLony again:

Turning adversity to advantage, ODOT has made significant progress ... in instilling a sense of awareness, appreciation, and responsibility within the transportation community and the public that historic bridges offer significant value to the built environment. Bridges not only are the most visible expression of the engineer's art, often serving as monumental gateways to cities as well as symbols of engineering prowess, but the more modest spans provide a harmonious scale and tranquility to country roads.[10]

ODOT has preserved many other bridges besides those on the Oregon Coast Highway, including the Willamette River bridges in Portland. Additional inland bridges are being preserved by the state highway department as well. ODOT is aided in the endeavor by its Bridge Preservation Unit, a group charged with developing bridge rehabilitation practices. The methods and solutions produced by this team are frequently more cost effective than new construction. ODOT has also benefited from the labors of far-sighted private citizens, people who see value in heritage and add their knowledge and enthusiasm to the mission of preserving Oregon's historic crossings.[11]

Oregon has demonstrated that historic bridge preservation can be a regular part of bridge management within state transportation agencies. Now perhaps other state highway departments will follow Oregon's lead. If so, a preservation ethic may filter to county and city public works agencies, since these are responsible for much of the nation's bridge care. To help things along, a group of professionals came together in Washington, D.C., in early December 2003. The Federal Highway Administration, the American Association of State Highway and Transportation Officials, the SRI Foundation (Statistical Research, Inc., is a nonprofit historic preservation organization), the NTHP, and the HAER of the NPS planned the workshop, which included individuals from the sponsoring organizations as well as bridge scholars, civil engineering educators, and various transportation, environmental, and preservation professionals from the pubic sector.[12] The resultant report detailed the workshop's goals:

In the spirit of stewardship, streamlining, and sound environmental and historic bridge management, the goal of the workshop was to provide federal and state transportation agencies, the Congress, and the interested public with recommendations and solutions on how to preserve this heritage at risk. Specifically, the purpose of the workshop was to articulate and define efficient and economical strategies for historic bridge preservation and management.[13]

The participants ultimately fashioned ten recommendations, which included mandating historic bridge management plans for each state, creating a national historic bridge task force composed of preservation officials in the public and private sectors, and developing a National Cooperative Highway Research Program synthesis to guide transportation departments through the regulatory process surrounding historic bridges while aiding the agencies when making decisions regarding historic bridge rehabilitation or replacement. Further recommendations included employing the national historic bridge task force to seek additional funding for historic bridge management, creating a Web site holding a national historic bridge glossary providing terms and nomenclature that would aid electronic database searches, and completing a national historic bridge context. Organizing the copious amount of bridge data that has been collected through the various statewide historic bridge surveys, developing a Web site dedicated to the preservation and management of historic bridges, improving knowledge of the status of historic bridges, and collecting and disseminating technical information covering the maintenance and rehabilitation of historic bridges completed the recommendations.[14]

It will take time for all of the recommendations to be implemented, certainly, but hopefully they will make historic bridge rehabilitation and maintenance prefer-

The physically suffering Long Meadow Bridge in Bloomington has been sealed from visitors for several years as the city wrestles with how to fund its rehabilitation. *Photograph taken in 2007.*

able to replacement, preserving important structural components of our past that help foster our sense of community heritage and our sense of place.

To this end, Minnesota recently took a giant stride forward. Mn/DOT has now formulated a "Management Plan for Historic Bridges in Minnesota." The plan is an extensive document detailing the state agency's current and future efforts regarding historic bridges in Minnesota. The plan is also intended for those responsible for historic bridges not maintained by the state. In other words, counties and cities and towns that own bridges that are either on the NRHP or are eligible for listing on the NRHP now have a document of guidelines that will help them manage these bridges. This is a big deal, because for many years there was no core tool that local governments could turn to for aid in addressing their historically significant bridges. The hope also is that the

management plan will spur local governments to more deeply consider the worthiness of preserving historic bridges rather than removing them.[15]

The management plan consists of several useful parts, including a section highlighting the laws and standards applicable to the maintenance and management of historic bridges. Another section provides background and analysis, essentially explaining how Mn/DOT got from there to here—that is, how the state agency's experience working with historic bridges over the last couple of decades has culminated in the "Management Plan for Historic Bridges in Minnesota." An especially useful section of the document focuses on preparing individual bridge management plans. The Mn/DOT has prepared several individual management plans for several historic bridges owned by the state. Each plan details how the historic bridge represented

The Stone Arch Bridge is a popular pedestrian and bicycle crossing. People often gather here to enjoy views of the Mississippi River near downtown Minneapolis. *Photograph taken in 2007.*

by the plan will be stabilized, preserved, and maintained. This section also explains how local governments can initiate similar plans for bridges in their cities or counties. The section on technical assistance will also prove helpful, as it will offer local governments guidance detailing how particular bridge types should be maintained, what techniques and materials should be employed, and so on.[16]

Funding for bridge preservation is always a primary concern. This is a problem exemplified by the city of Bloomington as it ponders how to acquire the dollars necessary to bring the closed Long Meadow Bridge back from the depths of decay. The bridge management plan presents potential funding sources, providing detailed information on each organization that may have monies available for the care of historic bridges. For instance, restoration of the Stone Arch Bridge span-

ning the Mississippi River in Minneapolis was aided with $2 million in Transportation Enhancement funds. Finally, the bridge management plan highlights several state and national agencies and organizations that are dedicated to providing information and expertise surrounding historic preservation issues, including the preservation of bridges.[17]

It is impractical to save every historic bridge, of course, and attempting to do so is silly. Still, we can preserve and reuse more than we currently do. Tools like the bridge management plan help us along, but we need more—we need private individuals, professionals, and organizations with a powerful sense of the role heritage plays in contemporary life to help alter the long-held societal belief that newer is always better. My grandmother disputes that, and so do I.

MINNESOTA'S HISTORIC

BRIDGES

All of Minnesota's extant historic bridges as of this writing are included here. These bridges are either listed in the National Register of Historic Places or have been determined eligible for listing. The National Register, the official list of the nation's historic places that reflect our history and are worthy of preservation, is administered by the National Park Service under the Secretary of the Interior. The photographs in this section appear courtesy of the Minnesota State Historic Preservation Office of the Minnesota Historical Society.

ANOKA COUNTY

Anoka–Champlin Mississippi River Bridge (Bridge No. 4380)
U.S. Highway 169 over Mississippi River, Anoka
This monumental reinforced-concrete, open-spandrel ribbed arch was designed by the Minnesota Department of Highways (MHD) and completed by the Minneapolis Bridge Company in 1929. A photograph of this bridge is on page 146.

BENTON COUNTY

Bridge No. L0077
Unpaved township road over St. Francis River, Glendorado Township
Completed circa 1910, this bridge is a relatively early example of a steel stringer.

BELTRAMI COUNTY

Nymore Bridge (Bridge No. 2366)
First Street over Mississippi River, Bemidji
This Classical Revival–style, reinforced-concrete arch was designed by the Standard Reinforced Concrete Company of Indianapolis, Indiana, and built by the Illinois Steel Bridge Company of Illinois in 1917. A photograph of this bridge is on page 129.

BIG STONE COUNTY

Bridge No. 3398
County Road 79 over Minnesota River
Completed in 1920, this is a rare reinforced-concrete Marsh arch designed by the Marsh Engineering Company of Des Moines, Iowa.

BLUE EARTH COUNTY

Bridge No. 1461
County Road 147 over Blue Earth River, Shelby Township
This pin-connected, Camelback through truss was completed circa 1900 by Lawrence Henry Johnson of Minneapolis.

Bridge No. L5658
Township Road 75 over Perch Creek
Completed in 1912, this is a rare concrete arch bridge built from a design patented by the Marsh Engineering Company of Des Moines, Iowa. (*Photograph by Shawn Rounds; Hess, Roise and Company*)

Kennedy Bridge (Bridge No. L5665)
Resting on Township Road 167 approach to Le Sueur River, Mankato Township
One of the oldest bridges in the state, this pin-connected, wrought iron, Pratt through truss was erected by the Wrought Iron Bridge Company of Canton, Ohio, in 1883. It has recently been pulled from its abutments. A photograph of this bridge is on page 161.

Kern Bridge (Bridge No. L5669)
Former route of Township Road 190 over Le Sueur River, Mankato and South Bend townships
Perhaps the rarest roadway bridge in Minnesota, this pin-connected, wrought iron, bowstring-arch through truss, which was completed by the Wrought Iron Bridge Company of Canton, Ohio, in 1873, has an uncertain future. A photograph of this bridge is on page 51.

Marsh Concrete Rainbow Arch Bridge (Bridge No. 90554)
Abandoned route of County Road 101 over the former course of Little Cottonwood River, Cambria Township
Erected in 1911, this is one of the earliest examples of a rare reinforced-concrete Marsh rainbow arch designed by the Marsh Engineering Company of Des Moines, Iowa. A photograph of this bridge is on page 123.

BRIDGE NO. L5658

Zieglers Ford Bridge (Bridge No. L5659)
Township Road 96 over Big Cobb River, Decoria Township
This steel, pin-connected, Pratt through truss was erected in 1904 by Mayer Brothers of Mankato. (*Photograph by Dale Martin*)

BRIDGE NO. L5659

BROWN COUNTY

Eden Bridge (Bridge No. 2110)
County State Aid Highway 8 over Minnesota River between Eden Township, Brown County, and Camp Township, Renville County
The Eden Bridge is an early example of a Warren pony truss with verticals. It was designed by the MHD and completed by Waddell and Hohle of Minneapolis in 1918. A photograph of this bridge is on page 66.

Stone Bridge
Roadway over stream, Flandreau State Park
This tiny metal culvert, which is faced in stone, was constructed by the state in 1935.

CARLTON COUNTY

Swinging Bridge
Pedestrian trail over St. Louis River, Jay Cooke State Park
Supported by reinforced-concrete pylons faced in native stone, this attractive structure constructed by the state in 1934 is a rare Minnesota example of a suspension span. (*Photograph by the Minnesota State Historic Preservation Office*)

CARVER COUNTY

Bridge No. 5837
County State Aid Highway 10 over abandoned line of the Burlington Northern Railroad, immediately north of Maple
This wood stringer was designed by the Great Northern Railway and completed by Fielding and Shepley of St. Paul in 1939. A photograph of this bridge is on page 5.

Bridge No. 5882
County State Aid Highway 10 over South Fork of the Crow River, Watertown
This decorative steel stringer was designed by the MHD and erected by Theodore Jensen Company of St. Cloud in 1939. (*Photograph by Jeffrey A. Hess; Hess, Roise and Company*)

BRIDGE NO. 5882

SWINGING BRIDGE

Bridge No. L2526
Fourth Street over Carver Spring, Carver
Part of the Carver Historic District, this small stone arch was
completed circa 1885.

Bridge No. L2783
Main Street over Carver Spring, Carver
Part of the Carver Historic District, this small stone arch was
completed circa 1910.

CASS COUNTY

Steamboat Bridge
*Abandoned line of the Great Northern Railway over Steamboat
River, adjacent to State Highway 371, twelve miles north of Walker*
In 1914, the Great Northern Railway built this plate girder as a
swing span so steamboats could float cut timber from Steamboat
Lake to Steamboat Bay on Leech Lake. It is now a pedestrian and
bicycle crossing. A photograph of this bridge is on page 100.

CHIPPEWA COUNTY

Bridge No. 5380
*Minnesota Trunk Highway 40 over Lac Qui Parle Lake, near
Milan*
A component of the Lac Qui Parle Project (a substantial water
conservation and flood control effort initiated in the mid-1930s),
this steel Parker through truss was designed by the MHD and
built in 1938 by Theodore Jensen Company of St. Cloud, Minnesota. (*Photograph by Jeffrey A. Hess; Hess, Roise and Company*)

BRIDGE NO. 5380

Bridge No. L8849
*Unpaved access road over Chippewa River, Lagoon Park,
Montevideo*
Completed by the Works Progress Administration (WPA) in
1938, this bridge is one of two exceptionally pleasing stone-faced,
reinforced-concrete arches designed by city engineer M. E.
Chamberlin.

BRIDGE NO. L8850

Bridge No. L8850
*Unpaved access road over Chippewa River, Lagoon Park,
Montevideo*
Completed by the WPA in 1938, this bridge is one of two
exceptionally pleasing stone-faced, reinforced-concrete arches
designed by city engineer M. E. Chamberlin. (*Photograph by
Jeffrey A. Hess; Hess, Roise and Company*)

CLAY COUNTY

Bridge No. 0961
Unpaved township road over the Buffalo River, Oakport Township
Constructed by Fargo Bridge and Iron Company of Fargo, North
Dakota, in 1913, this bridge is an early example of a steel Warren
pony truss designed by the Minnesota Highway Commission
(MHC). (*Photograph by Cynthia de Miranda; Hess, Roise and
Company*)

BRIDGE NO. 0961

Bridge No. 90818
County Road 96 over Buffalo River, Moland Township
Fargo Bridge and Iron Company of Fargo, North Dakota, fabricated and erected this steel, pin-connected, half-hip Pratt pony truss in 1907.

COOK COUNTY

Bridge No. 5132
Minnesota Trunk Highway 61 over Cascade River, Cascade River Wayside
Completed in 1932, this reinforced-concrete arch designed and built by the MHD is part of the striking Cascade River Wayside edging Lake Superior. (*Photograph by Jeffrey A. Hess; Hess, Roise and Company*)

BRIDGE NO. 5132

Bridge No. 7614
County State Aid Highway 17 over Grand Portage Creek, near Grand Portage
Probably a result of a New Deal federal relief effort, this attractive multiplate arch erected in 1941 is faced in stone and overlooks Lake Superior near the Canadian border. A photograph of this bridge is on page 84.

Spruce Creek Culvert (Bridge No. 8292)
Minnesota Trunk Highway 61 over Spruce Creek, Cascade State Park
Constructed in 1932 by the MHD, this reinforced-concrete culvert was redesigned into a striking stone-faced structure by landscape architect Arthur R. Nichols, whose plan was undertaken by the Civilian Conservation Corps (CCC) in 1935. (*Photograph by Jeffrey A. Hess; Hess, Roise and Company*)

CROW WING COUNTY

Bridge No. 5265
U.S. Highway 169 over a dry run, Garrison
Engineered by the National Park Service and built by the CCC near a picnic grounds in 1938, this handsome multiplate arch faced in stone edges Mille Lacs Lake and once served as a pedestrian underpass. (*Photograph by Shawn Rounds; Hess, Roise and Company*)

BRIDGE NO. 5265

Bridge No. L2878
City route over Little Pine River, Emily
This steel stringer was designed by the Minnesota Department of Conservation and erected in 1938 by the CCC.

BRIDGE NO. 8292

BRIDGE NO. L3942

Bridge No. L3942
Abandoned township road over Nokasippi River, near St. Mathias
Although no longer supporting a deck, the structure of this bridge remains. This rare example of a steel, pin-connected, half-hip Pratt pony truss was built by the Security Bridge Company in 1908. (*Photograph by Shawn Rounds; Hess, Roise and Company*)

DAKOTA COUNTY

Bridge No. L5773
City route over outlet of Black Dog Lake, Burnsville
Designed by Pioneer Service Engineering Company of Chicago, Illinois, and constructed in 1953 by Northern States Power Company as part of its Black Dog steam generating plant, this reinforced-concrete rigid frame has control gates built into its substructure to manipulate flow from Black Dog Lake into the Minnesota River. (*Photograph by Chad Perkins; Hess, Roise and Company*)

Waterford Bridge (Bridge No. L3275)
Township road over Cannon River, two miles northwest of Northfield
This Camelback through truss with bolted connections was designed by county surveyor Charles A. Forbes and built by the Hennepin Bridge Company of Minneapolis in 1909. A photograph of this bridge is on page 63.

FARIBAULT COUNTY

BRIDGE NO. 3130

Bridge No. 3130
Township Road 232 over Coon Creek, one-half mile south of Blue Earth
Completed in 1920, this bridge is the best surviving example of an early MHD standard design for a reinforced-concrete deck girder. (*Photograph by Denis P. Gardner; Hess, Roise and Company*)

Fort Snelling–Mendota Bridge (Bridge No. 4190)
Minnesota Highway 55 over Minnesota River, Mendota
Completed in 1926, this crossing was designed by prominent engineers Walter H. Wheeler and C. A. P. Turner and is the grandest of the monumental Twin Cities reinforced-concrete, open-spandrel ribbed arches. A photograph of this bridge is on page 138.

Hastings High Bridge (Bridge No. 5895)
U.S. Highway 61 over Mississippi River, Hastings
Designed by Sverdrup and Parcel of St. Louis, Missouri, this huge bridge, completed in 1951, has a main span that features a deck suspended beneath a steel arched truss. (*Photograph by Chad Perkins; Hess, Roise and Company*)

HASTINGS HIGH BRIDGE

BRIDGE NO. 89026

Bridge No. 89026
County State Aid Highway 21 over diversion channel to Minnesota Lake, Minnesota Lake Township
This reinforced-concrete deck girder was built in 1939 by the WPA. (*Photograph by Denis P. Gardner; Hess, Roise and Company*)

FILLMORE COUNTY

Bridge No. 5722
U.S. Highway 63 over Spring Valley Creek, Spring Valley
This unique reinforced-concrete triple box culvert was designed and completed by the MHD in 1936.

Bridge No. 6263
County Road 118 over Root River, Forestville Township
This steel pin-connected, Pratt through truss was fabricated and erected by Gillette-Herzog Manufacturing Company of Minneapolis in 1899. (*Photograph by Michael Koop*)

BRIDGE NO. 6263

Bridge No. 6662
Minnesota Trunk Highway 16 over Johnson Creek, near Peterson
This modernist-inspired steel stringer was designed by the MHD and completed in 1948. (*Photograph by Shawn Rounds; Hess, Roise and Company*)

BRIDGE NO. 6662

Bridge No. 7979
County Highway 15 over stream, Carimona Township
This double-span country stone arch was erected circa 1904.

Bridge No. 7980
County Highway 15 over stream, Carimona Township
This double-span country stone arch was erected circa 1904.

Bridge No. 9940
County Highway 29 over Riceford Creek, Newburg Township
Resting on stone abutments, this skewed steel stringer was completed in 1940 and is a fine example of WPA construction.

Bridge No. L4770
Township Road 213 over Mahoney Creek, two miles east of Fountain
Completed circa 1915, this bridge embodies design characteristics of a standard stone arch bridge plan that apparently was developed by the MHC about the second decade of the twentieth century. (*Photograph by Jeffrey A. Hess; Hess, Roise and Company*)

BRIDGE NO. L4770

Bridge No. L4885
Township Road 354 over Bear Creek, Fillmore Township
Alexander Y. Bayne and Company of Minneapolis erected this
steel pin-connected, Pratt through truss in 1906.

GOODHUE COUNTY

BRIDGE NO. 3481

Bridge No. 3481
*Unpaved city road over
Cannon River, western
outskirts of Red Wing*
Incorporating open-balus-
trade railings, this reinforced-concrete deck girder
completed by the MHD in
1921 is a fine example of the
state agency's aesthetic shift
away from heavy-looking railings to lighter, more visually
pleasing railings for many
concrete bridges. (*Photograph
by Denis P. Gardner; Hess,
Roise and Company*)

**Third Street Bridge
(Bridge No. L5391)**
Third Street North over Cannon River, Cannon Falls
This bridge is a steel Pennsylvania through truss, relatively
uncommon to Minnesota, designed by Louis P. Wolff of Loweth
and Wolff, St. Paul, and erected by Alexander Y. Bayne and
Company of Minneapolis in 1909. A photograph of this bridge is
on page 63.

Zumbrota Covered Bridge (Bridge No. 25580)
Pedestrian trail over North Branch of the Zumbro River, Zumbrota
Financed by the Stafford Western Immigration Company, the
enterprise that founded Zumbrota in 1856, this sheltered wood
truss completed in 1869 is the only covered roadway bridge in
Minnesota. A photograph of
this bridge is on page 5.

HENNEPIN COUNTY

Bridge No. 6247
*Plymouth Avenue over
Burlington Northern Railroad
tracks, Golden Valley*
Constructed in 1930, the Great
Northern Railway made this
utilitarian reinforced-concrete
deck girder appealing through
Classical Revival–style
detailing. (*Photograph by
Denis P. Gardner; Hess, Roise
and Company*)

BRIDGE NO. 6247

Bridge No. 6992
*Washington Avenue over line of the Burlington Northern Railroad,
Minneapolis*
This steel Pratt through truss, erected in 1891, was recently
substantially altered.

Bridge No. 90437
*Cedar Avenue over former line of Chicago, Milwaukee and St. Paul
Railway (CM&StP), Minneapolis*
Constructed in 1916, this Classical Revival–style reinforced-
concrete girder is part of the substantial CM&StP grade separa-
tion project completed in south Minneapolis in the 1910s. This
corridor now serves bicyclists and pedestrians as the Midtown
Greenway.

Bridge No. 90448
Pedestrian trail over Excelsior Boulevard, Minneapolis
Located within a potential historic district, this slightly arched,
steel stringer was constructed in 1936. (*Photograph by Chad
Perkins; Hess, Roise and Company*)

BRIDGE NO. 90448

Bridge No. 90449
Lake Street over Lake of the Isles Channel, Minneapolis
Completed in 1911, this Classical Revival–style reinforced-
concrete arch was designed by New York engineers H. Lincoln
Rogers and Guy Vroman.

Bridge No. 90482
Nokomis Avenue over Minnehaha Creek, Minneapolis
Designed and built by the city of Minneapolis, this reinforced-concrete deck girder resembles a Classical Revival–style reinforced-concrete arch. (*Photograph by Chad Perkins; Hess, Roise and Company*)

Bridge No. 90490
Penn Avenue South over Minnehaha Creek, Minneapolis
The small reinforced-concrete arch was completed circa 1902.

Bridge No. 90494
Portland Avenue over Soo Line Railway tracks, Minneapolis
Completed in 1915, this reinforced-concrete deck girder was designed by Charles F. Loweth, one of Minnesota's earliest professional engineers.

Bridge No. 90590
Nicollet Avenue over former line of CM&StP, Minneapolis
Constructed in 1914, this Classical Revival–style reinforced-concrete girder is part of the substantial CM&StP grade separation project completed in south Minneapolis in the 1910s. This corridor now serves bicyclists and pedestrians as the Midtown Greenway.

Bridge No. 90591
Nicollet Avenue over Minnehaha Creek, Minneapolis
Constructed in 1923, this large reinforced-concrete arch was designed by Minneapolis municipal engineers Kristoffer Olsen Oustad and N. W. Ellsberg.

Bridge No. 90592
28th Avenue South over Minnehaha Creek, Minneapolis
This small reinforced-concrete arch was built around 1904.

Bridge No. 90608
Minnetonka Boulevard over St. Albans Bay, Excelsior
This Art Deco–style reinforced-concrete deck girder was constructed by the WPA in 1941. (*Photograph by Chad Perkins; Hess, Roise and Company*)

Bridge No. 90646
Wooddale Avenue over Minnehaha Creek, Edina
Designed by the Hennepin County Highway Department, this stone-faced, multiplate arch was erected by the WPA in 1937. (*Photograph by Denis P. Gardner; Hess, Roise and Company*)

Bridge No. 90664
St. Anthony Boulevard over Burlington Northern Railroad line, Minneapolis
This large, skewed, steel Warren through truss was designed and built by the Northern Pacific Railway in 1925. (*Photograph by Denis P. Gardner; Hess, Roise and Company*)

Bridge No. 92321
Bloomington Avenue over Minnehaha Creek, Minneapolis
Erected in 1921, this Classical Revival–style reinforced-concrete deck girder was designed by Minneapolis municipal engineer Kristoffer Olsen Oustad.

Bridge No. 92322
12th Avenue South over Minnehaha Creek, Minneapolis
This reinforced-concrete deck girder, built in 1930, mimics a stone arch. (*Photograph by Chad Perkins; Hess, Roise and Company*)

Bridge No. 92324
Upton Avenue South over Minnehaha Creek, Minneapolis
Resembling a stone arch, this reinforced-concrete deck girder was designed by the city of Minneapolis and erected in 1926. (*Photograph by Chad Perkins; Hess, Roise and Company*)

Bridge No. 92347
First Avenue South over former line of CM&StP, Minneapolis
Constructed in 1914, this Classical Revival–style reinforced-concrete girder is part of the substantial CM&StP grade separation project completed in south Minneapolis in the 1910s. This corridor now serves bicyclists and pedestrians as the Midtown Greenway.

Bridge No. 92350
Bloomington Avenue South over former line of CM&StP, Minneapolis
Constructed in 1916, this Classical Revival–style reinforced-concrete girder is part of the substantial CM&StP grade separation project completed in south Minneapolis in the 1910s. This corridor now serves bicyclists and pedestrians as the Midtown Greenway.

Bridge No. 92643
Browndale Road over Minnehaha Creek, Edina
This small reinforced-concrete arch was constructed circa 1902.

Bridge No. L5722
28th Street over Lake of the Isles Channel, Minneapolis
Designed by William Pierce Cowles and Cecil B. Chapman of Minneapolis, this Classical Revival–style reinforced-concrete arch was constructed in 1911.

Bridge No. L5729
West Lake of the Isles Boulevard over channel, Minneapolis
This Classical Revival–style reinforced-concrete arch was designed by William Pierce Cowles and Cecil B. Chapman of Minneapolis and constructed in 1911.

Bridge No. L5735
Lake Nokomis Parkway over outlet of Lake Nokomis, Minneapolis
Designed by the city of Minneapolis and erected in 1926, this reinforced-concrete deck girder resembles a stone arch. (*Photograph by Chad Perkins; Hess, Roise and Company*)

Bridge No. L5736
Minnehaha Parkway over Minnehaha Creek, Minneapolis
Designed by the city of Minneapolis and erected in 1924, this reinforced-concrete deck girder is detailed in Second Egyptian Revival style and resembles a flat reinforced-concrete arch. (*Photograph by Chad Perkins; Hess, Roise and Company*)

Bridge No. L6393
Pedestrian trail over Minnehaha Creek, Minneapolis
This steel, cantilevered Pratt deck truss with an arched lower chord was designed by the Minneapolis Park Board and erected by the Minneapolis Steel Machinery Company of Minneapolis in 1926. (*Photograph by Chad Perkins; Hess, Roise and Company*)

Bridge No. L8898
4th Avenue North over Burlington Northern right-of-way, Minneapolis
Completed in 1891, this skewed Warren pony truss is an early example of a riveted bridge.

Bridge No. L8901
Fremont Avenue South over former line of CM&StP, Minneapolis
Constructed in 1913, this Classical Revival–style reinforced-concrete girder is part of the substantial CM&StP grade separation project completed in south Minneapolis in the 1910s. This corridor now serves bicyclists and pedestrians as the Midtown Greenway.

Bridge No. L8902
Colfax Avenue South over former line of CM&StP, Minneapolis
Constructed in 1913, this Classical Revival–style reinforced-concrete girder is part of the substantial CM&StP grade separation project completed in south Minneapolis in the 1910s. This corridor now serves bicyclists and pedestrians as the Midtown Greenway.

Bridge No. L8903
Bryant Avenue South over former line of CM&StP, Minneapolis
Constructed in 1913, this Classical Revival–style reinforced-concrete girder is part of the substantial CM&StP grade separation project completed in south Minneapolis in the 1910s. This corridor now serves bicyclists and pedestrians as the Midtown Greenway.

Bridge No. L8904
Aldrich Avenue South over former line of CM&StP, Minneapolis
Constructed in 1913, this Classical Revival–style reinforced-concrete girder is part of the substantial CM&StP grade separation project completed in south Minneapolis in the 1910s. This corridor now serves bicyclists and pedestrians as the Midtown Greenway.

Bridge No. L8906
Harriet Avenue South over former line of CM&StP, Minneapolis
Constructed in 1914, this Classical Revival–style reinforced-concrete girder is part of the substantial CM&StP grade separation project completed in south Minneapolis in the 1910s. This corridor now serves bicyclists and pedestrians as the Midtown Greenway.

Bridge No. L8907
Grand Avenue South over former line of CM&StP, Minneapolis
Constructed in 1914, this Classical Revival–style reinforced-concrete girder is part of the substantial CM&StP grade separation project completed in south Minneapolis in the 1910s. This corridor now serves bicyclists and pedestrians as the Midtown Greenway. (*Photograph by Chad Perkins; Hess, Roise and Company*)

Bridge No. L8908
Pleasant Avenue South over former line of CM&StP, Minneapolis
Constructed in 1913, this Classical Revival–style reinforced-concrete girder is part of the substantial CM&StP grade separation project completed in south Minneapolis in the 1910s. This corridor now serves bicyclists and pedestrians as the Midtown Greenway.

Bridge No. L8909
Pillsbury Avenue South over former line of CM&StP, Minneapolis
Constructed in 1914, this Classical Revival–style reinforced-concrete girder is part of the substantial CM&StP grade separation project completed in south Minneapolis in the 1910s. This corridor now serves bicyclists and pedestrians as the Midtown Greenway.

BRIDGE NO. L8915

Bridge No. L8910
Stevens Avenue South over former line of CM&StP, Minneapolis
Constructed in 1914, this Classical Revival–style reinforced-concrete girder is part of the substantial CM&StP grade separation project completed in south Minneapolis in the 1910s. This corridor now serves bicyclists and pedestrians as the Midtown Greenway.

Bridge No. L8911
Oakland Avenue South over former line of CM&StP, Minneapolis
Constructed in 1915, this Classical Revival–style reinforced-concrete girder is part of the substantial CM&StP grade separation project completed in south Minneapolis in the 1910s. This corridor now serves bicyclists and pedestrians as the Midtown Greenway.

Bridge No. L8913
Columbus Avenue South over former line of CM&StP, Minneapolis
Constructed in 1915, this Classical Revival–style reinforced-concrete girder is part of the substantial CM&StP grade separation project completed in south Minneapolis in the 1910s. This corridor now serves bicyclists and pedestrians as the Midtown Greenway.

Bridge No. L8914
Elliot Avenue South over former line of CM&StP, Minneapolis
Constructed in 1915, this Classical Revival–style reinforced-concrete girder is part of the substantial CM&StP grade separation project completed in south Minneapolis in the 1910s. This corridor now serves bicyclists and pedestrians as the Midtown Greenway.

Bridge No. L8915
Tenth Avenue South over former line of CM&StP, Minneapolis
Constructed in 1915, this Classical Revival–style reinforced-concrete girder is part of the substantial CM&StP grade separation project completed in south Minneapolis in the 1910s. This corridor now serves bicyclists and pedestrians as the Midtown Greenway. (*Photograph by Chad Perkins; Hess, Roise and Company*)

Bridge No. L8916
Eleventh Avenue South over former line of CM&StP, Minneapolis
Constructed in 1915, this Classical Revival–style reinforced-concrete girder is part of the substantial CM&StP grade separation project completed in south Minneapolis in the 1910s. This corridor now serves bicyclists and pedestrians as the Midtown Greenway.

Bridge No. L8917
Twelfth Avenue South over former line of CM&StP, Minneapolis
Constructed in 1915, this Classical Revival–style reinforced-concrete girder is part of the substantial CM&StP grade separation project completed in south Minneapolis in the 1910s. This corridor now serves bicyclists and pedestrians as the Midtown Greenway.

Bridge No. L8918
Thirteenth Avenue South over former line of CM&StP, Minneapolis
Constructed in 1915, this Classical Revival–style reinforced-concrete girder is part of the substantial CM&StP grade separation project completed in south Minneapolis in the 1910s. This corridor now serves bicyclists and pedestrians as the Midtown Greenway.

Bridge No. L8919
Fourteenth Avenue South over former line of CM&StP, Minneapolis
Constructed in 1916, this Classical Revival–style reinforced-concrete girder is part of the substantial CM&StP grade separation project completed in south Minneapolis in the 1910s. This corridor now serves bicyclists and pedestrians as the Midtown Greenway.

Bridge No. L8920
Fifteenth Avenue South over former line of CM&StP, Minneapolis
Constructed in 1916, this Classical Revival–style reinforced-concrete girder is part of the substantial CM&StP grade separation project completed in south Minneapolis in the 1910s. This corridor now serves bicyclists and pedestrians as the Midtown Greenway.

Bridge No. L8921
Sixteenth Avenue South over former line of CM&StP, Minneapolis
Constructed in 1916, this Classical Revival–style reinforced-concrete girder is part of the substantial CM&StP grade separation project completed in south Minneapolis in the 1910s. This corridor now serves bicyclists and pedestrians as the Midtown Greenway.

Bridge No. L8922
Seventeenth Avenue South over former line of CM&StP, Minneapolis
Constructed in 1916, this Classical Revival–style reinforced-concrete girder is part of the substantial CM&StP grade separation project completed in south Minneapolis in the 1910s. This corridor now serves bicyclists and pedestrians as the Midtown Greenway.

Bridge No. L8923
Eighteenth Avenue South over former line of CM&StP, Minneapolis
Constructed in 1916, this Classical Revival–style reinforced-concrete girder is part of the substantial CM&StP grade separation project completed in south Minneapolis in the 1910s. This corridor now serves bicyclists and pedestrians as the Midtown Greenway.

Bridge No. L9327
Theodore Wirth Parkway over Bassett Creek, Golden Valley
Imitating a stone arch, this reinforced-concrete arch, completed in 1940, was designed by the Minneapolis Park Board. (*Photograph by Denis P. Gardner; Hess, Roise and Company*)

Broadway Bridge (Bridge No. 27664)
Merriam Street over East Channel of Mississippi River, Minneapolis
This bridge features a preserved component of the original Pratt truss bridge that was built over the Mississippi River at Broadway Avenue in 1887 by the King Iron Bridge Company of Cleveland, Ohio.

Cappelen Memorial Bridge (Bridge No. 2441)
Franklin Avenue over the Mississippi River, Minneapolis
Finished in 1923, the monumental reinforced-concrete, open-spandrel ribbed arch was designed by Minneapolis municipal engineers Frederick William Cappelen and Kristoffer Olsen Oustad. A photograph of this bridge is on page 133.

Cedar Avenue Bridge (Bridge No. 2796)
Cedar Avenue over the Mississippi River, Minneapolis
This monumental reinforced-concrete, open-spandrel ribbed arch was designed by Minneapolis municipal engineer Kristoffer Olsen Oustad and completed in 1929. A photograph of this bridge is on page 144.

Columbia Park Bridge (Bridge No. 93844)
Pedestrian trail over trackage of Soo Line Railway, Columbia Park, Minneapolis
Gillette-Herzog Manufacturing Company of Minneapolis constructed this steel ribbed, lattice arch in 1896. (*Photograph by Chad Perkins; Hess, Roise and Company*)

BRIDGE NO. 93844

BRIDGE NO. L9327

Electric Short Line Bridge No. 14.51 (Bridge No. 27136)
Luce Line Trail over line of the Burlington Northern Railroad, Orono
The wrought iron, pin-connected Pratt through truss was completed by the Chicago and Alton Railroad over the Illinois River near Pearl, Illinois, in 1885. It was disassembled and then reinstalled at its current location in 1914.

Hanover Bridge (Bridge No. 92366)
Pedestrian trail over the Crow River, Hanover
Erected by the Morse Bridge Company of Youngstown, Ohio, in 1885, this pin-connected Pratt through truss is one of Minnesota's few remaining wrought iron bridges. A photograph of this bridge is on page 52.

Intercity Bridge (Ford Bridge, Bridge No. 3575)
Ford Parkway over Mississippi River, Minneapolis and St. Paul
This monumental reinforced-concrete, open-spandrel ribbed arch was designed by St. Paul municipal engineer Martin Sigvart Grytbak and completed in 1927. A photograph of this bridge is on page 143.

Interlachen Bridge (Bridge No. L9328)
William Berry Drive over former Como-Interurban-Harriet trolley line, Minneapolis
Employing the patented reinforcing method developed by Viennese engineer Josef Melan, William S. Hewett of Minneapolis constructed this stone-faced concrete arch in 1900, which makes it possibly the oldest reinforced-concrete bridge in Minnesota. A photograph of this bridge is on page 120.

Long Meadow Bridge (Bridge No. 3145)
Cedar Avenue over Long Meadow Lake, Bloomington
This steel Camelback through truss was fabricated by Minneapolis Steel and Machinery Company and constructed by Illinois Bridge Company of Chicago, Illinois, in 1920.

Minnesota Soldiers Home Bridge (Bridge No. 5756)
Access road over Minnehaha Creek, Minnesota Soldiers Home, Minneapolis
Fabricated by Minneapolis Steel and Machinery Company, this substantial steel, three-hinged, open-spandrel arch was assembled in 1908 by Alexander Y. Bayne and William S. Hewett of Minneapolis. (*Photograph by Dale Martin*)

MINNESOTA SOLDIERS HOME BRIDGE

Northern Pacific Railway Bridge No. 9 (Bridge No. 94246)
Pedestrian trail over the Mississippi River, University of Minnesota, Minneapolis
Engineered and erected by the Northern Pacific Railway in 1887, this large, steel deck truss was greatly strengthened in 1923 but eventually evolved into a pedestrian and bicycle crossing. A photograph of this bridge is on page 76.

Queen Avenue Bridge (Bridge No. L9329)
West Lake Harriet Boulevard over former Como-Interurban-Harriet trolley line, Minneapolis
Designed by Charles R. Shepley of Minneapolis and built by the Minneapolis Street Railway Company in 1905, this early example of a reinforced-concrete arch exhibits Classical Revival–style detailing. (*Photograph by Robert M. Frame III*)

QUEEN AVENUE BRIDGE

Stone Arch Bridge (Bridge No. 27004)
Pedestrian crossing over the Mississippi River, near the Falls of St. Anthony, Minneapolis
Completed by the Minneapolis Union Railway in 1883, this monumental bridge is one of America's most impressive stone arches. A photograph of this bridge is on page 29.

Third Avenue Bridge (Bridge No. 2440)
Third Avenue over the Mississippi River, Minneapolis
Finished by 1917, this reinforced-concrete, open-spandrel ribbed arch designed by municipal engineer Frederick William Cappelen was the first of the monumental arches erected in the Twin Cities metropolitan region. A photograph of this bridge is on page 130.

HOUSTON COUNTY

Bridge No. 6679
Minnesota Trunk Highway 76 over South Fork of the Root River, two miles south of Houston
This early example of a cantilevered, deep-section steel I beam bridge was designed by the MHD and constructed by Leon Joyce of Rochester, Minnesota, in 1949. A photograph of this bridge is on page 82.

BRIDGE NO. L4005

Bridge No. L4005
Township Road 124 over Riceford Creek, three miles north of Spring Grove
Engineered and constructed by the Joliet Bridge and Iron Company of Joliet, Illinois, in 1905, this Pratt pony truss is one of the state's earliest and best examples of the half-hip design. (*Photograph by Shawn Rounds; Hess, Roise and Company*)

Bridge No. L4013
Township Road 126 over dry run, Black Hammer Township
Completed in 1915, this bridge embodies the design characteristics of a standard stone arch bridge plan that apparently was developed by the MHC about the second decade of the twentieth century. A photograph of this bridge is on page 38.

ITASCA COUNTY

Bridge No. 7423
County Road 446 over Swan River, four miles north of Warba
Completed in 1917, this is a rare concrete arch type designed by the Marsh Engineering Company of Des Moines, Iowa, and erected by Lofberg Cement Company of Grand Rapids, Minnesota.

JACKSON COUNTY

Bridge No. 2628
Township Road 183 over Okabena Creek, Alba Township
This unusually long-span reinforced-concrete through girder was designed by the MHD and constructed in 1917. (*Photograph by Jeffrey A. Hess; Hess, Roise and Company*)

Bridge No. L5245
Township Road 187 over Okabena Creek, Alba Township
This pin-connected Pratt pony truss may be the oldest such bridge in Minnesota. Its designer and builder are unknown. A photograph of this bridge is on page 58.

BRIDGE NO. 2628

KITTSON COUNTY

Drayton Bridge (Bridge No. 6690)
Minnesota Trunk Highway 11 over Red River of the North, near Drayton, North Dakota
Soon to be replaced, this large Warren through truss designed by Clifford Johnson of Denver, Colorado, and built by Helseth Engineering Company of St. Paul in 1954, features unique engineering adaptations to a problematic site. A photograph of this bridge is on page 91.

Kennedy Bridge (Bridge No. 5728)
Fifth Street over County Ditch No. 27, Kennedy
This rubble-faced, multiplate arch was designed by E. L. Lium and constructed by the WPA. (*Photograph by Jeffrey A. Hess; Hess, Roise and Company*)

KENNEDY BRIDGE

LAKE BRONSON DAM

Lake Bronson Dam (Bridge No. 7498)
County State Aid Highway 28 over South Branch of Two Rivers, Lake Bronson State Park
This combination reinforced-concrete deck girder and reinforced-concrete dam was designed by the division of drainage and waters and erected by the WPA in 1937. (*Photograph by Jeffrey A. Hess; Hess, Roise and Company*)

KOOCHICHING COUNTY

Bridge No. 5721
Minnesota Trunk Highway 65 over Little Fork River, near Silverdale
Fabricated in the late 1800s, this wrought iron, pin-connected Camelback through truss was erected at an unknown location, deconstructed and stored at Sauk Centre, and then re-erected over the Little Fork River by the MHD in 1937. A photograph of this bridge is on page 53.

Bridge No. 5804
County State Aid Highway 1 over Big Fork River, near Lindford
Designed by the MHD and finished by Teberg and Berg of St. Paul in 1939, this is an intriguing-looking crossing formed of a steel Pennsylvania through truss approached at either end by a steel Warren pony truss with verticals and a polygonal top chord. A photograph of this bridge is on page 81.

LAC QUI PARLE COUNTY

Bridge No. 6391
County State Aid Highway 33 over Minnesota River, Lac Qui Parle State Park
Built as part of the Lac Qui Parle Project, a substantial water conservation and flood control effort initiated in the mid-1930s, this relatively large dam and bridge formed of reinforced concrete was completed by the WPA in 1938. (*Photograph by Shawn Rounds; Hess, Roise and Company*)

LAKE COUNTY

Bridge No. 3459
State Forest road over Baptism River, Tettegouche State Park, near Silver Bay
This large, steel deck truss was constructed in 1923. (*Photograph by Jeffrey A. Hess; Hess, Roise and Company*)

BRIDGE NO. 3459

Bridge No. 3589
U.S. Highway 61 over Stewart River, immediately north of Two Harbors
This Classical Revival–style reinforced-concrete arch was designed by the MHD and finished in 1924 by Adams Construction Company of Minneapolis and August Laine of Kettle River, Minnesota. A photograph of this bridge is on page 128.

BRIDGE NO. 6391

ENCAMPMENT FOREST ASSOCIATION BRIDGE

Encampment Forest Association Bridge

Private path at Encampment Forest Association, near Two Harbors
Completed in the 1930s by the Encampment Forest Association, an association of families that created a private vacation getaway adjacent to Lake Superior in the 1920s, this is the only known timber king post in Minnesota. (*Photograph by Michael Koop*)

LAKE OF THE WOODS COUNTY

Bridge No. 5557

Minnesota Trunk Highway 11 over Rapid River, Clementson
Situated amid a stunning landscape, this reinforced-concrete, open-spandrel ribbed arch was designed by the MHD and built by L. M. Feller Company of Rochester, Minnesota, in 1950. A photograph of this bridge is on page 148.

LE SUEUR COUNTY

Bridge No. 4846

Pedestrian trail over Shanaska Creek, Washington Lake Park, near St. Peter
This rare, wrought iron, pin-connected Pratt through truss was raised over the Blue Earth River in Blue Earth County in 1875, removed and re-erected on County Road 102 over Minnesota Trunk Highway 22 in Le Sueur County in 1929, then again removed and re-erected over Shanaska Creek in Washington Lake Park in 1984. (*Photograph by Britta Bloomberg.*)

Broadway Bridge (Bridge No. 4930)

Minnesota Trunk Highway 99 over Minnesota River, St. Peter
One of Minnesota's most handsome trusses, this skewed, steel Pennsylvania through truss was designed by the MHD and built by the Minneapolis Bridge Company in 1931. A photograph of this bridge is on page 79.

LYON COUNTY

Bridge No. 5083

Minnesota Trunk Highway 19 over Redwood River, Marshall
One of two virtually identical, ornamental reinforced-concrete deck girders, this bridge was designed by the MHD and completed by the Guaranty Construction Company of Minneapolis in 1931.

Bridge No. 5151

Minnesota Trunk Highway 19 over Redwood River, Marshall
One of two virtually identical, ornamental reinforced-concrete deck girders, this bridge was designed by the MHD and completed by the Guaranty Construction Company of Minneapolis in 1931. A photograph of this bridge is on page 150.

Camden State Park Bridge

Park road over the Redwood River, Camden State Park
Part of the Camden State Park Historic District, this stone-faced reinforced-concrete slab was erected by the WPA circa 1938.

BRIDGE NO. 4846

MARSHALL COUNTY

Bridge No. L9372
Pedestrian trail over Middle River, Old Mill State Park, Foldahl Township
Completed in 1940 and supported by attractive stone pylons, this rare Minnesota example of a suspension crossing was designed and built by the state. (*Photograph by Rolf T. Anderson*)

BRIDGE NO. L9372

MARTIN COUNTY

Bridge No. 661
Township Road 38 over Elm Creek, Westford Township
Erected in 1912 by O. C. Gould and Sons of Fairmont, Minnesota, this reinforced-concrete deck girder was designed by William Pierce Cowles of Minneapolis with design approval from the MHC. (*Photograph by Jeffrey A. Hess; Hess, Roise and Company*)

BRIDGE NO. 661

MEEKER COUNTY

Bridge No. 5388
Minnesota Trunk Highway 24 over North Fork of the Crow River, near Kingston
Representing the final evolution of this bridge type in Minnesota, this steel Warren pony truss with verticals and a polygonal top chord was designed by the MHD and constructed by Teberg and Berg of St. Paul in 1935. A photograph of this bridge is on page 80.

Bridge No. 90990
Township Road 161 over Washington Creek, Dassel Township
Made of granite fieldstone, this small stone arch was constructed in 1908.

Salisbury Bridge (Bridge No. 90980)
County Road 190 over North Fork of the Crow River, near Kingston
Constructed by the Hewett Bridge Company of Minneapolis in 1899, this pin-connected Pratt through truss is one of Minnesota's earliest steel trusses. A photograph of this bridge is on page 57.

MILLE LACS COUNTY

Bridge No. 3355
U.S. Highway 169 over Whitefish Creek, near Onamia
This stone-faced reinforced-concrete slab was designed by the National Park Service and completed by the Civilian Conservation Corps in 1939. A photograph of this bridge is on page 154.

Dunn Memorial Bridge (Bridge No. 4936)
County State Aid Highway 29 over West Branch of Rum River, Princeton
Christened for former state legislator Robert C. Dunn, this Classical Revival–style reinforced-concrete deck girder, which was designed by the MHD and completed in 1931, mimics a reinforced-concrete arch. A photograph of this bridge is on page 149.

MORRISON COUNTY

Camp Ripley Bridge (Bridge No. 4969)
Minnesota Trunk Highway 115 over Mississippi River, near Camp Ripley
Constructed by the Minneapolis Bridge Company in 1930, this steel deck girder was designed by the MHD.

MOWER COUNTY

Bridge No. 5368
Fourth Street over Cedar River, Austin
This stone-faced reinforced-concrete arch was designed by Alvin C. White of the Mower County Highway Department and built by the Civil Works Administration in 1934.

Bridge No. 5374
Abandoned rail line over Oakland Avenue, Austin
The Art Deco–style steel deck girder was designed by the Chicago Great Western Railway and erected in 1937 as part of a transportation corridor now known as the Austin Underpass Historic District. (*Photograph by Jeffrey A. Hess; Hess, Roise and Company*)

Bridge No. 5699
Southeast Second Street over Oakland Avenue, Austin
A rare bridge type in Minnesota, this Art Deco–style reinforced-concrete rigid frame was designed by the MHD and erected in 1937 as part of a transportation corridor now known as the Austin Underpass Historic District. A photograph of this bridge is on page 157.

Bridge No. 5700
Southeast Third Street over Oakland Avenue, Austin
This Art Deco–style steel deck girder was designed by the Chicago Great Western Railway and erected in 1937 as part of a transportation corridor now known as the Austin Underpass Historic District. (*Photograph by Jeffrey A. Hess; Hess, Roise and Company*)

OLMSTED COUNTY

Bridge No. 448
County State Aid Highway 18 over Middle Fork of the Zumbro River
This reinforced-concrete, open-spandrel ribbed arch was constructed by N. M. Stark and Company of Des Moines, Iowa, in 1917. (*Photograph by Shawn Rounds; Hess, Roise and Company*)

Bridge No. 89182
County Road 125 over South Branch of the Zumbro River, Rochester Township
Surmounting a dam, this handsome steel stringer, constructed in 1934, features a shallow-arched concrete fascia.

Frank's Ford Bridge (Bridge No. L6322)
County Road 121 over South Branch of the Zumbro River, Oronoco Township
One of the state's oldest truss bridges, this steel, pin-connected Pratt through truss was erected in 1895 by Horace E. Horton of Chicago Bridge and Iron of Chicago, Illinois. (*Photograph by Robert M. Frame III*)

OTTER TAIL COUNTY

Bridge No. 5453
U.S Highway 59 over line of the Burlington Northern Railroad
Constructed in 1939 by L. M. Feller Company of Rochester, Minnesota, this skewed concrete slab was designed by the MHD and the Great Northern Railway. A photograph of this bridge is on page 155.

Phelps Mill Bridge (Bridge No. L0885)
Township Road 970 over Otter Tail River, Phelps Mill, Maine Township
The Security Bridge Company erected this steel, pin-connected Pratt pony truss at Phelps Mill in 1907. A photograph of this bridge is on page 59.

Waterstreet Bridge (Bridge No. L0884)
Gravel roadway over Otter Tail River, West Lost Lake,
Maine Township
One of the state's oldest truss bridges, this steel, pin-connected Pratt through truss was constructed in 1895, possibly by Milwaukee Bridge and Iron Works of Milwaukee, Wisconsin. It has an unpromising future. A photograph of this bridge is on page 56.

PINE COUNTY

Kettle River Bridge (Bridge No. 5718)
Minnesota Trunk Highway 123 over Kettle River, Sandstone
This cantilevered, steel Pratt deck truss with an arched lower chord was designed by the MHD and constructed by A. Guthrie and Company of St. Paul in 1948. A photograph of this bridge is on page 90.

PIPESTONE COUNTY

Split Rock Bridge (Bridge No. 5744)
County Road 54 over Split Rock Creek, Split Rock Creek State
Recreational Reserve, Eden Township
Made of pink Sioux quartzite, a beautiful stone common to southwestern Minnesota, this finely crafted stone arch was designed by Pipestone County highway engineer Elmer Keeler and New Ulm architect Albert G. Plagens and built by the WPA in 1938. A photograph of this bridge is on page 40.

POLK COUNTY

Sorlie Memorial Bridge (Bridge No. 4700)
DeMers Avenue over Red River of the North, East Grand Forks,
Minnesota, and Grand Forks, North Dakota
Designed by the North Dakota State Highway Department and constructed by the Minneapolis Bridge Company in 1929, this steel Parker through truss rests on circular bearings that allow it to compensate for the shifting river banks. A photograph of this bridge is on page 77.

POPE COUNTY

Bridge No. 1816
County State Aid Highway 21 over East Branch of the Chippewa
River, Chippewa Falls Township
Part of the Terrace Mill Historic District, this steel stringer was constructed in 1940.

Stone Arch Bridge (Bridge No. R0437)
Near Minnesota Trunk Highway 104, Chippewa Falls Township
Part of the Terrace Mill Historic District, this stone arch was constructed in 1903 and was recently rehabilitated. (*Photograph by Michael Koop*)

RAMSEY COUNTY

Bridge No. 62075
Pedestrian trail over Montreal Avenue, St. Paul
This Art Moderne–style reinforced-concrete arch was completed in 1927.

Bridge No. 92247
Lexington Avenue over Como Park path, St. Paul
Featuring the pioneering reinforcing system developed by Viennese engineer Josef Melan, this early example of a reinforced-concrete arch was designed and built by William S. Hewett and Company in 1904. (*Photograph by Robert M. Frame III*)

BRIDGE NO. 92247

Bridge No. L5852
Sterk Road over Como Park Lagoon, St. Paul
Constructed in 1894, this small stone arch with Classical Revival–style detailing was designed by the St. Paul city engineer's office.

STONE ARCH BRIDGE

Bridge No. L5853
Pedestrian trail over Como Park path, St. Paul
Featuring the pioneering reinforcing system developed by Viennese engineer Josef Melan, this early example of a reinforced-concrete arch was designed and built by William S. Hewett and Company in 1904. (*Photograph by Robert M. Frame III*)

Bridge No. L8560
Phalen Drive over South Canal, Phalen Park, St. Paul
This reinforced-concrete arch was constructed in 1923 and features Classical Revival–style and Medieval Revival–style detailing.

Bridge No. L8789
Pedestrian trail over Phalen Park Channel, St. Paul
Featuring vertical end posts embedded in a foundation, this rare Pratt bedstead pony truss was fabricated by the St. Paul Foundry Company and erected in 1906.

Bridge No. L8804
Edgecumbe Road over ravine, St. Paul
This reinforced-concrete deck girder was designed by St. Paul municipal engineer Martin Sigvart Grytbak and constructed in 1916.

Bridge No. L9218
Drewry Lane over pedestrian trail, St. Paul
This small reinforced-concrete arch was erected in 1905. (*Photograph by Shawn Rounds; Hess, Roise and Company.*)

Chicago Great Western Railway Aerial Lift Bridge
Former line of the Chicago Great Western Railway over the Mississippi River, St. Paul
Completed by the Chicago Great Western Railway in 1913, this steel crossing is one of a small number of vertical-lift bridges erected in Minnesota. A photograph of this bridge is on page 135.

Colorado Street Bridge (Bridge No. L8803)
East side of South Wabasha Street, near Terrace Park, St. Paul
Completed in 1888, this decorative stone arch is formed of various stone types. It was built by O'Brien Brothers of St. Paul employing an innovative construction method devised by St. Paul municipal engineer Andreas W. Munster, the bridge's designer. (*Photograph by Jeffrey A. Hess; Hess, Roise and Company*)

Intercity Bridge (Ford Bridge, Bridge No. 3575)
Ford Parkway over Mississippi River, Minneapolis and St. Paul
This monumental reinforced-concrete, open-spandrel ribbed arch was designed by St. Paul municipal engineer Martin Sigvart Grytbak and completed in 1927. A photograph of this bridge is on page 143.

Mendota Road Bridge (Bridge No. 90401)
Water Street over Pickerel Lake outlet, St. Paul
Designed by the St. Paul city engineer's office and constructed in 1894, this small, modestly ornamented stone arch is formed of gray limestone, a material that was often used for foundations for nineteenth-century St. Paul buildings. (*Photograph by Jeffrey A. Hess; Hess, Roise and Company*)

Robert Street Bridge (Bridge No. 9036)
Robert Street over Mississippi River, St. Paul
Designed by Toltz, King, and Day of St. Paul, and finished in 1926, this monumental reinforced-concrete arch formed of three different arch types was a joint undertaking between St. Paul and Ramsey County. A photograph of this bridge is on page 135.

Seventh Street Improvement Arches (Bridge No. 90386)
East Seventh Street over pedestrian and bicycle trail, St. Paul
Featuring a helicoid design, this exceptionally rare stone arch was designed by consulting engineer William Albert Truesdell and completed in 1884 as part of a major improvement of Seventh Street. A photograph of this bridge is on page 36.

REDWOOD COUNTY

Bridge No. 1238
Unpaved municipal road over Cottonwood River, Sanborn
This rare reinforced-concrete through girder with a cellular, or cavitated, deck was designed by the MHD and erected by Milo A. Adams and Company of Minneapolis in 1918. A photograph of this bridge is on page 151.

Bridge No. 1238A
Unpaved municipal road over Cottonwood River, Sanborn
This rare reinforced-concrete slab with a cellular, or cavitated, deck was designed by the MHD and erected by Milo A. Adams and Company of Minneapolis in 1918. A photograph of this bridge is on page 152.

Bridge No. 89850
County Road 17 over Minnesota River, Delhi Township
This steel, pin-connected Parker through truss was constructed by Lawrence Henry Johnson of Minneapolis in 1903.

Ramsey Park Swayback Bridge (Bridge No. 89859)
Park road over Redwood River, Ramsey Park, Redwood Falls
Constructed by the WPA in 1938, this reinforced-concrete slab is embellished with granite sidewalls and railings and exhibits the unique swayback design. A photograph of this bridge is on page 153.

RICE COUNTY

Bridge No. 8096
Minnesota Trunk Highway 19 over Spring Creek, Northfield
Built in 1918, this reinforced-concrete arch was enlarged by the MHD in 1947, at which time it was also dressed in stone and given Gothic Revival–style detailing. (*Photograph by Jeffrey A. Hess; Hess, Roise and Company*)

Faribault Viaduct (Bridge No. 5370)
Division Street over Straight River, Faribault
This large, decorative, reinforced-concrete, open-spandrel ribbed arch was designed by Sverdrup and Parcel of St. Louis, Missouri, and completed by Okes Construction Company of St. Paul in 1937. (*Photograph by Robert M. Frame III*)

ROCK COUNTY

Bridge No. 1482
Pedestrian trail between Schoneman Park ponds, Schoneman Park, off U.S. Highway 75, immediately south of Luverne
Built in 1908 by the Hewett Bridge Company, this is the only known steel, pin-connected, king-post pony truss remaining in Minnesota. A photograph of this bridge is on page 60.

Bridge No. L2162
Former route of County Road 51 over tributary of Split Rock Creek, Rose Dell Township
Now overgrown with grasses, this mildly classical reinforced-concrete elliptical arch, completed circa 1907, was a staple design of Perley N. Gillham's. Gillham was a local contractor who dotted southwestern Minnesota with his modest, yet charming, bridges. A photograph of this bridge is on page 122.

Bridge No. L2194
Township Road 8 over stream, Magnolia Township
Completed in 1928, this Classical Revival–style reinforced-concrete box culvert is the latest known crossing attributed to Perley N. Gillham.

Bridge No. L2210
Township Road 20 over Ash Creek, Clinton Township
This mildly classical reinforced-concrete elliptical arch, completed in 1911, was a staple design of Perley N. Gillham's. Gillham was a local contractor who dotted southwestern Minnesota with his modest, yet charming, bridges.

Bridge No. L2257
City road over stream, Luverne
This mildly classical reinforced-concrete elliptical arch, completed in 1910, was a staple design of Perley N. Gillham's. Gillham was a local contractor who dotted southwestern Minnesota with his modest, yet charming, bridges.

Bridge No. L2340
Township Road 108 over Spring Water Creek, Beaver Creek Township
Completed in 1906, this reinforced-concrete arch with simple aesthetics is one of the earliest bridges constructed by Perley N. Gillham.

Bridge No. L4646
Sixth Street over Spring Brook, Beaver Creek
This mildly classical reinforced-concrete elliptical arch, completed in 1911, was a staple design of Perley N. Gillham's. Gillham was a local contractor who dotted southwestern Minnesota with his modest, yet charming, bridges. A photograph of this bridge is on page 122.

ST. LOUIS COUNTY

Aerial Lift Bridge (Bridge No. L6116)
Lake Avenue over Duluth Ship Canal, Duluth
Minnesota's most celebrated vertical-lift bridge began as a ferry bridge designed by city engineer Thomas F. McGilvray and completed in 1905 by Modern Steel Structural Company of Waukesha, Wisconsin. The steel crossing was reengineered into its current form in 1929 by the Kansas City–based firm of Harrington, Howard and Ash. A photograph of this bridge is on page 106.

Blatnik Bridge (Bridge No. 9030)
Interstate Highway 535 over outlet to Superior Bay, Duluth, Minnesota, and Superior, Wisconsin
A joint project between Minnesota and Wisconsin, this exceptionally long bridge was completed in 1961. Its main span features a deck suspended beneath a steel arched truss.

Bridge No. 5757
Minnesota Trunk Highway 23 over Mission Creek, Duluth
This fieldstone-faced multiplate arch was designed by the MHD and built by A. A. Bodin and Son of Minneapolis in 1937. (*Photograph by Shawn Rounds; Hess, Roise and Company*)

BRIDGE NO. 5757

Bridge No. 7626
Duluth, Missabe and Iron Range Railway line over Minnesota Trunk Highway 23, Duluth
A component of a large rail viaduct reaching to an ore-handling facility on St. Louis Bay, this steel deck plate girder was designed by the Duluth, Missabe and Northern Railway and completed circa 1925. (*Photograph by Jeffrey A. Hess; Hess, Roise and Company*)

Bridge No. 7627
Duluth, Missabe and Iron Range Railway (DM&IR) line over Minnesota Trunk Highway 23, Duluth
A component of a large rail viaduct reaching to an ore-handling facility on St. Louis Bay, this steel deck plate girder was designed by the Duluth, Missabe and Northern Railway and completed circa 1904.

Bridge No. 7631
DM&IR line over city route, Duluth
This steel deck plate girder was constructed in 1925.

Bridge No. 7632
Abandoned DM&IR line over city route, Duluth
This steel deck plate girder was constructed in 1925.

Bridge No. 7645
County State Aid Highway 5 over Bearskin River, unorganized township
Designed by the St. Louis County Highway Department and built by E. W. Coons of Hibbing, Minnesota, in 1934, this modest-looking crossing is one of the first to be erected with thirty-six-inch-deep steel rolled I beams, a significant technological advancement in bridge building in Minnesota. A photograph of this bridge is on page 81.

Bridge No. 7753
Unpaved county road over unnamed stream, about eight miles east of Chisholm
Designed by the St. Louis County Highway Department, this steel stringer erected by the Great Northern Bridge Company of Minneapolis nevertheless adhered to a standard plan developed by the MHD. (*Photograph by Jeffrey A. Hess; Hess, Roise and Company*)

Bridge No. 88557
Wallace Avenue over Tischers Creek, Duluth
This stone-faced reinforced-concrete arch was designed and built by the city of Duluth in 1932. (*Photograph by Shawn Rounds; Hess, Roise and Company*)

Bridge No. 89451
Skyline Parkway over Amity Creek, Duluth
This Classical Revival–style, stone-faced reinforced-concrete arch was completed circa 1911.

Bridge No. L6113
East Fourth Street over Tischers Creek, Duluth
This stone-faced reinforced-concrete arch was designed by the city of Duluth and built in 1925 by Salo and Wiinamaki, apparently a local contractor. (*Photograph by Shawn Rounds; Hess, Roise and Company*)

Bridge No. L6137
DM&IR line over Superior Street, Duluth
This steel deck plate girder was constructed in 1925. (*Photograph by Jeffrey A. Hess; Hess, Roise and Company*)

Bridge No. L6138
DM&IR line over Superior Street, Duluth
This steel deck plate girder was constructed in 1925.

Bridge No. L8477
Tenth Street over Miller Creek, Duluth
This Classical Revival–style, stone-faced reinforced-concrete arch was constructed in 1927.

Bridge No. L8501
Snively Boulevard over Amity Creek, Duluth
This Classical Revival–style, stone-faced reinforced-concrete arch was constructed circa 1911.

Bridge No. L8503
Snively Boulevard over Amity Creek, Duluth
This Classical Revival–style, stone-faced reinforced-concrete arch was constructed circa 1911.

Bridge No. L8505
Snively Boulevard over Amity Creek, Duluth
This Classical Revival–style, stone-faced reinforced-concrete arch was constructed circa 1911.

Bridge No. L8506
Snively Boulevard over Amity Creek, Duluth
This Classical Revival–style, stone-faced reinforced-concrete arch was constructed circa 1911.

Bridge No. L8507
Snively Boulevard over Amity Creek, Duluth
This Classical Revival–style, stone-faced reinforced-concrete arch was constructed circa 1911.

Bridge No. L8515
Lewis Street over Tischers Creek, Duluth
This stone-faced reinforced-concrete arch was designed and built by the city of Duluth in 1922. (*Photograph by Shawn Rounds; Hess, Roise and Company*)

Bridge No. L8796
Township Road 883 over West Swan River, Lavell Township
This reinforced-concrete slab was constructed circa 1910.
(*Photograph by Jeffrey A. Hess; Hess, Roise and Company*)

Lester River Bridge (Bridge No. 5772)
Minnesota Trunk Highway 61 over Lester River, Duluth
This Classical Revival–style, reinforced-concrete ribbed arch
is faced in randomly coursed ashlar. It was designed primarily
by Morell and Nichols of Minneapolis and finished by Duluth
contractor Charles Russell McLean in 1925. A photograph of this
bridge is on page 127.

Oliver Bridge (Bridge No. 6544)
*Minnesota Trunk Highway 39 over St. Louis River, Duluth,
Minnesota, and Oliver, Wisconsin*
Engineered to carry both railroad and automobile traffic, this
huge steel bridge has a main swing span formed of a Warren
truss that serves as a deck truss for the rail line and a through
truss for the roadway. It was completed by the Interstate
Transfer Railway and the Spirit Lake Transfer Railway in 1917.
A photograph of this bridge is on page 96.

Railroad Bridge
Rail line over Skyline Parkway, Duluth
This is a reinforced-concrete-faced bridge.

Stewart Creek Stone Arch Bridge (Bridge No. L6007)
Skyline Parkway over Stewart Creek, Duluth
Although the engineer and builder are unknown, this somewhat
brutal-looking crossing, finished circa 1925, is one of Minnesota's
most impressive stone arches. A photograph of this bridge is on
page 39.

SCOTT COUNTY

Bridge No. 4175
Pedestrian trail over Minnesota River, Shakopee
This handsome, steel Warren deck truss with verticals was
designed by the MHD and constructed by Widell Company of
Mankato in 1927. (*Photograph by Chad Perkins; Hess, Roise and
Company*)

**Jordan Fair Grounds Bridge
(Bridge No. 5704)**
Rice Street over Sand River, Jordan
Designed by the MHD and constructed in 1936 by M. E. Souther
of St. Paul, this is one of Minnesota's most ornamental steel
deck plate girders. (*Photograph by Chad Perkins; Hess, Roise and
Company*)

STEARNS COUNTY

Great Northern Railway Bridge
South Main Street at South Eighth Street, Sauk Centre
This site held a railroad bridge as early as 1878, but by 1924 the Great Northern Railway reengineered the site as a grade separation (a depressed automobile roadway beneath the bridge). In 1931, the railroad company rebuilt the steel girder crossing.

STEELE COUNTY

Clinton Falls Bridge (Bridge No. L5573)
Township Road 95 over Straight River, Clinton Falls Township
One of Minnesota's oldest steel trusses, this pin-connected Pratt through truss was built in 1894 by the George E. King Bridge Company of Des Moines, Iowa. (*Photograph by David Anderson*)

SWIFT COUNTY

Bridge No. 3858
Township Road 25 over Pomme de Terre River, Moyer Township
This steel Pratt through truss was constructed in 1923. (*Photograph by Shawn Rounds; Hess, Roise and Company*)

BRIDGE NO. 3858

TODD COUNTY

Bridge No. L7069
Township Road 357 over Turtle Creek, Turtle Creek Township
This multiplate arch faced in fieldstone was designed by the Todd County Highway Department and constructed by the WPA in 1940. (*Photograph by Chad Perkins; Hess, Roise and Company*)

Bridge No. L7075
Township Road 411 over Turtle Creek, Hartford Township
Addressing Classical Revival style in a rudimentary fashion, this multiplate arch faced in fieldstone was designed by the Todd County Highway Department and constructed by the WPA in 1940. A photograph of this bridge is on page 83.

WABASHA COUNTY

Bridge No. 5827
Minnesota Trunk Highway 60 over coulee, Zumbro Falls
Designed by the MHD and erected by the WPA in 1938, this multiplate arch is faced in randomly coursed ashlar. A photograph of this bridge is on page 83.

Walnut Street Bridge (Bridge No. R0412)
Pedestrian trail over North Branch of the Zumbro River, Mazeppa
This steel, pin-connected Pratt through truss was built in 1904 by William S. Hewett and Company of Minneapolis. (*Photograph by the Minnesota State Historic Preservation Office*)

WALNUT STREET BRIDGE

BRIDGE NO. L7069

ZUMBRO PARKWAY BRIDGE

Zumbro Parkway Bridge
(Bridge No. 3219)
County Road 68 over branch of Zumbro River, Hyde Park Township
One of the finest examples of its type, this stone-faced multiplate arch with limited Gothic Revival–style detailing was designed by local engineer J. M. Evans and constructed by the WPA in 1937. (*Photograph by Jeffrey A. Hess;, Hess, Roise and Company*)

WADENA COUNTY

Bridge No. L7120
Abandoned township road over Partridge River, Thomastown Township
Representing a bridge type never popular on Minnesota's road-ways but extremely popular on railroad lines, this steel plate through girder was designed by the MHD and erected in 1913. (*Photograph by Shawn Rounds; Hess, Roise and Company*)

BRIDGE NO. L7120

WASHINGTON COUNTY

Point Douglas–St. Louis River Road Bridge
Abandoned road over Brown's Creek, Stillwater
Perhaps the oldest bridge in the state, this small stone arch was constructed in 1863 as part of Minnesota's military road network. A photograph of this bridge is on page 32.

Soo Line High Bridge
Minneapolis, St. Paul and Sault Ste. Marie Railway line over St. Croix River, Washington County, Minnesota, and St. Croix County, Wisconsin
Designed by celebrated engineer C. A. P. Turner and completed by the Minneapolis, St. Paul and Sault Ste. Marie Railway in 1911, this monumental three-hinged open-spandrel arch is one of the most impressive steel bridges in America. A photograph of this bridge is on page 47.

SOUTH ST. PAUL BELT RAILWAY BRIDGE

South St. Paul Belt Railway Bridge
(Bridge No. 5600)
Abandoned rail and roadway line over the Mississippi River between St. Paul Park and Inver Grove Heights
Engineered to carry both railroad and automobile traffic, this huge steel bridge with a main span formed of a pin-connected through-truss swing span was designed by Charles F. Loweth of St. Paul and built by the Pittsburgh Bridge Company of Pittsburgh, Pennsylvania, in 1895. (*Photograph by Jeffrey A. Hess; Hess, Roise and Company*)

Stillwater Bridge (Bridge No. 4654)
Minnesota Trunk Highway 36 over St. Croix River, Stillwater, Minnesota, and Houlton, Wisconsin
Engineered by Ash, Howard, Needles, and Tammen, as well as the MHD, this crossing, completed in 1931, is one of a small number of vertical-lift bridges erected in Minnesota. A photograph of this bridge is on page 106.

WATONWAN COUNTY

Bridge No. 6527
Pedestrian trail over Watonwan River, Madelia
Built in 1909 by the Minneapolis Bridge and Iron Company, this bridge is a steel Warren through truss with verticals.

WINONA COUNTY

The Arches (Bridge No. L1394)
Dakota, Minnesota and Eastern Railroad line over Garvin Brook, Warren Township
Constructed in 1882 by the Winona and St. Peter Railroad, this is one of Minnesota's most impressive stone arches. A photograph of this bridge is on page 26.

Bridge No. L1393
Dakota, Minnesota and Eastern Railroad line over County Road 20, Warren Township
Completed in 1910, this steel deck plate girder replaced the earlier wrought iron deck plate girder that was built at this site in 1882 by the Winona and St. Peter Railroad. A photograph of this bridge is on page 50.

Bridge No. L1409
Township Road 62 over Garvin Brook, Hillsdale Township
Completed in 1895, this stone arch was designed by county engineer Fred H. Pickles and constructed by local stonemason Charles Butler. A photograph of this bridge is on page 37.

Dam and Footbridge
Pedestrian trail over manmade lake, Whitewater State Park
Part of the Whitewater State Park Historic District, this attractive dam and footbridge erected by the CCC in 1935 is made of reinforced concrete and faced in stone. (*Photograph by Rolf T. Anderson*)

DAM AND FOOTBRIDGE

FOOTBRIDGE

Footbridge
Pedestrian trail over Whitewater River, Whitewater State Park
Part of the Whitewater State Park Historic District, this handsome timber stringer was erected by the CCC in 1935 and modified in 1938. (*Photograph by Rolf T. Anderson*)

Main Channel Bridge (Bridge No. 5900)
Minnesota Trunk Highway 43 over the Mississippi River, Winona
This huge, cantilevered steel through truss was designed by the MHD and the Wisconsin State Highway Commission and finished by Industrial Contracting Company of Minneapolis in 1942. A photograph of this bridge is on page 88.

YELLOW MEDICINE COUNTY

Bridge No. L7897
Township Road 27 over Ditch No. 53, Normania Township
This small, attractive reinforced-concrete culvert was designed by the MHD and the Yellow Medicine County Highway Department and constructed in 1925. A photograph of this bridge is on page 156.

Bridge No. L7898
Township Road 27 over Ditch No. 53, Normania Township
This small, attractive reinforced-concrete culvert was designed by the MHD and the Yellow Medicine County Highway Department and constructed in 1925. A photograph of this bridge is on page 156.

Prestegard Bridge (Bridge No. L7969)
Township Road 115 over Yellow Medicine River, Minnesota Falls Township
This steel Pratt pony truss was erected in 1909 by Milo A. Adams of Minneapolis. A photograph of this bridge is on page 65.

AFTERWORD

ERIC DeLONY

AFTER READING THIS BOOK, one cannot help being impressed by the diversity, number, and types of bridges in Minnesota. From the Hennepin Avenue suspension bridge to the rare bowstring-truss Kern Bridge, from the unusual Hastings Spiral Bridge and Duluth's Aerial Lift Bridge to the solid stone arches, the state obviously has a rich cultural and architectural heritage in its bridges.

Yet the most famous bridge incident in Minnesota happened quite recently, when the Interstate Highway 35W Bridge in Minneapolis collapsed into the Mississippi River on August 1, 2007. The collapse was the worst bridge disaster since the 1967 failure of the Silver Bridge spanning the Ohio River, and the entire bridge-engineering industry responded. Collapse of an interstate bridge focuses priorities and puts pressure on all bridge and highway funding; those of us involved in historic bridge preservation can only hope that historic bridges will continue to be rehabilitated and saved as other critical situations are addressed.

The tragedy highlighted the aging state of our nation's infrastructure. Of interest to the historic bridge community is that the bridges of the early interstate era are those most at risk—not the bridges built in the late nineteenth and early twentieth centuries that are the subject of this book and of bridge preservation. I am not aware of a single rehabilitated historic bridge injuring an individual or endangering personal property during the thirty years I have been studying historic bridges.

The Eisenhower Interstate System celebrated its fiftieth anniversary in 2006. After World War II, bridges were constructed by the thousands during rapid expansion of the nation's highway system; highway departments developed steel beams and cantilevers, concrete slabs and girders, reinforced- and prestressed-concrete beams for overpasses, short and mid-length spans. Many bridges of this generation are now eligible for the National Register of Historic Places.

As the interstate highway system aged, the U.S. Department of Transportation's Federal Highway Administration (FHWA) and state transportation offices grew increasingly concerned about how the interstate system could be managed under potential constraints of the National Historic Preservation Act (NHPA) and Section 4(f) of the U.S. Department of Transportation Act. The consensus was an exemption whereby most roads, bridges, tunnels, interchanges, and ramps located within the interstate's 46,876-mile right-of-way were excluded as historic properties under national preservation laws. Certain elements of the interstate system clearly are historically valuable, so states were requested by FHWA to identify features of national or exceptional significance that would be excluded from the exemption and subject to preservation guidelines. States were asked to submit to FHWA lists of bridges and other interstate features such as tunnels, interchanges, and ramps—a good first step in designating preservation priorities.[1] Components of the highway system that would not be covered by the exemption and still would be subject to historic preservation review include (1) elements that are at least fifty years old, possess national significance, and meet the National Register eligibility criteria; (2) elements that are less than fifty years old, possess national significance, meet the National Register eligibility criteria, and are of exceptional importance; and (3) elements that were listed in the National Register or were determined eligible for the National Register prior to the effective date of the exemption.

We are only beginning to review these postwar, early interstate bridges. To build the interstate, engineering design guidelines and standards were developed by the U.S. Bureau of Public Roads, but bridge engineers in each state could develop their own innovative designs for state bridges if they complied with national standards; the federal-state transportation partnership permitted that guidelines developed at the national level could be interpreted and executed by the states. More outstanding historic bridges designed by state bridge engineers will continue to be identified, since the exemption likely omitted some important bridges.

Bridge scholarship in Minnesota, exemplified by Jeff Hess, Charlene Roise, Bob Frame, Fred Quivik, and Denis Gardner, is reinforced by a rich collection of historic photographs and a sampling of bridge artifacts, as demonstrated in this book. There have been significant preservation successes in the state: the Seventh Street Improvement Arches, a helicoid arch built in 1884, was declared a National Historic Civil Engineering Landmark in 2000 by the American Society of Civil Engineers; the Hanover Bridge, from 1885, was converted to pedestrian use; Rock County Bridge No. 1482, a rare king-post pony truss near Luverne, was moved and protected; and the Stillwater Bridge spanning the St. Croix National Scenic River was the subject of a national preservation effort that involved local residents, the departments of transportation of Minnesota and Wisconsin, and the National Park Service. But why hasn't Minnesota—and the rest of the country—been more successful in saving its bridges? A fundamental flaw of historic bridge legislation, management, and preservation plans is that most states, including Minnesota, do not assume responsibility for non-state-owned or federally owned bridges, leaving this to local communities, which rarely have the funds to care for old bridges; a seminal rule of historic bridge rehabilitation is involvement by local citizen groups and interested local governments. What is the relationship between local, state, and federal authorities regarding historic bridges?

Primary reasons for replacement of historic bridges are new technologies and materials, poor maintenance, and an apathetic public. The risk extends beyond the bridge to the larger context: road, village, countryside, cityscape (both urban and rural) threatened with suburbanization, congestion, and subsequent development. All of these changes require increased infrastructure, which includes preservation of historic bridges. Recent statistics suggest that more than half the historic bridges in America have been destroyed during the past twenty-five years—a period when preservation awareness about all types of historic structures has been at its highest and most sophisticated level.[2]

Minnesota began working on statewide historic bridge surveys in 1985, and in 2006 Mn/DOT completed its new "Management Plan for Historic Bridges in Minnesota."[3] Though "intended to aid owners of historic bridges, including the state, counties, cities, and towns," the report also declares that "Mn/DOT is committed to preserving and performing a higher level of maintenance on selected state-owned historic bridges and working to encourage preservation efforts for bridges controlled by local agencies." The state is responsible for twenty-six state-owned historic bridges, 15 percent of the historic bridges in Minnesota; it is not responsible for the remaining 85 percent, which include many one-of-a-kind potentially nationally or regionally significant bridges. This restriction to only state-owned historic bridges is common to other states: state DOTs have relieved themselves of responsibility for the majority of historic bridges owned by municipalities or on secondary farm-to-market roads. Though the Minnesota management plan is designed (through the twenty-six case studies) to provide guidance and direction to local communities, I question its effectiveness in dealing with the other historic bridges in the state.

The authors of the management plan, engineer Steve Olson and historian Bob Frame, addressed my criticism with blunt reality of the actual situation regarding historic bridges not only in Minnesota but throughout the country. Olson said, "I believe Mn/DOT has made a good faith effort and will preserve the couple dozen historic bridges on the Trunk Highway system that were part of our earlier project. Beyond the Mn/DOT-owned bridges, I'm afraid the results will not be positive for at least the next five years. There is nothing more than a hope that local community groups will stand up and lobby to protect their local resources." Hope is not a strategy, but that seems to be our current resource.

Frame, now actively working for historic bridges in Indiana, concurred with Olson on the lack of available funding. He responded, "I'd probably call funding the carrot instead of the stick. When it comes to sticks, Indiana has a pretty big one in its citizen advocacy organizations lobbying for historic bridge preservation. Few states have such a well-organized, well-funded cadre of bridge-savvy citizens." Indiana is an outstanding example of the power of public advocacy to create change, and the results of statewide advocacy are demonstrated in its "Programmatic Agreement Regarding the Management and Preservation of Indiana's Historic Bridges."[4] One item of note is the designation of "select" and "non-select" bridges, establishing a new category of bridge preservation beyond the National Register for state funding from FHWA. This is the focus of county highway departments, which own two-thirds of the state's historic bridges, when reviewing the Indiana Historic Bridge Inventory. Funding remains an issue, but dollars are more likely to flow to the squeaky wheel, backed up by organized citizens who know what they want. Indiana's Historic Spans Task Force received a National Trust Preservation Honor Award in October 2007.

Charlene Roise, a Minneapolis consultant who has worked on many historic bridges, emphasizes the lack of funding and the challenge to create political advocacy and a public constituency for historic bridges: "It is hard to get people really worked up about any preservation issue, and bridges are often a much harder sell than buildings. No advocates, no money." It is difficult to change policy and increase funding with little public support.

Preservation has not permeated our local culture as much as I'd like. The only incentive to encourage preservation is federal project dollars, but federal support for projects in Minnesota is becoming increasingly scarce. The Minnesota preservation community tried unsuccessfully in 2007 to secure a state tax credit for historic buildings, and to my knowledge there are no additional state laws pertaining to the preservation of historic bridges on a local level. Some counties have given up their efforts to obtain federal dollars for their projects: no federal dollars, no preservation stick.

A national historic bridge funding program for local governments similar to what is available for covered bridges would be ideal. We have only one historic covered bridge of note in Minnesota, in Zumbrota, and there were never many in the state, so we are ineligible for that source of funding.

Most statewide historic bridge survey and management plans are limited to bridges currently in service on public roads for which state DOTs have management responsibility, so some of the best and most significant non-DOT bridges never get preservation consideration because they are abandoned, privately owned, or not on the federal or state aid systems. Strengthening the national Historic Bridge Program, Title 23, Section 144(o), may offer a partial solution.

It is pitiful to watch some local bridges disappear, such as the Kern Bridge spanning the Le Sueur River south of Mankato, now impossible to access through dense foliage along the river. The local section of the American Society of Civil Engineers is becoming more astute with respect to history and heritage efforts, and our committee continues to grow and generate interest among the civil engineering community. We have a long way to go, but we've begun our journey. Minnesota's historic bridge management plan is premised on integrating the engineer and the historian, but suggests that further interdisciplinary collaboration among local leaders, preservationists, and the public is sorely needed. As three of the state's bridge experts have reiterated, without further incentives of funding, appreciation, and awareness, historic bridges remain an endangered heritage. Despite heroic efforts in all parts of the country, more than half the historic bridges in the United States were destroyed during the past twenty-five years. Ignorance and lack of interest coupled with ineffective laws and regulations and insufficient funding at all levels of government render these bridges at extreme risk.

N O T E S

PREFACE

1. Charles Filteau, letter to K. Nelson, likely a county official in Alexandria, Minnesota, May 1, 1876, copy in the possession of the author.

2. The first part of this introduction is drawn primarily from two sources: Fredric L. Quivik and Dale L. Martin's "Iron and Steel Bridges in Minnesota," July 1988, National Register of Historic Places Multiple Property Documentation Form, available at the State Historic Preservation Office (hereafter SHPO), Minnesota Historical Society (hereafter MHS), St. Paul; and Robert M. Frame III's "Historic Bridge Project," March 31, 1985, prepared for the SHPO and the Minnesota Department of Transportation, available at the SHPO, MHS, St. Paul.

3. The federally established criteria for determining that a property—any property—is historic can be found in U.S. Department of Interior, *National Register Bulletin: How to Apply the National Register Criteria for Evaluation*, rev. ed. (Washington, D.C.: Government Printing Office, 1997), 2.

WOOD BRIDGES

1. "The First Suspension Bridge," *Hennepin History* (July 1952): 2.

2. "Grand Celebration," *St. Anthony Express*, January 27, 1855; Penny A. Petersen, *Hiding in Plain Sight* (Minneapolis: Marcy-Holmes Neighborhood Association/NRP, 1999), 10–13, 18–19; Warren Upham, *Minnesota Place Names: A Geographical Encyclopedia* (St. Paul: Minnesota Historical Society Press, 2001), 229–30.

3. "Grand Celebration"; Jeffrey A. Hess, "Final Report of the Minnesota Historic Bridge Survey: Part 1," August 1988, prepared for the MHS and the Minnesota Department of Transportation (hereafter Mn/DOT), available at SHPO, MHS, St. Paul, 77.

4. Robert M. Frame III, "Historic Bridge Project," March 31, 1985, prepared for the SHPO and the Mn/DOT, available at the SHPO, MHS, St. Paul, 8–9; Nicholas Westbrook, ed., *A Guide to the Industrial Archeology of the Twin Cities* (St. Paul and Minneapolis: Society for Industrial Archeology, 1983), 16; "Background and History of the Wabasha Street Bridge River Crossing," in "Wabasha Street Bridge Project Information," August 2002, Division of Bridges, Department of Public Works, City of St. Paul, http://bridges.ci.stpaul.mn.us/Construct/WABASHA/wabasha.html.

5. David Plowden, *Bridges: The Spans of North America* (New York: W. W. Norton and Company, 1974), 33; Demian Hess, "Minnesota Military Roads," July 1989, National Register of Historic Places Multiple Property Documentation Form, available at SHPO, MHS, St. Paul, E.7; Fredric L. Quivik and Dale L. Martin, "Iron and Steel Bridges in Minnesota," July 1988, National Register of Historic Places Multiple Property Documentation Form, available at SHPO, MHS, St. Paul, E.0; Denis P. Gardner, *Minnesota Treasures: Stories Behind the State's Historic Places* (St. Paul: Minnesota Historical Society Press, 2004), 23; "George Washington Campground," in "New England Mountain Bike Association," May 10, 2004, www.nemba.org/ridingzone/GeorgeWashingtonRI.html.

6. "Canal Bridge at Detroit Lakes," 1895, photo available in library photographic file, MHS, St. Paul; Frame, "Historic Bridge Project," 7; Plowden, *Bridges*, 33.

7. Jeffrey A. Hess and Chad Perkins, "Historic Highway Bridge Inventory: The Survey Sample," 1995, copy of study available at SHPO, MHS, St. Paul, 15, 34.

8. Frame, "Historic Bridge Project," 74; Gardner, *Minnesota Treasures*, 64; Jeffrey A. Hess, "Bridge No. 5837," in "Minnesota Historic Highway Bridge Inventory," 1997, available at SHPO, MHS, St. Paul, n.p.

9. The best history of federal relief efforts in Minnesota is Rolf T. Anderson's, "Federal Relief Construction in Minnesota, 1933-1941," August 30, 1993, National Register of Historic Places Multiple Property Documentation Form, available at SHPO, MHS, St. Paul; Hess, "Bridge No. 5837."

10. R. H. Nelson, "The Story of Goodhue County: Part IV," *Goodhue County News*, June 1977, 1–2; "Waite's Crossing on the Red River Trail," *Crossings*, December 1987, 5–6; "Mill on Vermillion Falls, Covered Bridge in Background, Hastings," ca. 1869, photo available in library photographic file, MHS, St. Paul.

11. Fred Kniffen, "The American Covered Bridge," *Geographical Review* 41 (January 1951): 114, 118–119; Robert Fletcher and J. P. Snow, "A History of the Development of Wooden Bridges," *Proceedings of the American Society of Civil Engineers* (October 1934): 335.

12. William H. Shank, *Historic Bridges of Pennsylvania* (York, Penn.: American Canal and Transportation Center, 1966), 17; Plowden, *Bridges*, 37; Fletcher and Snow, "Wooden Bridges," 333.

13. Zumbrota Valley Historical Society, Centennial Book Committee, *Zumbrota: The First 100 Years* (Zumbrota, Minn.: Zumbrota Valley Historical Society, 1956), 247–249;

David Nystuen, "Zumbrota Covered Bridge," October 1974, National Register of Historic Places Registration Form, available at SHPO, MHS, St. Paul, n.p.; "The Only Zumbrota in the World," n.d., pamphlet sponsored by the city of Zumbrota and various promotional agencies and printed by Sommers Printing, Inc., Zumbrota, available at MHS, St. Paul, n.p.

14. "Historic Bridge Is Moved," *Zumbrota Covered Bridge Society*, September 1970, n.p.; "Homecoming for Zumbrota's History-spanning Bridge," *Minneapolis Star Tribune*, March 4, 1997; Nystuen, "Zumbrota Covered Bridge," n.p.; Zumbrota Valley Historical Society, 249.

15. Gardner, *Minnesota Treasures,* 45–46.

16. Ibid., 45, 47–48; Carl Zapffe, *Brainerd, Minnesota, 1871–1946* (Brainerd, Minn.: Brainerd Civic Association, 1946), 3–4.

17. Theodore C. Blegen, *Minnesota: A History of the State* (Minneapolis: University of Minnesota Press, 1963), 97–98, 110–114; Shank, *Bridges of Pennsylvania*, 17–18; Plowden, *Bridges,* 38–39.

18. Carl W. Condit, *American Building: Materials and Techniques from the First Colonial Settlements to the Present* (Chicago and London: University of Chicago Press, 1982), 59–61; Plowden, *Bridges,* 38–39.

19. Ingolf Dillan, *Brainerd's Half Century* (Brainerd, Minn.: self-published, 1923), 18–20; Gardner, *Minnesota Treasures,* 47–48.

20. Plowden, *Bridges,* 39.

21. Richard S. Prosser, *Rails to the North Star* (Minneapolis: Dillon Press, 1966), 20–21, 142–143; George E. Warner and Charles M. Foote, comp., *History of the Minnesota Valley: Carver County* (Minneapolis: North Star Publishing Company, 1882), i, 6; Lucie K. Hartley, *The Carver Story* (n.p., 1971), 151; Upham, *Minnesota Place Names,* 552.

22. "View of Carver, Minnesota," October 1893, photo available in library photographic file, MHS, St. Paul.

23. Don L. Hofsommer, *Minneapolis and the Age of Railways* (Minneapolis: University of Minnesota Press, 2005), 11, 85–86; Peter L. Wilson, Senior Engineering Specialist, Bridge Inspection Unit, e-mail to Denis P. Gardner, January 19, 2007, in possession of Denis P. Gardner, n.p.; "Fort Snelling at Junction of the Mississippi and Minnesota," ca. 1867, photograph by Rodolph W. Ransom, photo available in library photographic file, MHS, St. Paul; Prosser, *Rails,* 140.

24. Hazel M. Jacobson, *Hastings from River to Rails on the H&D* (n.p., 1975), 3–5; Warner and Foote, *Minnesota Valley,* 6; Gardner, *Minnesota Treasures,* 40; Upham, *Minnesota Place Names,* 168; Prosser, *Rails,* 137.

25. Prosser, *Rails,* 137; Jacobson, *Hastings,* 5, 7–8; "Hastings and Dakota Railway Company Train on Bridge over the Dalles of the Vermillion River, Dakota County," circa 1870, photo available in library photographic file, MHS, St. Paul.

26. "Railroad Bridge, Undine's Basin, Vermillion River, Dakota County," circa 1900, photo available in library photographic file, MHS, St. Paul; Prosser, *Rails,* 21, 137.

27. *Pioneer Faces and Places* (Grand Marais, Minn.: Cook County Historical Society, 1979), 54; Rotary Club of Fort William, *The Outlaw Bridge: A Record of Rotary Achievement, 1917–1987* (Thunder Bay, Ont.: Rotary Club of Fort William, 1987), n.p.

28. Ibid.

29. Harold Severson, *We Give You Kenyon: A Bicentennial History of a Minnesota Community* (Kenyon, Minn.: Security Bank of Kenyon, 1976), 18.

30. Ibid., 17.

31. Ibid., 18, 20; Prosser, *Rails,* 123, 125, 149; "Chicago, Milwaukee and St. Paul Railway," 1978, Minnesota Architecture-History Inventory Form, available at SHPO, MHS, St. Paul, n.p.; Christian A. Rasmussen, *A History of Goodhue County, Minnesota* (n.p., 1935), 166.

32. "Duluthian Recalls Building Lester Park Rustic Bridge," *Duluth News Tribune*, October 14, 1931. Additional information can be found in "Lester Park Trail" on the Web site of the City of Duluth Parks and Recreation Department, www. ci.duluth.mn.us/city/parksandrecreation/Secondarypages/lesterparktrail.htm.

33. Plowden, *Bridges,* 57.

STONE BRIDGES

1. "The New Bridge," *Minneapolis Tribune*, March 12, 1875; "The Second Suspension Bridge," *Hennepin History* (April 1953): 2; untitled typescript of newspaper article in *St. Paul Daily Press*, November 20, 1873; Lucile M. Kane, "Minneapolis' Wire Suspension Bridge: First Bridge over the Mississippi," *Gopher Historian* (Spring 1964): 16; Hess, "Final Report," 77, 86; Upham, *Minnesota Place Names,* 233.

2. "The Bridge Question," *Minneapolis Tribune*, April 7, 1875; "Bridge on Fire," *Minneapolis Tribune*, January 29, 1877.

3. "Condensed History," *Minneapolis Tribune*, October 6, 1876; "Bridge on Fire."

4. Gardner, *Minnesota Treasures,* 34–35.

5. Condit, *American Building,* 71.

6. As quoted in Jeffrey A. Hess, "Minnesota Masonry-Arch Highway Bridges," July 1988, National Register of Historic Places Multiple Property Documentation Form, available at SHPO, MHS, St. Paul, E.1.

7. Hess, "Minnesota Masonry-Arch Highway Bridges," E.1–E.2; Plowden, *Bridges,* 9.

8. Plowden, *Bridges,* 9; Charles K. Hyde, *Historic Highway Bridges of Michigan* (Detroit: Wayne State University Press, 1993), 50.

9. Architectural and Historical Research, LLC, and Hess, Roise and Company, "Section 106 Evaluation of Architectural and

Structural Resources: The Existing Rail Line of the Dakota, Minnesota and Eastern Railroad Powder River Basin Expansion Project in Minnesota," June 2000, prepared for the Surface Transportation Board and Burns and McDonnell, available at SHPO, MHS, St. Paul, 22–23; Condit, *American Building*, 75.

10. Prosser, *Rails,* 13, 169; Mary Garder, "Century Old: The Arches," *Winona Daily News*, November 29, 1982; Architectural and Historical Research, LLC, and Hess, Roise and Company, "Section 106," 10, 12, 23.

11. Garder, "Century Old"; Architectural and Historical Research, LLC, and Hess, Roise and Company, "Section 106 Evaluation," 23–24.

12. "Series of Stone Arch Railroad Bridges in Southern Minnesota," *Minnesota Preservationist* 4 (May/June 2001): n.p.

13. Plowden, *Bridges,* 31–32.

14. St. Anthony Falls Heritage Board et al., *Historic Stone Arch Bridge: The Reopening of a Landmark* (Minneapolis: St. Anthony Falls Heritage Board, ca. 1995), 1; Gardner, *Minnesota Treasures,* 46, 61–62; Prosser, *Rails,* 135–136, 146, 161–162.

15. Ray Lowry, "'Hill's Folly': The Building of the Stone Arch Bridge," *Hennepin County History* 47 (Winter 1988): 8; Petersen, *Hiding in Plain Sight,* 92; Prosser, *Rails,* 146.

16. "The Stone Arch Bridge," *Gopher Historian* (Spring 1971): n.p.; Lowry, "Hill's Folly," 20–21, 24; Petersen, *Hiding in Plain Sight,* 92, 94.

17. The state railroad commissioner is quoted in St. Anthony Falls Heritage Board et al., 3. The length of the arch spans is found in the same source, 2. For other sources see Daniel L. Schodek, *Landmarks in American Civil Engineering* (Cambridge: MIT Press, 1987), 144, as well as "The Stone Arch Bridge."

18. St. Anthony Falls Heritage Board et al., 4, 6–8.

19. John J. Hackett, "Point Douglas–St. Louis River Road Bridge," September 30, 1974, National Register of Historic Places Registration Form, available at SHPO, MHS, St. Paul, 7.1.

20. Demian Hess, "Minnesota Military Roads," E.1–E.3.

21. Ibid., E.2–E.3.

22. Ibid., E.3–E.4.

23. Ibid., E.3–E.4; Hackett, Registration Form, 8.0.

24. Linda Picone, "Town Board Gets a Bill for 110-Year-Old Bridge," *Minneapolis Tribune*, November 11, 1974; Hackett, Registration Form, 8.0–8.1.

25. Hackett, Registration Form, 8.0–8.1.

26. Gardner, *Minnesota Treasures,* 81–84.

27. Ibid.; "William Albert Truesdell," *Association of Engineering Societies* 28 (June 1909): 371; Karl J. Karlson, "Bridge a Marvel of Engineering," *St. Paul Pioneer Press*, May 28, 2001.

28. Jeffrey A. Hess, "Bridge No. L1409," August 1988, National Register of Historic Places Registration Form, available at SHPO, MHS, St. Paul, 7.0, 8.0.

29. Ibid., 8.1; Hess, "Minnesota Masonry-Arch Highway Bridges," E.3, E.7–E.9, E.11.

30. Hess, "Minnesota Masonry-Arch Highway Bridges," E.5–E.6.

31. Ibid., E.3; Hess, "Bridge No. L1409," 8.0.

32. Jeffrey A. Hess, "Bridge No. L4013," August 1988, National Register of Historic Places Registration Form, available at SHPO, MHS, St. Paul, 7.0, 8.0.

33. Ibid.; Hess, "Minnesota Masonry-Arch Highway Bridges," E.7.

34. Ibid.

35. Jeffrey A. Hess, "Bridge No. L6007 (Stewart Creek Stone Arch Bridge)," August 1988, National Register of Historic Places Registration Form, available at SHPO, MHS, St. Paul, 8.1.

36. Ibid.

37. Ibid.

38. Ibid., 7.1.

39. Jeffrey A. Hess, "Split Rock Bridge," August, 1988, National Register of Historic Places Registration Form, available at SHPO, MHS, St. Paul, 7.1, 8.1.

40. Anderson, "Federal Relief Construction," E.48; Hess, "Split Rock Bridge," 7.1, 8.1.

41. Hess, "Split Rock Bridge," 7.1, 8.1.

IRON AND STEEL BRIDGES

1. Kenneth Broas, "Steel Arch Bridge (Hennepin Avenue Bridge)," February 1987, Historic American Engineering Record, available at Library of Congress, Washington, D.C., 2–4.

2. Ibid., 4–5.

3. Ibid., 5; Frame, "Historic Bridge Project," 79.

4. Broas, "Steel Arch Bridge," 13, 15; Frame, "Historic Bridge Project," 102; Gardner, *Minnesota Treasures,* 70.

5. Broas, "Steel Arch Bridge," 1, 14, 16–17.

6. Quivik and Martin, "Iron and Steel Bridges," E.0.

7. Gardner, *Minnesota Treasures,* 67–70.

8. Ibid.; Robert M. Frame III, "Reinforced-Concrete Highway Bridges in Minnesota," August 15, 1988, National Register of Historic Places Multiple Property Documentation Form, available at SHPO, MHS, St. Paul, E.7–E.8; Frame, "Historic Bridge Project," 99; Plowden, *Bridges,* 177.

9. Gardner, *Minnesota Treasures,* 68–69.

10. Parsons Brinckerhoff and Engineering and Industrial Heritage, "A Context for Common Historic Bridge Types," October 2005, prepared for the National Cooperative

Highway Research Program, the Transportation Research Council, and the National Research Council, 3.73; Gardner, *Minnesota Treasures,* 69.

11. Condit, *American Building,* 229.

12. Plowden, *Bridges,* 177.

13. J. A. L. Waddell, *Bridge Engineering*, vol. 1 (New York: John Wiley and Sons, Inc., 1916), 409–410; Architectural and Historical Research, LLC, and Hess, Roise and Company, "Bridge No. M 31," in "Section 106 Evaluation," n.p.; Jeffrey A. Hess, "Bridge No. L1393," in "Minnesota Historic Highway Bridge Inventory," 1997, available at SHPO, MHS, St. Paul, n.p.

14. Jeffrey A. Hess, "Bridge No. 0523," in "Minnesota Historic Highway Bridge Inventory," 1997, available at SHPO, MHS, St. Paul, n.p.

15. Plowden, *Bridges,* 171.

16. Ibid., 57; Quivik and Martin, "Iron and Steel Bridges," E.6–E.8.

17. Ibid.; Dennis Gimmestad, "Kern Bridge," January 1980, National Register of Historic Places Registration Form, available at SHPO, MHS, St. Paul, n.p.

18. Gimmestad, "Kern Bridge," n.p.; Condit, *American Building,* 98; Schodek, *American Civil Engineering* 101, 103; Quivik and Martin, "Iron and Steel Bridges," E.7.

19. Condit, *American Building,* 96; Quivik and Martin, "Iron and Steel Bridges," E.7.

20. A good description of Pratt bridges is located in American Association for State and Local History (AASLH), technical leaflet 95, "Bridge Truss Types: A Guide to Dating and Identifying," *History News* 32 (May 1977): n.p.

21. Victor C. Darnell, *Directory of American Bridge Companies, 1840–1900* (Washington, D.C.: Society for Industrial Archeology, 1984), 56; John J. Hackett, "Hanover Bridge," April 1978, National Register of Historic Places Registration Form, available at SHPO, MHS, St. Paul, n.p.; Upham, *Minnesota Place Names,* 640.

22. Jeffrey A. Hess, "Bridge No. 5721," September 1997, National Register of Historic Places Registration Form, available at SHPO, MHS, St. Paul, 7.1; AASLH, "Bridge Truss Types," n.p.

23. Hess, "Bridge No. 5721," 8.1–8.2.

24. Quivik and Martin, "Iron and Steel Bridges," E.6; Condit, *American Building,* 125; Ruth Schwartz Cowan, *A Social History of American Technology* (New York: Oxford University Press, 1997), 132–133; Jack El-Hai, *Lost Minnesota: Stories of Vanished Places* (Minneapolis: University of Minnesota Press, 2000), 164–165.

25. "Hastings Bridge Has Fallen Down," *Minnesota Highways* 1 (January 1952): 3; Parsons Brinckerhoff and Engineering and Industrial Heritage, 3.34; AASLH, "Bridge Truss Types," n.p.; El-Hai, *Lost Minnesota,* 164–165.

26. El-Hai, *Lost Minnesota,* 164–165.

27. Ibid., 164.

28. "New Highway 61 Bridge Opened Wednesday," *Hastings Gazette*, February 23, 1951; "Time Draws Near for Disposal of Spiral Approach," *Hastings Gazette*, February 16, 1951; Jeffrey A. Hess, "Bridge No. 5895," in "Minnesota Historic Highway Bridge Inventory," 1997, available at SHPO, MHS, St. Paul, n.p.; Ibid., 165.

29. Denis P. Gardner, "People's Union Church," May 2004, National Register of Historic Places Registration Form, available at SHPO, MHS, St. Paul, 8.1.

30. "Waterstreet Bridge: Its Past, Present, and Its Future," in "Otter Chapter, Izaak Walton League of America," June 5, 1979, available at SHPO, MHS, St. Paul, n.p.; "Historical Information Concerning the Waterstreet Bridge and Surrounding Area in Maine Township, Otter Tail County, MN," n.d., typescript available at SHPO, MHS, St. Paul, n.p.; untitled newspaper and untitled article concerning Waterstreet Bridge, July 15, 1895, clipping available at SHPO, MHS, St. Paul; Darnell, *American Bridge Companies,* 74.

31. Interview with Peter L. Wilson, Senior Engineering Specialist, Mn/DOT Bridge Division, by the author, January 18, 2007; "Waterstreet Bridge," n.p.; "Historical Information Concerning the Waterstreet Bridge," n.p.

32. David C. Anderson, "Bridge No. 90980 (Salisbury Bridge)," July 31, 1995, National Register of Historic Places Registration Form, available at SHPO, MHS, St. Paul, 8.1–8.3; Meeker County Historical Society, *Meeker County Memories* (Litchfield, Minn.: Meeker County Historical Society, 1987), 17–18.

33. Fredric L. Quivik, "Montana's Minneapolis Bridge Builders," *The Journal of the Society for Industrial Archeology* 10 (1984): 38–39; Frame, "Historic Bridge Project," 67, 75, 78–79, 88; Anderson, "Bridge No. 90980," 8.3.

34. Jeffrey A. Hess, "Bridge No. L5245," in "Minnesota Historic Highway Bridge Inventory," 1997, available at SHPO, MHS, St. Paul, n.p.

35. Rosanne Bergantine, *Phelps: A Peek into Its Past* (n.p., 1970), 3; John J. Hackett, "Phelps Mill," November 20, 1974, National Register of Historic Places Registration Form, available at SHPO, MHS, St. Paul, n.p.

36. Ibid.

37. Maurice W. Hewett, "William Sherman Hewett: A Biography," unpublished typescript available in the William S. Hewett file at the Northwest Architectural Archives, Anderson Library, University of Minnesota, Minneapolis.

38. Ibid; Eric Kudalis, "Harry Wild Jones," in "Historic Profiles through the Decades," *Architecture Minnesota* 18 (November-December 1992): 40; Thomas W. Balcom, "A Tale of Two Water Towers: Washburn Park and Its Water Supply," *Minnesota History* 49 (Spring 1984): 21; Camille Kudzia, "Washburn Park Water Tower," August 1981, National Register of Historic Places Registration Form, available at SHPO, MHS, St. Paul, 7.0, 8.0.

39. Charlene K. Roise and Robert M. Hybben, "Bridge No. 1482," September 1991, National Register of Historic Places Registration Form, available at SHPO, MHS, St. Paul, 8.1.

40. Ibid.; Jeffrey A. Hess, "Bridge No. L7560," in "Minnesota Historic Highway Bridge Inventory," 1997, available at SHPO, MHS, St. Paul, n.p.; Frame, "Historic Bridge Project," 22–24.

41. Susan Granger, "Bridge No. 6527," Minnesota Architecture-History Inventory Form, available at SHPO, MHS, St. Paul, n.p.; Gerald A. Engstrom, highway engineer, letter to Susan Roth, Minnesota National Register Historian, October 20, 1987, available at SHPO, MHS, St. Paul, 2; Upham, *Minnesota Place Names,* 624.

42. Frame, "Historic Bridge Project," 87–88; Condit, 100.

43. Perhaps the best general discussion of the Minnesota Highway Commission is found in Frame's "Historic Bridge Project," 22–28.

44. Ruth Anderson, Watonwan County Historical Society Museum Director, letter to Susan Roth, Minnesota National Register Historian, n.d., available at SHPO, MHS, St. Paul, n.p.

45. Dale Martin and Fredric Quivik, "Third Street Bridge," July 1988, National Register of Historic Places Registration Form, available at SHPO, MHS, St. Paul, 7.0; Parsons Brinckerhoff and Engineering and Industrial Heritage, 3–37; AASLH, "Bridge Truss Types," n.p.

46. Gardner, *Minnesota Treasures,* 168; Frame, "Historic Bridge Project," 85.

47. The quote from the Dakota County Board of Commissioners, as well as additional information in this paragraph, is found in Jeffrey A. Hess, "Bridge No. L3275," in "Minnesota Historic Highway Bridge Inventory," 1997, available at SHPO, MHS, St. Paul, n.p.

48. The quote from the Waterford Township resident, as well as additional information in this paragraph is found in Hess, "Bridge No. L3275," n.p.; Quivik and Martin, "Iron and Steel Bridges," E.11; Frame, "Historic Bridge Project," 78.

49. The quote from the *Granite Falls Journal* is found in Jeffrey A. Hess, "Bridge No. L7969," in "Minnesota Historic Highway Bridge Inventory," 1997, available at SHPO, MHS, St. Paul, n.p.

50. "Milo A. Adams, Pioneer Bridge Builder, Dies," *Minneapolis Tribune,* June 12, 1922.

51. Hess, "Bridge No. L7969," n.p.

52. Frame, "Historic Bridge Project," 24–26; Hess, "Bridge No. L7969," n.p.; Hess and Perkins, "Bridge Inventory," 22.

53. Hess and Perkins, "Bridge Inventory," 12–13; Frame, "Historic Bridge Project," 27.

54. Jeffrey A. Hess, "Bridge No. 2110," in "Minnesota Historic Highway Bridge Inventory," 1997, available at SHPO, MHS, St. Paul, n.p.; Frame, "Historic Bridge Project," 100.

55. Hess, "Bridge No. 2110."

56. Frances P. Alexander and Andrew J. Schmidt, The 106 Group Ltd., "Determination of Eligibility for Bridge Number 3145, Long Meadow Bridge, Bloomington, Hennepin County (Draft)," September 1994, architecture-history study completed for the Mn/DOT, copy available at the SHPO, MHS, St. Paul, 6, 8, 10–12; Frame, "Historic Bridge Project," 80.

57. Darril and Timothy Wegscheid, longtime residents near the Long Meadow Bridge, e-mails to Denis P. Gardner, May 22–23, 2007, in possession of Denis P. Gardner, n.p.; Alexander and Schmidt, "Bridge Number 3145," 6, 8, 10–12.

58. Mary Lynn Smith, "For Trail Users, Old Bridge Is a Missed Link," *Minneapolis Star Tribune,* April 16, 2005.

59. Marcia Ohlhausen, "Northern Pacific Bridge Number 9," June 24, 1994, Minnesota Architecture-History Inventory Form, available at SHPO, MHS, St. Paul, 8.2; El-Hai, *Lost Minnesota,* 4.

60. F. B. Maltby, "The Mississippi River Bridges," *Journal of the Western Society of Engineers* 8 (July-August 1903): 425–427; Albert W. Morse, "N.P. Bridge Nearing Completion," *Minnesota Techno-Log* 3 (January 1923): 5; Ohlhausen, "Bridge Number 9," 8.4; Hofsommer, *Age of Railways,* 80, 123, 149–151; Lucile M. Kane and Alan Ominsky, *Twin Cities: A Pictorial History of Saint Paul and Minneapolis* (St. Paul: Minnesota Historical Society Press, 1983), 73; Prosser, *Rails,* 29, 146.

61. Westbrook, *Industrial Archeology of the Twin Cities,* 16, 26–27; Denis P. Gardner, "A History of the Southeast Heating Plant," March 2002, architectural-historical study prepared for the University of Minnesota, copy in possession of the author, 13; Prosser, *Rails,* 146; "Background and History of the Wabasha Street Bridge River Crossing."

62. Morse, "N.P. Bridge Nearing Completion," 32; Ohlhausen, "Bridge Number 9," 8.4; Maltby, "The Mississippi River Bridges," 427.

63. Ohlhausen, "Bridge Number 9," 8.4.

64. *Souvenir Historical Program: The Sorlie Memorial Bridge, 1929* (Grand Forks: Page Printing Company, 1929), n.p.

65. Ibid.; Denis P. Gardner and Charlene K. Roise, "Northern Pacific Bridge No. 95," July 2000, Historic American Engineering Record documentation completed for United States Army Corps of Engineers (USACOE), available at USACOE, St. Paul, 26.

66. Quivik and Martin, "Iron and Steel Bridges," E.10; Frame, "Historic Bridge Project," 87–88; *Sorlie Memorial Bridge,* n.p.

67. The quotation concerning the roller bearings for the Sorlie Memorial Bridge is found in E. J. Budge, "The Grand Forks Bridge," *North Dakota Highway Bulletin* (December 1928): 7. For other source see *Sorlie Memorial Bridge,* n.p.

68. *Sorlie Memorial Bridge,* n.p.

69. Warren H. Strandell, Polk County Commissioner, District 2, letter to Susan Roth, Minnesota National Register Historian, October 16, 1997, available at SHPO, MHS, St. Paul, n.p.

70. Ibid.

71. Jeffrey A. Hess, "Broadway Bridge," September 1997, National Register of Historic Places Registration Form, available at SHPO, MHS, St. Paul, 7.1.

72. Ibid, 8.1–8.2; "Babcock to Open St. Peter Bridge Bids October 14," *St. Peter Herald*, September 26, 1930.

73. Hess, "Broadway Bridge," 7.1.

74. "Broadway Bridge to Be Opened to Traffic at Once," *St. Peter Herald*, June 26, 1931.

75. Jeffrey A. Hess, "Bridge No. 5388," September 1997, National Register of Historic Places Registration Form, available at SHPO, MHS, St. Paul, 8.1–8.2.

76. Ibid.

77. Ibid.

78. "County to Receive $118,250 in Highway and Bridge Aid," *International Falls Press*, May 13, 1937; Jeffrey A. Hess, "Bridge No. 5804," in "Minnesota Historic Highway Bridge Inventory," 1997, available at SHPO, MHS, St. Paul, n.p.

79. Upham, *Minnesota Place Names,* 299; Hess, "Bridge No. 5804."

80. The quotation from the *Engineering News-Record* is found in Hess, "Bridge No. 5804."

81. Quivik and Martin, "Iron and Steel Bridges," E.19–E.20; Plowden, *Bridges,* 296.

82. Jeffrey A. Hess, "Bridge No. 7645," in "Minnesota Historic Highway Bridge Inventory," 1997, available at SHPO, MHS, St. Paul, n.p.

83. Jeffrey A. Hess, "Bridge No. 6779," in "Minnesota Historic Highway Bridge Inventory," 1997, available at SHPO, MHS, St. Paul, n.p.

84. Quivik and Martin, "Iron and Steel Bridges," E.19–E.20.

85. Ibid.

86. Jeffrey A. Hess, "Bridge No. 5827," National Register of Historic Places Registration Form, available at SHPO, MHS, St. Paul, 7.1, 8.1–8.2.

87. Jeffrey A. Hess, "Bridge No. L7075," in "Minnesota Historic Highway Bridge Inventory," 1997, available at SHPO, MHS, St. Paul.

88. Jeffrey A. Hess, "Bridge No. 7614," in "Minnesota Historic Highway Bridge Inventory," 1997, available at SHPO, MHS, St. Paul, n.p.

89. Gardner, "People's Union Church," 8.12; Quivik and Martin, "Iron and Steel Bridges," E.19.

90. "Survey Report: History/Architecture: Minnesota Trunk Highway Archaeological Reconnaissance Survey," January 17, 1992, copy of study available at SHPO, MHS, St. Paul, 1–4; Larry Oakes, "Spanning the Years," *Minneapolis Star Tribune*, June 24, 1994.

91. "New Wabasha-Nelson Bridge Will Be Opened to Traffic Either Friday or Saturday," *Wabasha County Herald-Standard*, January 1, 1931; "New Wabasha-Nelson Bridge Opened to Traffic Jan. 1; Ferry Ceases Operation," *Wabasha County Herald-Standard*, January 8, 1931; Frame, "Historic Bridge Project," 80.

92. Jeffrey A. Hess, "Evaluation of National Register Eligibility: Winona Highway Crossing (Bridge Nos. 5900 and 5930)," September 1996, available at SHPO, MHS, St. Paul, 1, 5.

93. Ibid., 1–2.

94. Ibid., 2–3; George A. Hool and W. S. Kinne, *Movable and Long-Span Steel Bridges* (New York: McGraw-Hill Book Company, Inc., 1923), 288.

95. Frame, "Historic Bridge Project," 80; Ibid., 5–6, 8.

96. Hess, "Winona Highway Crossing," 7–8.

97. Kachelmyer, Clement P., Mn/DOT, letter to Leslie D. Peterson, trunk highway archaeologist, MHS, June 13, 1983, copy available at SHPO, MHS, St. Paul, n.p.

98. Jeffrey A. Hess, "Kettle River Bridge," September 1997, National Register of Historic Places Registration Form, available at SHPO, MHS, St. Paul, 8.1–8.3.

99. Ibid.

100. Ibid.; Steven R. Brown, "Substructure Movement at Bridge 5718: A Case History," September 1983, study completed for a civil engineering internship through the University of Minnesota, Minneapolis, copy available at SHPO, MHS, St. Paul, 5; Mn/DOT, "Bridge No. 5718: General Plan and Elevation," January 13, 1984, drawing created for deck reconstruction of Kettle River Bridge, available at Mn/DOT, St. Paul, n.p.

101. Brown, "Substructure Movement at Bridge 5718," 5.

102. Jeffrey A. Hess, "Bridge No. 6690," in "Minnesota Historic Highway Bridge Inventory," 1997, available at SHPO, MHS, St. Paul, n.p.; Gardner, *Minnesota Treasures,* 255–258.

103. Hess, "Bridge No. 6690."

104. "New Drayton Bridge Open to Traffic Monday," *Kittson County Enterprise*, November 24, 1954; Ibid.

105. "Bridge No. 6690: General Plan and Elevation," November 19, 1991, drawing created for repair of Drayton Bridge, available at Mn/DOT, St. Paul, n.p.; Hess, "Bridge No. 6690."

106. "River Bridge Floats on a Sea of Plastic," *Engineering News-Record* 171 (October 3, 1963): 26; Frame, "Historic Bridge Project," 78; Hess, "Bridge No. 6690."

107. Quivik and Martin, "Iron and Steel Bridges," E.19–E.20; Plowden, *Bridges,* 296.

108. David C. Anderson, "Redstone Bridge," July 31, 1995, National Register of Historic Places Registration Form (Draft), available at SHPO, MHS, St. Paul, 7.1; Gardner, *Minnesota Treasures,* 168–170.

109. Jeffrey A. Hess, "Stillwater Bridge," August 1988, National Register of Historic Places Registration Form, available at

SHPO, MHS, St. Paul, 8.1; Anderson, "Redstone Bridge," 7.1–7.3, 8.7.

110. Parsons Brinckerhoff and Engineering and Industrial Heritage, 3.43.

111. Ibid., 8.5.

112. Jeffrey A. Hess, "Bridge No. 6544," in "Minnesota Historic Highway Bridge Inventory," 1997, available at SHPO, MHS, St. Paul, n.p.

113. Frank A. King, *The Missabe Road* (San Marino, CA: Golden West Books, 1972), 92; Ibid.

114. Blegen, *Minnesota: A History of the State,* 369; Ibid.

115. Hess, "Bridge No. 6544."

116. Robert M. Frame III, "Great Northern Railway Company Bridge," April 1980, National Register of Historic Places Registration Form, available at SHPO, MHS, St. Paul, n.p.; Gardner, *Minnesota Treasures,* 61–64.

117. Ibid.

118. Hess, "Stillwater Bridge," 8.5.

119. Gardner, *Minnesota Treasures,* 107–110.

120. Tom Lutz, "Aerial Lift Bridge," March 1973, National Register of Historic Places Registration Form, available at SHPO, MHS, St. Paul, n.p.; Ibid.

121. Dwight E. Woodbridge and John S. Pardee, eds., *History of Duluth and St. Louis County: Past and Present,* vol. 2 (Chicago: C. F. Cooper and Company, 1910), 507–508.

122. Richard M. Johnson, "Transporter to Vertical Lift: Duluth's Aerial Lift Bridge," in *Proceedings of the Seventh Historic Bridges Conference* (Cleveland: Cleveland State University, 2001), 135; Gardner, *Minnesota Treasures,* 107–110.

123. Hess, "Stillwater Bridge," 8.6.

124. E. J. Miller, MHD Bridge Engineer, letter to C. M. Babcock, Commissioner of Highways, April 13, 1926, copy available at SHPO, MHS, St. Paul, n.p.

125. Interview with Dennis Gimmestad, Government Compliance Officer, SHPO, November 29, 2006, by the author. Several photos of the predecessor to the Stillwater Bridge are available in the photographic collection of the MHS, St. Paul. For other sources see Britta L. Bloomberg, "Future is brighter for Historic Stillwater Lift Bridge," *Minnesota Preservation Planner* 16 (Spring 2005): 1, 3, and Hess, "Stillwater Bridge," 8.6.

126. Gimmestad interview; Bloomberg, "Historic Stillwater Lift Bridge," 1, 3.

127. Ibid.

128. Charles Birnstiel, "Popular Obsolete Movable Bridges," in *Proceedings of the Seventh Historic Bridges Conference,* 142–143; interview with Peter L. Wilson, Senior Engineering Specialist, Mn/DOT Bridge Division, by the author, January 18, 2007; Stephen P. Hall, "Duluth-Superior Harbor Cultural Resources Study," August 1976, authorized by the Department of the Army, Corps of Engineers, St. Paul District, available at SHPO, MHS, St. Paul, 41; Pete Mohs, "Disassembled Lift-bridge Was Part of Man's Life," *Grand Rapids Herald-Review,* October 2, 1983; Hess, "Stillwater Bridge," 8.1–8.2.

129. Considerable information on Scherzer movable bridges is found in *Scherzer Rolling Lift Bridges: Their Inception, Development and Use* (Chicago: Scherzer Rolling Lift Bridge Company, ca. 1915).

130. Ted Hall, *Drumbeat: A Report from the Northland* (Ranier, Minn.: Rainy Lake Chronicle, 1974), 37.

131. *Scherzer Rolling Lift Bridges,* 36–38; Prosser, *Rails,* 43, 131; Upham, *Minnesota Place Names,* 300.

CONCRETE BRIDGES

1. Mike Kaszuba, "It's a Beauty of a Bridge, with a Beauty of a Price," *Minneapolis Star Tribune,* September 19, 1989; Don Nelson, "Critics Hope to Sink Plans to Replace Hennepin Av. Bridge," *Minneapolis Star Tribune,* July 19, 1982; Joe Kimball, "Panel Approves Bridge Funds," *Minneapolis Star Tribune,* July 1, 1984; Martha S. Allen, "Hennepin Av. Bridge Design Evokes an Older Time Span," *Minneapolis Star Tribune,* March 23, 1984.

2. Joe Kimball, "County Board Chooses 'Cadillac' Bridge Design," *Minneapolis Star Tribune,* April 6, 1984; Kaszuba, "Beauty of a Bridge."

3. Steve Olson, HNTB engineer, e-mail to Denis P. Gardner, June 22, 2006, in possession of Denis P. Gardner, n.p.; *Father Louis Hennepin Bridge: Dedication,* September 12, 1990, pamphlet produced for dedication of Hennepin Avenue Bridge, available at Hennepin County History Museum, Minneapolis, n.p.; "New Bridge Gets First-class Plaques," *Minneapolis Star Tribune,* January 5, 1991; "Later a Bridge, Now a Catwalk," *Minneapolis Star Tribune,* February 1, 1989; George Monaghan, "Maestro of Suspension has gotten Hang of Hennepin Bridge Just Right," *Minneapolis Star Tribune,* October 17, 1989; Kaszuba, "Beauty of a Bridge"; Blegen, *Minnesota: A history of the State,* 50.

4. Condit, *American Building,* 155–156; Plowden, *Bridges,* 297.

5. Frame, "Reinforced-Concrete Highway Bridges," E.2–E.3; Robert M. Frame III, "Interlachen Bridge," August 15, 1988, National Register of Historic Places Registration Form, available at SHPO, MHS, St. Paul, 8.1; Parsons Brinckerhoff and Engineering and Industrial Heritage, 2.17; Condit, *American Building,* 174–175; Plowden, *Bridges,* 297.

6. Maria Elena Baca, "Retro Rail," *Minneapolis Star Tribune,* July 7, 2006; Frame, "Interlachen Bridge," 7.1, 8.1–8.2; Plowden, *Bridges,* 298.

7. Plowden, *Bridges,* 300–303, 317.

8. Ibid., 318.

9. Robert M. Frame III, "Bridge No. L2162," August 15, 1988, National Register of Historic Places Registration Form, available at SHPO, MHS, St. Paul, 8.1–8.2; Robert M. Frame III, "Bridge No. L4646," August 15, 1988, National Register of Historic Places Registration Form, available at SHPO, MHS, St. Paul, 8.1–8.2; The 106 Group, "Evaluation of 27 Bridges in Rock County, Minnesota, for the National Register of Historic Places," August 1994, study completed for the Mn/DOT, copy available at SHPO, MHS, St. Paul, 14–16.

10. Arthur P. Rose, *An Illustrated History of the Counties of Rock and Pipestone, Minnesota* (Luverne, Minn.: Northern History Publishers Company, 1911), 112; The 106 Group, 14–16.

11. This quote is found in Frame, "Bridge No. L4646," 8.2.

12. Ibid., 8.1–8.2; Frame, "Bridge No. L2162," 8.1–8.2.

13. Dennis Gimmestad, "Marsh Concrete Rainbow Arch Bridge," January 1980, National Register of Historic Places Registration Form, available at SHPO, MHS, St. Paul, n.p.; James B. Marsh, "Reinforced Arch Bridge," Patent Number 1,035,026, filed with United States Patent Office November 1, 1911, approved August 6, 1912, n.p; James C. Hippen, *Marsh Rainbow Arch Bridges in Iowa* (Boone County, Iowa: Boone, Iowa, 1997), 5.

14. Peter L. Wilson, Senior Engineering Specialist, Mn/DOT Bridge Division, e-mail to Denis P. Gardner, January 19, 2006, in possession of Denis P. Gardner, n.p.

15. URS Corporation et al., "Skyline Parkway Corridor Management Plant (Draft)," February 2003, study available at SHPO, MHS, St. Paul, 1.

16. Mark Ryan, "Snively's Road," *Minnesota History* (Winter 1994): 147, 149–152, 159; Ibid., 4–5.

17. Chuck Frederick, "Two of the Seven Bridges to get Summer Makeover," *Duluth News Tribune*, May 31, 2002; Ryan, 150–151.

18. Mary Ann Nord, comp., *The National Register of Historic Places in Minnesota: A Guide* (St. Paul: Minnesota Historical Society, 2003), 222; Ryan, 152–153; URS Corporation et al., "Skyline Parkway," 5, 9, 15, 18.

19. Frederick, "Summer Makeover"; Ryan, "Snively's Road," 163.

20. Susan Granger, Scott Kelly, and Kay Grossman, "Lester River Bridge," January 17, 2002, National Register of Historic Places Registration Form, available at SHPO, MHS, St. Paul, 7.1–7.2.

21. Ibid.

22. Ibid., 8.1–8.7.

23. The quote from Shawn Perich is found in Granger, Kelly, and Grossman, "Lester River Bridge," 8.5.

24. This quote is found in Jeffrey A. Hess, "Bridge No. 3589," September 1997, National Register of Historic Places Registration Form, available at SHPO, MHS, St. Paul, 8.1.

25. Ibid., 7.1, 8.1–8.3.

26. Ibid.

27. Robert M. Frame III, "Nymore Bridge," August 15, 1989, National Register of Historic Places Registration Form, available at SHPO, MHS, St. Paul, 7.1.

28. Ibid., 7.1, 8.1.

29. George M. Cheney, "Concrete Bridge Reinforcement," Patent Number 820,921, filed with United States Patent Office February 26, 1906, approved May 15, 1906, n.p.; Ibid.

30. Cheney patent application.

31. "New Bridge over Mississippi River Inlet to Cost $22,772; Work Will Commence Soon," *Bemidji Pioneer*, August 22, 1916; Frame, "Historic Bridge Project," 80; Frame, "Nymore Bridge," 8.1.

32. Robert M. Frame III, "Cappelen Memorial Bridge," May 12, 1978, National Register of Historic Places Registration Form, available at SHPO, MHS, St. Paul, n.p.; Frame, "Historic Bridge Project," 69.

33. Kenneth Bjork, *Saga in Steel and Concrete: Norwegian Engineers in America* (Northfield, Minn.: Norwegian-American Historical Association, 1947), 148–149.

34. Westbrook, *Industrial Archeology of the Twin Cities,* 23; Ibid.

35. Frame, "Reinforced-Concrete Highway Bridges," E.12–E.13.

36. Ibid., E.13–E.14; Plowden, *Bridges,* 299.

37. Frame, "Cappelen Memorial Bridge," n.p.

38. Bjork, *Saga in Steel and Concrete,* 150.

39. "Design of 400-Ft. Concrete Arch of the Cappelen Memorial Bridge," *Engineering News-Record* (January 25, 1923): 148–152; Frame, "Cappelen Memorial Bridge," n.p.

40. "Design of 400-Ft. Concrete Arch," 148–149, 151; Plowden, *Bridges,* 299.

41. Robert M. Frame III, "Robert Street Bridge," August 15, 1988, National Register of Historic Places Registration Form, available at SHPO, MHS, St. Paul, 7.1, 8.1; "Robert Street Bridge—1896," photograph available in photographic collection of the MHS, St. Paul; "Heavy Traffic Made First Robert Street Span Obsolete," *St. Paul Pioneer Press*, August 1, 1926; Frame, "Historic Bridge Project," 90.

42. Frame, "Robert Street Bridge," 8.1–8.2; Frame, "Historic Bridge Project," 99, 142.

43. W. E. King and Roy Childs Jones, "Engineering and Architectural Design of a Long Concrete Bridge," *Engineering News-Record* (November 4, 1925): 732–733; Frame, "Robert Street Bridge," 7.1–7.2.

44. Westbrook, *Industrial Archeology of the Twin Cities,* 27–28; King and Jones, "Long Concrete Bridge," 732–733; Frame, "Robert Street Bridge," 8.1–8.2.

45. Frame, "Robert Street Bridge," 7.1; King and Jones, "Long Concrete Bridge," 737.

46. "Artistry and Utility Combined in Magnificent New Bridge," *St. Paul Pioneer Press*, August 1, 1926; Ibid., 7.1–7.2.

47. Walter H. Wheeler, "Long Concrete-Arch Road Bridge

Over Minnesota River," *Engineering News-Record* (March 31, 1927): 514–519; Robert M. Frame III, "Fort Snelling-Mendota Bridge," May 12, 1978, National Register of Historic Places Registration Form, available at SHPO, MHS, St. Paul, n.p.; Plowden, *Bridges,* 299; Frame, "Historic Bridge Project," 101.

48. Elizabeth A. Gales, "Cream of Wheat Building," n.d., City of Minneapolis Heritage Preservation Commission Registration Form, available at Minneapolis Heritage Preservation Commission, Minneapolis, 7.1–7.2; John Mecum and Muriel Nord, "Minneapolis Armory," May 1985, National Register of Historic Places Registration Form, available at SHPO, MHS, St. Paul, 8.2; Design Center for American Urban Landscape and College of Architecture and Landscape Architecture, University of Minnesota, "The Minneapolis Armory Reuse Study," March 1990, copy available at SHPO, MHS, St. Paul, 25, 27.

49. Don Spavin, "Ferry Good Enough, Bridge's Critics Said," *St. Paul Pioneer Press,* September 10, 1978; Wheeler, "Long Concrete-Arch Road Bridge," 514–515.

50. Undated typescript research notes in Fort Snelling-Mendota Bridge file, available at SHPO, MHS, St. Paul, n.p.; Spavin, "Bridge's Critics"; Frame, "Fort Snelling-Mendota Bridge," n.p.

51. Don Ahern, "Bridge Reopening Cheered," *St. Paul Pioneer Press,* October 15, 1994.

52. Condit, *American Building,* 255.

53. Robert M. Frame III, "Intercity Bridge," August 15, 1988, National Register of Historic Places Registration Form, available at SHPO, MHS, St. Paul, 7.1, 8.1–8.2.

54. Frame, "Historic Bridge Project," 30, 66; Ibid., 8.1.

55. Martin S. Grytbak, "Concrete Arch Bridge over the Mississippi," *Engineering News-Record* (November 10, 1927): 756, 758; Bjork, *Saga in Steel and Concrete,* 153–154.

56. Grytbak's quote is found in Bjork, *Saga in Steel and Concrete,* 153–154.

57. Ibid., 154; Frame, "Intercity Bridge," 8.2; Frame, "Historic Bridge Project," 77.

58. Frame, "Intercity Bridge," 8.2.

59. Virginia Rybin, "Panel Makes Recommendation on Ford Bridge Repair," *St. Paul Pioneer Press,* November 15, 1998; Jackie Sluss, Historian, Mn/DOT, letter to Dennis Gimmestad, Government Compliance Officer, SHPO, October 8, 1999, available at SHPO, MHS, St. Paul; Frame, "Intercity Bridge," 7.1.

60. Robert M. Frame III, "Cedar Avenue Bridge," August 15, 1988, National Register of Historic Places Registration Form, available at SHPO, MHS, St. Paul, 7.1, 8.1–8.2; Lynne VanBrocklin Spaeth and Robert M. Frame III, "Anoka-Champlin Mississippi River Bridge," May 1979, National Register of Historic Places Registration Form, available at

SHPO, MHS, St. Paul, n.p.; Minnesota Department of Highways, "Proposal for Bridge No. 4380 on State Project 3-49," 1928, proposal copy available at SHPO, MHS, St. Paul, 1.

61. "Cedar Bridge to be Finished by January 1," circa 1929 newspaper clipping in the Cedar Avenue Bridge file, available at SHPO, MHS, St. Paul; Frame, "Cedar Avenue Bridge," 7.1, 8.1–8.2.

62. R. B. Johnson, "History on the Mississippi," July 1998, unpublished brief history in the Anoka-Champlin Mississippi River file, available at SHPO, MHS, St. Paul, 3; Dennis A. Gimmestad, Government Compliance Officer, SHPO, letter to Clement P. Kachelmyer, Mn/DOT, February 12, 1991, available at SHPO, MHS, St. Paul; Frame, "Cedar Avenue Bridge," 8.2.

63. Edith A. Dunn, "A History of the Anoka-Champlin Bridge 4380," January 1997, cultural resource study prepared for Mn/DOT, copy available at SHPO, MHS, St. Paul, 1–2; MHD, *Biennial Report of the Minnesota Commissioner of Highways, 1929–1930* (St. Paul: MHD, 1930), 6; Robert M. Frame III, memorandum to SHPO regarding the Anoka-Champlin Mississippi River Bridge, October 25, 1984, available at SHPO, MHS, St. Paul, n.p.

64. "Anoka-Champlin Bridge Dedication Ceremony Program," August 1, 1998, copy of dedication program available at SHPO, MHS, St. Paul, n.p.; "Bridge No. 4380," October 1971, engineering drawing of elevation of Anoka-Champlin Mississippi River Bridge, copy available at SHPO, MHS, St. Paul; Johnson, "History on the Mississippi," 3; Dunn, "Bridge 4380," 3; Spaeth and Frame, "Anoka-Champlin Bridge," n.p.

65. Kristen Zschomler, Historian-Archaeologist, and Peter L. Wilson, Senior Engineering Specialist, both of Mn/DOT, e-mail to Denis P. Gardner, September 19, 2006, in possession of Denis P. Gardner, n.p.

66. Michael T. Sheehan, "Oronoco Bridge," May 5, 1982, National Register of Historic Places Registration Form (draft), available at SHPO, MHS, St. Paul, n.p.

67. Jeffrey A. Hess, "Bridge No. 5557," in "Minnesota Historic Highway Bridge Inventory," 1997, available at SHPO, MHS, St. Paul, n.p.

68. Lloyd Larson, Engineering Coordinator, Mn/DOT, letter to R. E. Wolfe, District Engineer, Mn/DOT, June 14, 1983, copy available at SHPO, MHS, St. Paul, n.p.; Hess, "Bridge No. 5557," n.p.

69. Leonard R. Dickinson, State Representative, letter to M. J. Hoffman, MHD, February 23, 1948, copy available at SHPO, MHS, St. Paul, n.p.; the date for the erection of the truss bridge over the Rapid River is drawn from labeling on an undated photograph of the bridge in the possession of SHPO, MHS, St. Paul; the highway department quote is found in Hess, "Bridge No. 5557," n.p.

70. Frame, "Reinforced-Concrete Highway Bridges," E.6.

71. Robert M. Frame III, "Dunn Memorial Bridge," November 22, 1987, Statewide Bridge Survey Inventory Form, available at SHPO, MHS, St. Paul, n.p.

72. Jeffrey A. Hess, "Bridge No. 5083" and "Bridge No. 5151," September 1997, National Register of Historic Places Registration Forms, available at SHPO, MHS, St. Paul, 8.1–8.2; "Business Men Hear Report on Highway Status," *Marshall News-Messenger*, January 9, 1931; Upham, 337.

73. "Pavement Fete Draws Crowd of Over 10,000," *Marshall News-Messenger*, October 30, 1931.

74. The comments of Hess are found in "Bridge No. 5083," 8.2.

75. Jeffrey A. Hess, "Bridge No. 1238," in "Minnesota Historic Highway Bridge Inventory," 1997, available at SHPO, MHS, St. Paul, n.p.

76. Frame, "Reinforced-Concrete Highway Bridges," E.9.

77. Jeffrey A. Hess, "Bridge No. 1238A," in "Minnesota Historic Highway Bridge Inventory," 1997, available at SHPO, MHS, St. Paul, n.p.

78. Frame, "Reinforced-Concrete Highway Bridges," E.7.

79. Hess, "Bridge No. 1238A," n.p.

80. The quote of the state highway commission, as well as additional information, is found in Hess, "Bridge No. 1238A," n.p.

81. Hess, "Bridge No. 1238," n.p.

82. Dennis Gimmestad, "Ramsey Park Swayback Bridge," September 1978, National Register of Historic Places Registration Form, available at SHPO, MHS, St. Paul, n.p.

83. Albert H. Good, *Park and Recreation Structures* (n.p.: United States Department of the Interior, National Park Service, 1938), 175.

84. Ibid., 175.

85. Gimmestad, "Ramsey Park Swayback Bridge"; Good, *Park and Recreation Structures,* 200.

86. Good, *Park and Recreation Structures,* 200.

87. Anderson, "Federal Relief Construction," E.11–E.12, E.23–E.24; Jeffrey A. Hess, "Bridge No. 3355," National Register of Historic Places Registration Form, available at SHPO, MHS, St. Paul, 7.1, 8.1.

88. Hess, "Bridge No. 3355," 7.1, 8.1.

89. Ibid.

90. Jeffrey A. Hess, "Bridge No. 5453," in "Minnesota Historic Highway Bridge Inventory," 1997, available at SHPO, MHS, St. Paul, n.p.

91. Waddell, *Bridge Engineering,* 1043; Jeffrey A. Hess, "Bridge No. L7897," and "Bridge No. L7898," in "Minnesota Historic Highway Bridge Inventory," 1997, available at SHPO, MHS, St. Paul, n.p.

92. Hess, "Bridge No. L7897," and "Bridge No. L7898."

93. Arthur G. Hayden and Maurice Barron, *The Rigid-Frame Bridge* (New York: John Wiley and Sons, Inc., 1950), 1–2;
Jeffrey A. Hess, "Bridge No. 5699," in "Minnesota Historic Highway Bridge Inventory," 1997, available at SHPO, MHS, St. Paul, n.p.; Frame, "Reinforced-Concrete Highway Bridges," E.10.

94. Condit, *American Building,* 259; Plowden, *Bridges,* 320; Frame, "Reinforced-Concrete Highway Bridges," E.10; Hess, "Bridge No. 5699," n.p.

95. Hess, "Bridge No. 5699," n.p.

96. Ibid.

97. Frame, "Reinforced-Concrete Highway Bridges," E.12.

BRIDGE PRESERVATION

1. A companion to the HAER is the HABS, or Historic American Buildings Survey, a study, or historical record, for a building determined historic but facing demolition or substantial alteration.

2. For discussion of all major Minnesota bridge studies up to 1995, see Hess and Perkins, "Historic Highway Bridge Inventory," 2–7.

3. Fredric L. Quivik, "Kennedy Bridge," July 1988, National Register of Historic Places Registration Form, available at SHPO, MHS, St. Paul, n.p.

4. Samuel I. Schwartz, "Catch Me, I'm Falling," *New York Times*, August 13, 2007. A study commissioned for the New York City Department of Transportation in 1989 concluded that the city's 840 bridges could be "maintained in near pristine condition" for an annual cost of $150 million. In contrast, the city at that time was completing little routine maintenance on bridges and was spending roughly $400 million to replace sections of bridges and often entire bridges.

5. The approximate number of highway bridges in Minnesota is drawn from Hess, Roise and Company, "The Preservation of Historic Bridges in Minnesota: Preparation of a List of Bridges for Field Survey Final Project Report," August 1991, study prepared for the SHPO and the Mn/DOT, copy available at SHPO, MHS, St. Paul, 6. The final number of bridges determined eligible for the National Register of Historic Places through the Minnesota Historic Highway Bridge Inventory, as well as the number actually added to the historic listing, can be found in Charlene K. Roise and Jeffrey A. Hess, "Management Plan for Minnesota's Historic Bridges," November 1997, prepared for the Mn/DOT, copy available at SHPO, MHS, St. Paul, 3.

6. Interview with Dave Killdahl, Crookston City Engineer, summer 2005, by the author; Jeffrey A. Hess, "Bridge No. L8471," in "Minnesota Historic Highway Bridge Inventory," 1997, available at SHPO, MHS, St. Paul, n.p.

7. A good source for regulations related to historic resources is Thomas F. King's *Cultural Resource Laws and Practice: An Introductory Guide* (New York: AltaMira Press, 2004). For other source see Roise and Hess, "Management Plan," 1.

8. Eric DeLony and Terry H. Klein, "Historic Bridges: A Heritage at Risk: A Report on a Workshop on the Preservation and Management of Historic Bridges," June 2004, report of bridge preservation workshop held December 3–4, 2003, funded by the Federal Highway Administration's Office of Project Development and Environmental Review, 1; Roise and Hess, "Management Plan," 1.

9. DeLony's quote, as well as information on Oregon's Historic Bridge Preservation Program, is found in Eric DeLony, "Oregon DOT Receives National Honor for Historic Bridge Program," in *Society for Industrial Archeology Newsletter* 35 (Spring 2006): 16–17.

10. Ibid.

11. Ibid.

12. DeLony and Klein, "A Heritage at Risk," 1.

13. Ibid.

14. Considerably more detailed information concerning these recommendations is found in DeLony and Klein, "A Heritage at Risk," 3–9.

15. "Management Plan for Historic Bridges in Minnesota," June 2006, study prepared by Mead and Hunt and HNTB for the Mn/DOT, copy available at the Mn/DOT, St. Paul.

16. Ibid.

17. Ibid.

AFTERWORD

1. For a list of nationally and exceptionally significant features of the interstate highway system, see www.environment. fhwa.dot.gov/histpres/highways_list.asp.

2. Eric DeLony and Terry H. Klein, *Historic Bridges: A Heritage at Risk. A Report on a Workshop on the Preservation and Management of Historic Bridges*, Washington, D.C., December 3–4, 2003, SRI Preservation Conference Series 1 (June 2004), 18; see www.srifoundation.org/index.html.

3. Report prepared by Mead and Hunt and HNTB for the Minnesota Department of Transportation, June 2006.

4. This report can be accessed from the Web sites www.in.gov/ dot/programs/bridges/inventory/index.html and www. in.gov/indot/files/HistoricBridgePA.pdf.

INDEX

Y

Z

DENIS P. GARDNER is a historical consultant and writer. He is author of *Minnesota's Treasures: Stories Behind the State's Historic Places*.

ERIC DELONY, former chief of the Historic American Engineering Record (HAER), is a consultant and activist working for the preservation of historic bridges.